POPULATION,

RESOURCES,

AND THE FUTURE:

NON-MALTHUSIAN PERSPECTIVES

POPULATION,

RESOURCES,

AND THE FUTURE:

NON-MALTHUSIAN PERSPECTIVES

Contributors:

Harold J. Barnett
R. W. Behan
Arthur J. Dyck
W. Farrell Edwards
R. Buckminster Fuller
B. Delworth Gardner
Elvis J. Holt
Phillip R. Kunz
Philip F. Low
Evan Tye Peterson
Ben Wattenberg

EDITED BY HOWARD M. BAHR/BRUCE A. CHADWICK/DARWIN L. THOMAS
BRIGHAM YOUNG UNIVERSITY PRESS

The views expressed in this book are solely those of the contributors and should not be interpreted as the official or unofficial position of the contributor's institution, Brigham Young University, Brigham Young University Press, or any other organization, either religious or secular.

Library of Congress Card Catalog Number: 72-86043
ISBN: 0-8425-1523-2

Brigham Young University Press, Provo, Utah 84601
© 1972 by Brigham Young University Press. All rights reserved
Printed in the United States of America

1972 5 M 4773

CONTENTS

v

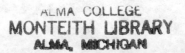

―――

*Previously published

vi

PREFACE

The papers in this volume represent a variety of personal and intellectual perspectives. Each author is responsible for the views which appear under his name. The selection of pieces and their arrangement into sections is the sole responsibility of the editors. Some of the papers present personal values as well as scientific evidence. The views expressed in these papers are solely those of the contributors and should not be interpreted as the official or unofficial position of the contributor's institution, Brigham Young University, Brigham Young University Press, or any other organization, either religious or secular.

We are indebted to the scholars who have contributed original pieces in the belief that non-Malthusian perspectives on population growth and resource utilization are not receiving the attention they deserve, and to the authors and copyright holders of articles previously published for permission to reprint their work in this anthology. In addition, valuable assistance was rendered at various stages in the writing by several scientists who read the manuscript and made critical suggestions. The generous contributions of Spencer J. Condie, Homer S. Ellsworth, George Jarvis, J. Joel Moss, Phillip Smith, and John S. Staley are acknowledged with thanks.

We are especially indebted to Neal A. Maxwell, whose enthusiasm for the project encouraged us to persevere, and whose suggestions about the manuscript as a whole and the original papers in particular were extremely helpful. Finally, we wish to express appreciation to Ernest L. Olson, director of BYU Press, who willingly accepted and completed an almost impossible production schedule.

I.
ARE PROPOSALS FOR POPULATION CONTROL PREMATURE ?

Introduction

At the outset let us identify this collection of papers as a plea for "equal time," and set down some of the values that have guided us in selecting pieces for inclusion. Many serious problems face lodgers on "spaceship earth" in the last decades of the twentieth century, including mass malnutrition, environmental pollution, depletion of natural resources, deteriorating cities, and international tensions; we believe that the resolution of these problems depends upon (1) man's belief in his capacity to devise and manage solutions; (2) continued development of valid scientific knowledge and of the ability to apply that knowledge in technological and social engineering; and (3) concentration of our limited human resources on seeking solutions to the underlying causes of social and ecological ills, rather than to their symptoms. In short, we must ask the right questions, devote adequate resources to finding answers to them, and set in motion appropriate action.

We are impressed by the complexities of the problems that face modern societies in terms of both the potential consequences for the earth's ecosystem and the absolute numbers of people whose lives may be affected. In light of these complexities and of the far-reaching ramifications of the acts of both individuals and governments, we are skeptical of easy solutions or simplistic *rendering of complex problems into easily understood slogans and, to judge by experience, into frequently misdirected and even harmful public programs based on such "self-evident" solutions.*

Scientists in many disciplines and a sizable proportion of the general public have identified the "population explosion" and the "ecological crisis" as critical problems requiring immediate attention. Some have suggested, and these views have been well received, that population size is "causing" the ecological imbalance. But the impact of human population growth on the problems mentioned above depends upon a vast number of factors, including the level of technology in a society, the nature of its social organization, its values concerning the use and re-use of natural resources, its power relative to other human societies, its marital and reproductive practices, and its institutions of socialization.

It is valid and commendable to urge an assessment of the effect of population size as one of the dimensions which may contribute to the various "crises" which confront our civilization. But the premature identification of population growth as the critical problem, and the subsequent design of far-reaching action programs based upon that premise, is scientifically irresponsible. We are also cognizant of fads in science and in politics, and of the political implications of the scientific theses popular at a given time. Both politically and scientifically, population control is a "now" idea. Only a small minority urge caution or otherwise question the attack on the larger-than-two-child family, or even raise the possibility that accepting population size as the critical causal variable brings premature closure on the causal relationships in a very complex system.

We are not unduly concerned over the fact that such voices are in the minority, but our understanding of how the scientific community functions causes us to wonder whether such voices can be heard. The brilliant analyst, Thomas Kuhn (1962), has documented what happens in scientific circles when the majority of scientists accept, as given, the basic (often implicit) assumptions underlying their particular scientific paradigm and proceed to solve the particular set of problems suggested by that paradigm. Kuhn calls this activity of "agreed" scientists normal science, *and demonstrates that the purpose of normal science is anything but the generation of innovative breakthroughs (novel theoretical*

4

formulations). Indeed, he (Kuhn, 1962:24) maintains that "no part of the aim of normal science is to call forth new sorts of phenomena; indeed those that will not fit . . . are often not seen at all." Not only will the community of "agreed" scientists be blind to novelties around them but "they often suppress fundamental novelties because they (the novelties) are necessarily subversive" (Kuhn, 1962:5) to the basic commitments of the community of scientists. A classic example of the failure to perceive anomalies as well as of suppression of novel explanations of scientific "fact" is the Velikovsky affair (Grazia et al., 1967). The blatant and successful attempts to suppress the results of Velikovsky's scholarly work, and the intense public pressure generated by internationally renowned scientists in that case is vivid documentation of the accuracy of Kuhn's analysis.

It would be devastating to scientific advancement should the scientific community agree that the population growth was the cause of most of our social and ecological problems to the point that no one was even asking what the advantages of large families were, if there were beneficial effects of high density, how more food could be supplied, how the distribution system could be refined to serve a growing population better, how new sources of energy might be developed, or what new forms of world government could be created to reduce the problems of starvation, pollution, or depletion of resources. If the scientific community develops such unanimity of thought because of the failure to perceive novel issues and the tendency to suppress different theoretical perspectives, man's future will indeed be bleak. As Kuhn (1962:5) maintains, "competition between segments of the scientific community is the only historical process that ever actually results in the rejection of one previously accepted theory or in the adoption of another." Man does not now have all the necessary answers to solve the problems discussed above. He must develop them through rejecting current ideas that prove untenable, regardless of their popularity, and through testing new and as yet undeveloped theories about his own nature and the nature of his physical environment. This necessity calls for active developing and testing of a multitude of differing theoretical perspectives.

In our view, a basic premise of the most visible recent neo-Malthusian movement, Zero Population Growth, is just the kind of assumption likely to prevent us from reaching solutions to the

5

problems that confront us. That premise, recently summarized as "the gloomy faith that an ecological doomsday is not far away unless the number of earth dwellers stops growing, including, or especially, Americans" (Greene, 1972:43), has also been questioned by Ansley Coale, director of the Office of Population Research at Princeton University, who writes:

> Even if our population should rise to a billion, our average density would not be very high by European standards. It seems to me that we must attack the problems of pollution, urban deterioration, juvenile delinquency, and the like directly, and if sensible programs are evolved, continued population growth on the order of the present would not make the programs less effective (Greene, 1972:43).

In addition to the nature of the scientific community, there is another reason why we fear that the "minority voices crying in the wilderness" may not be heard. That is the sheer power generated by a combining of the political establishment with the scientific. Presidential commissions and vocal activists, citizen groups and learned societies all buttress the scientific hypothesis that the presence of too many people is causing the problems. There seems to be a feeling in some circles that even if the more alarmist predictions are incorrect, even if the outlook is not as gloomy as it is said to be, the negative pronouncements and cries of impending disaster serve the useful function of sensitizing us to the problem and motivating us into action. Unfortunately, the inaccurate assessment has other consequences as well. The unsettling fact is that the consequences of identifying the wrong causal factor and devising solutions appropriate to that factor, or of "overkill" with respect to the influence of family size on national problems and the attendant "underkill" with respect to aspects of our family and community organization that are perhaps more important, are not known to us.

The end of improving man's use of the earth and the quality of his life does not justify the means of exaggerating or falsifying the seriousness of his present condition or of the outlook for the future. We have had enough of managed news and of pronouncements which distort or underreport in the presumably well-meaning interest of making us better faster. This is not the way to solve our environmental and social problems.

In August 1971, a conference of the Center for the Study of

Democratic Institutions brought together food scientists and social scientists in a discussion of the environment. The 1971 conference was described by the president of the Center as a kind of rebuttal to one sponsored the year before. The earlier conference had served as a forum for those whom the agricultural experts identified as "doomsday ecologists," and had produced a book containing this theme:

> Each day brings to light a new ecological crisis. Our dense, amber air is a noxious emphysema agent; farming—anti-husbandry—turns fertile soil into a poisoned wasteland; rivers are sewers, lakes cesspools, and our oceans are dying (Fadiman and White, 1971).

The agricultural experts assembled in 1971 disagreed. Their position:

> The land is in better shape than it ever has been; pollution of air and waterways is the byproduct of urban industrialization, not husbandry; and there is no credible evidence that the chemical/genetic/mechanical revolution has affected the chain of life in ways any more drastic than those common to nature's evolutionary change (Ashmore, 1971:2).

They also had heartening things to say about food production and population:

> If it were solely a matter of increasing production on existing acreage, and bringing in new land, there would be no real threat of an imbalance between population and food supply in the foreseeable future. But, of course, there is the matter of distribution, of making one area's abundance available to meet another area's scarcity (A Center Conference, 1971:3).

This statement is a prime example of the point we seek to emphasize about perceiving the critical components of the problem. According to the agriculturalists, neither term of the Malthusian equation—not population size nor food supply—is the critical element. Instead, it is the distribution system that deserves immediate attention. To the degree that programs aimed at reducing population size use resources which might have been directed at improving distribution systems, or deflect creative thinking from the latter problem, they may prove not merely neutral in their consequences but positively harmful.

People have been frightened by future projections which

7

suggest, or have been interpreted to show, that as population growth continues, so will pollution and resource depletion, until war, famine, pestilence or the poisoning of the earth bring mass death or even the end of mankind. Yet, as most model builders know, how a theoretical model turns out depends upon the assumptions and parameters built into it. The projected future is alarming or attractive, depending upon who does the constructing and on the components and limiting principles he uses.

Another "fact" accepted without question in many quarters is that high human density is bad. A few animal studies on crowding, of questionable generality for other animal species, let alone for human population, are quoted ad nauseum *to make the point that overcrowding produces pathological behavior. Yet still people crowd to the cities, because on balance they find life there more rewarding than in other locales. In fact, there is evidence that from a number of points of view, urban life—high density living—is good for people. Many of the anti-human-density statements are anticity pronouncements, and represent a continuation of the anti-urban bias of much of western thought of the past centuries. Yet we should not confuse the consequences of poor organization, corruption, or inefficiency in urban areas with the consequences of human density per se. Is high density bad? It depends on the setting and the indicator of "quality." In terms of economic vitality, Otto Fredrich (1971:58) has observed:*

> *England and Germany prosper even though they have a population density greater than that of India. And the Japanese are demonstrating that the world's most thickly populated nation may also become its richest.*

Many assert in alarmist tones that our resources are being used up. Yet in point of fact the "using up" usually means being converted from easily usable to somewhat more difficult-to-use forms. One of the advantages of "spaceship earth" is that little escapes from the spaceship, although the form may be changed. Moreover, even in terms of more conventional calculus, the sustaining power of the earth's resources as we now know them are fantastic almost beyond belief.

Let us affirm here in the strongest terms that we are not saying that there are no problems of pollution or pesticide contamination, nor are we saying that uncontrolled population growth is a

8

good thing. Instead, we urge that the reader recognize the mythological, ideological, and even religious character of much that passes for scientific fact in the arena of population and ecology. More than that: we urge that scientists and others honestly examine the evidence and attempt to separate the passion of cooperating in a common "cause" and the fulfillment of winning "converts" to one's intellectual hobby from the evaluation of the cold, stark facts (or, unfortunately, often the absence of such facts) about what is, and the responsible assessments of what may be.

Research on better methods of using water, air, land, and other resources is needed; and so are better studies of alternative modes of organizing high concentrations of human beings to maximize the advantages of metropolitan living. Vast changes are needed in the consumption habits of a people used to wasting water, paper, electricity, and many other resources. Research is needed to identify under what conditions large families are "good" for children, and when small families may be "bad." But we need the solid, irrefutable evidence in hand before the power of government is brought to bear on the values and priorities of so fundamental an institution as the family. Too many times we have been rushed, psychologically converted but intellectually misled, into "doing something before it's too late," only to find that our precipitate action has exacerbated the problem, or created history that we are not proud of and whose costly and unjust consequences resonate for generations.

Talk of injustices and consequences for the future brings us to the ethical problem involved in proposals for population limitation. Some of these are raised in the final section of this book. But it seems appropriate at the beginning to reaffirm Daniel Callahan's (1972:494) conclusion to an extensive and careful treatment of the ethical implications of population control:

> A strong indication that freedom of choice will be ineffective [in limiting population growth] does not establish grounds for rejecting it. Only if it can be shown that the failure of this freedom to reduce population growth threatens other important human values, thus establishing a genuine conflict of values, would the way be open to remove it from the place of primacy. . . .
>
> In this sense, to predicate human rights at all is to take a risk. It is to assert that the respect to be accorded human beings ought not to be

9

dependent upon majority opinion, cost-benefit analysis, social utility, governmental magnanimity, or popular opinion. While it is obviously necessary to adjudicate conflicts among rights, and often to limit one right in order to do justice to another, the pertinent calculus is that of rights, not of utility. A claim can be entered against the primacy of one right only in the name of one or more other important rights. The proper route to a limitation of rights is not directly from social facts (demographic, economic, and so on) to rights, as if these facts were enough in themselves to prove the case against a right. The proper route is from showing that the social facts threaten rights, and in what way, to showing that a limitation of one right may be necessary to safeguard or enhance other rights. To give primacy to the right of free choice is to take a risk. The justification for the risk is the high value assigned to the right, a value that transcends simply utilitarian considerations.

The selections which follow have been chosen and organized with the intent of highlighting and documenting the point that the neo-Malthusian perspective on population growth and the attribution of social and environmental problems to "overpopulation" is only one of several hypothetical approaches to the problem. From the standpoint of available scientific knowledge, there is little evidence that it is the soundest perspective. Furthermore, governmental population control programs which derive from this perspective may not only solve the "wrong problem," but create other problems perhaps more serious in their impact upon human dignity and well-being than the population growth they are designed to stem. For example, in the wake of the campaign to convince people to have two or fewer children, will parents come to regard their children as less valuable than they otherwise might? What will be the consequence for a third or fourth child's self concept when the people around him affirm, via strong emphasis on the morality of the two-child norm, that his parents were remiss in allowing him to be born, or that he is a "surplus" child? Will an extended "educational" program on "overpopulation" reduce our respect for the individual human life? Will we adopt a set of values which exalt natural resources at the expense of human resources?

In the end, the energies, idealism, and resources devoted to altering people's ideas about family size in order to produce zero population growth, particularly in the more developed societies, may be in vain. It is not that they will not succeed; but even if zero population growth is achieved, many of the problems which supposedly derive from population size will still exist. Life is

10

short; *human energy and talent are limited; it is tragic that solutions to many of our most pressing problems will be postponed because despite the neo-Malthusian ideologies, the variance in social conditions attributable to population size alone proves to be so small. If our assessment of the evidence is correct, millions of well-meaning, talented people will have been caught up in a movement which focused on the wrong variable. In our opinion, the greater problem—we would not go so far as to say the greatest—as far as present knowledge will take us, is summarized beautifully in the following statement:*

> After all, children are not just transients in the world's boardinghouse, to be welcomed or turned away at the convenience of the older boarders. And if it is true that every newborn child should have a right to its share of food, it is also true that those who control the food supply should think twice before declaring that they no longer have enough for strangers and newcomers. In other words, the essence of the population problem—so far, at least—is not that mankind has propagated too many children but that it has failed to organize a world in which they can grow in peace and prosperity. Rich nations and poor alike have grossly misused the world's resources, both material and intellectual; neglected them, wasted them, and fought each other over how to share them. Thus the basic question is not how many people can share the earth, but whether they can devise the means of sharing it at all (Fredrich, 1971:59).

References

Ashmore, Harry
1971   "The day before doomsday." Center Report 4 (October):2.

Callahan, Daniel
1972   "Ethics and population limitation." Science 175 (February):494.

Center Conference
1971   "Population, world needs for food and fiber, and protection of the ecosystem." Center Report 4 (October):3.

Fadiman, Clifton, and Jean White
1971   "Introduction," by Harvey Wheeler in Eco-
            cide—And Thoughts Toward Survival. Santa
            Barbara: Fund for the Republic, Inc.

Fredrich, Otto
1971   "Population explosion: is man really doomed?"
            Time (September 13):58-59.

Grazia, Alfred de, Ralph E. Juergens, and Livio C. Stecchine
1967   The Velikovsky Affair: Scientism vs. Science.
            New York: University Books.

Greene, Wade
1972   "The militant Malthusians." Saturday Review
            (March 11):72.

Kuhn, Thomas S.
1962   The Structure of Scientific Revolution. Chicago:
            University of Chicago Press.

II.
"OVERPOPULATION":
THE WRONG PROBLEM

Introduction

Of course the gloomy wizards with their magical slide-rules may be right, but only a madman would surrender to their counsel of despair, with its brutal wrenching of social patterns and values, without exhausting every alternative. . . .

The goal is not survival but survival as human beings. The decisions are not technical, reserved to experts, but political and moral, demanding the intelligent participation of all of us. . . . The outcome of the human drama depends in large part upon whether, in the next decade, we devote our primary energies to multiplying and redistributing the bread or to reducing the number of guests at the table (Neuhaus, 1971:268-269).

The last sentence in the quotation nicely summarizes the fundamental difference between the Malthusian or neo-Malthusian approach to population problems and the non-Malthusian perspectives presented in this book. In the latter view, social problems derive primarily from the nature of social organization, rather than from such externalities as a built-in limit to the earth's capacity to provide human sustenance. Hopefully, a consequence of this approach will be increased attention to finding and using social structures or cultural patterns which will prove more effective than our present systems for feeding, educating, healing, pacifying, and uniting mankind. In contrast, the neo-Malthusians highlight population size as a chief, if not dominant, cause of present and

15

future woes, and too frequently their programs for resolving or preventing crises boil down to attempts to limit or reduce population size, or to fostering a fatalistic resignation that for at least part of the earth's population—usually the poorer part—war, famine, or pestilence are inevitable.

It is a major theme of this book, and of this chapter in particular, that this identification of population growth as the critical problem of our time is a misplaced alarm that threatens us in at least two ways. First, it diverts attention and resources from other problems, and solutions to those problems may not be discovered because they were cast in Malthusian terms. Second, there are the drastic costs to human freedom and dignity if many of the proposals for widespread population control are taken seriously and adopted. These threats are particularly disturbing in light of the questionable scientific status of the entire Malthusian argument. At best, it is an unsupported theory about the relationship between man and his environment. At worst, it is an untestable ideological dogma sold to an unsuspecting public in the name of science.

Both of the papers in Chapter 2 carry forth the introductory theme set in chapter 1, taking issue with the premature or simply incorrect identification of overpopulation as the critical problem. In chapter 1, we viewed some of the premises of modern neo-Malthusian movements as more than mere diversions, and suggested that adoption of the "overpopulation" ideology actually may impede the solution of pressing social problems. We questioned the wisdom of those who would "oversell" the gloomy view of the future in the name of saving men from themselves, and we questioned value systems which appear to exalt natural resources at the expense of human resources. Even if zero population growth were achieved, many of the problems presently said to derive from population growth would still be with us. Richard Neuhaus has made the same point in his book, In Defense of People:

> *Reducing population as the way to preserve a quality environment is an easy surrender in the face of historical challenge, a reversal of the process by which we have achieved our present level of civilization (which, for all its faults, has its advantages over what any other group of 200 million has ever enjoyed). Only a little reflection reveals the absurdity of thinking that we can have the present per capita use of*

resources but lower the total use by reducing population. It has been pointed out, for example, that if we were to use as much electricity per person as we did in 1960 without lifting the total produced above the 1940 level, the population of the United States would have to be cut back to 25 million. The prospect makes the goal of population growth zero appear ridiculously modest.

The specious but seductive logic of "People cause pollution, ergo fewer people = less pollution" suggests catchy slogans for the picket signs of the frightened affluent and also suggests disastrous social policies (Neuhaus, 1971:243).

In Chapter 2, "The Nonsense Explosion" by Ben Wattenberg describes the "overpopulation" crisis" as a political smokescreen which, in the U.S. at least, obscures many more legitimate concerns. By international standards the United States is not a crowded country, and many of the problems linked to population size really have to do with population redistribution. Population growth rates in this country are declining, and projections of the future population have recently been revised downward. Wattenberg agrees that the population will continue to grow. But, in contrast to the premise of the "Explosionists," he does not think that a larger U. S. population would necessarily be a bad thing. Social facilities depend on humans to create and staff them; more Americans will mean more teachers, more librarians, more nurses, and more construction workers. He also rejects the argument that it is the well-to-do who must limit their family size, pointing out that in the U.S. relatively affluent parents already produce barely enough children to replace themselves. In fact, given current patterns, "if the entire population were entirely affluent, we certainly would not be talking about a population explosion." Concern over population size as one aspect of the problems of the future is commendable, he writes, but to make a crisis of population growth is wrong, even foolhardy, because it allows politicians to sidestep the major problems of our time—including the massively expensive changes necessary to clean up the environment, reduce racial discrimination, and make our cities livable—by attributing the problems to too many people.

In his article, Harold Barnett assesses elements of Malthusian theory from the standpoint of modern economics and economic history. Among his conclusions: (1) In virtually all of the developed or developing nations for which adequate data are available to chart long-term trends, increasing population has been ac-

companied by increasing economic output per capita. (2) "Future generations are not adversely affected by the increase in numbers. When grown up, the extra bodies work as well as consume." (3) Fertility in advanced countries is likely to reflect families' realistic assessments of their economic capacity to care for their children. (4) The economic interest of future generations is better served by increasing economic production and improving the lot of the living rather than trying to hoard resources for the future. (5) Population growth is not likely to be restrained by environmental deterioration. (6) The cry that "there is not time" is not appropriate; the so-called "population bomb" does not have a short fuse. With increasing modernization, the world population will eventually level off or rise only slowly. "We have enough to do in sensibly managing our own birthrates and our own environments without presuming we are or should be making these decisions for future generations."

Thus, contrary to the Malthusian thesis, there is no reason to believe that in technologically advanced countries diminishing returns will accompany population growth, that there will be a shortage of natural resources, or that per capita income will be low. There will be problems of alleviating congestion and environmental deterioration, and these, like the problems of arms limitation or preventing nuclear catastrophes, will require capabilities for more effective world government.

Reference

Neuhaus, Richard
    1971   In Defense of People. New York: The Macmillan Co.

Overpopulation as a Crisis Issue*

Ben Wattenberg

As the concern about the environment has swept across the nation, the ghost of the "population explosion"—recently haunting only India and other ugly foreign places—has suddenly been domestically resurrected and we are again hearing how crowded it is in America.

Life magazine, for example, chose to launch the new decade with the headline "Squeezing into the '70s," announcing that, because of the crowds, "the despair of yesterday's soup line has been replaced by today's ordeal of the steak line." Two months later *Life* featured a story about a young New Jersey mathematician who had himself sterilized because he is "deeply worried by this country's wildly expanding population."

Crowded, crowded, crowded, we are told. Slums are crowded, suburbs are crowded, megalopolis is crowded, and more and more and more people are eating up, burning up, and using up the beauty and wealth of America—turning the land into a polluted, depleted sprawl of scummy water and flickering neon, an ecologi-

---

*Reprinted from *The New Republic*, April 4 and 11, 1970, pages 18-23. Copyright 1970 by Ben Wattenberg. Reprinted by permission of Harold Matson Company, Inc.

19

cal catastrophe stretching from the Everglades to the Pacific Northwest. Crisis. Crisis. Crisis.

That so very much of this is preposterous, as we shall see, should come as no real surprise to those who follow the fads of crisis in America. There are no plain and simple problems any more. From poverty to race to crime to Vietnam all we face are crises which threaten to bring down the world upon our heads. And now it is ecology/environment—which is a perfectly good problem to be sure—but with its advent comes dragged in by the heels our old friend the super crisis of the population explosion, which is not nearly as real or immediate a problem in America, and ends up serving unfortunately as a political smokescreen that can obscure a host of legitimate concerns.

While the rhetoric rattles on about where will we ever put the next hundred million Americans, while the President tells us that the roots of so many of our current problems are to be found in the speed with which the last hundred million Americans came upon us, while the more apocalyptic demographers and biologists (like Dr. Paul Ehrlich) are talking about putting still nonexistent birth control chemicals in the water supply, and about federal licensing of babies—the critical facts in the argument remain generally unstated and the critical premises in the argument remain largely unchallenged.

The critical facts are that America is not by any standard a crowded country and that the American birth rate has recently been at an all-time low.

The critical premise is that population growth in America is harmful.

In not stating the facts and in not at least challenging the premises, politicians, and planners alike seem to be leaving themselves open to both bad planning and bad politics. This happens by concentrating on what the problem is not, rather than on what the problem is. Let's, then, first look at the facts. The current population of the United States is 205 million. That population is distributed over 3,615,123 square miles of land, for a density of about 55 persons per square mile. In terms of density, this makes the United States one of the most sparsely populated nations in the world. As measured by density, Holland is about 18 times as "crowded" (at 975 persons per square mile), England is 10 times as dense (588 persons per square mile), scenic Switzerland seven

20

times as dense (382), tropical Nigeria three times as dense (174) and even neighboring Mexico beats us out with 60 persons per square mile. The U.S., by international standards, is not a very "crowded" country.

But density in some cases can be very misleading in trying to judge "crowdedness." The Soviet Union, for example, is less dense than the U.S. (29 per square mile), but has millions of square miles of uninhabitable land, just as do Brazil and Australia, two other nations also less densely populated than the U.S.

Of course, the U.S. also has large areas of land that are equally uninhabitable: the Rockies, the Western deserts, parts of Alaska and so on.

But while it is of interest to know that America has some land that is uninhabitable, what is of far more importance is that we have in the United States vast unused areas of eminently habitable land, land that in fact was inhabited until very recently. In the last eight years one out of three counties in America actually *lost* population. Four states have lost population: North and South Dakota, West Virginia, and Wyoming; and another two states, Maine and Iowa, gained less than one percent in the eight years. Furthermore, three out of five counties had a net out-migration; that is, more people left the county than came in.

These counties, the net-loss counties and the net-out-migration counties, are the areas in America where the current hoopla about the population sounds a bit hollow. These are the areas, mostly rural and small town, that are trying to attract industry, areas where a smokestack or a traffic jam signifies not pollution but progress, areas that have more open space around them for hunting and fishing than before, and areas where the older people are a little sad because, as they tell you, "the young people don't stay around here anymore."

This human plaint tells us what has been happening demographically in the United States in recent years. It has not been a population explosion, but a population redistribution. And the place people have been redistributing themselves to is a place we call "suburb."

In less than two decades the proportion of Americans living in suburbs has gone from less than a quarter to more than a third.

But even the total increase in population—rural, city, and suburb—is misleading. The big gains in population occurred 10 and

American Population by Residence

| | Population | | Increase |
	1950	1968	1950-1968
Residing in central city	35%	29%	6 million
Residing in suburb	24%	35%	32 million (!)
Residing in small cities, towns and rural	41%	36%	9 million
	100%	100%	47 million

15 years ago; today growth is much slower. Thus, in calendar year 1956, the U.S. population grew by 3.1 million, while in calendar year 1968 population went up by 2.0 million—and in a nation with a larger population base.

What has happened, simply, is that the baby boom has ended. When the G.I.'s came home after World War II, they began begetting large numbers of children, and Americans went on begetting at high rates for about 15 years. The best index of population growth in the U.S. is the fertility rate, that is, the number of babies born per thousand women aged 15-44. In 1940, the fertility rate was 80, just a few points above the 1936 Depression all-time low of 76. Ten years later, in 1950, the baby boom had begun and the fertility rate had soared to 106, an increase of 32 percent in just ten years. It kept climbing. In 1957, it reached 123, up more than 50 percent in two decades.

But since 1957, the rate has gone steadily down: to 119 in 1960, to 98 in 1965, to 85.7 in 1968, not very much higher now than in Depression times. The estimated fertility rate for 1969 was down slightly to 85.5 and there is no reason now to think it will go up, although, as we shall see, it may sink further.

When measured by another yardstick, the "percent national population growth" (birth plus immigration less deaths), the American population is now growing by about 1.0 percent per year; just a decade ago it was growing by 1.8 percent per year. That may not sound like much of a difference, .8 percent, but in a nation of 200 million people it means 16 million fewer people over a single decade!

With all this, however, comes another important set of facts: our population *is* still growing. At the reduced growth rate there are now about two million people being added to our popu-

22

lation each year. This may even go up somewhat in the next few years as the baby-boom babies become young adults and—roughly simultaneously—parents. Moreover, a growing population, even a slowly growing population, grows by larger numbers as it grows. As the two hundred million Americans become two hundred and fifty million Americans there is a proportionately greater number of potential mothers, more babies, and the incremental two million new Americans per year can rise to 2½ or 3 million new Americans even with a relatively low growth *rate*.

The current, most likely projection of the Census Bureau of the U.S. population in the year 2000—three decades hence—hovers somewhere in the 280-290 million range. That means there will be about 75-85 million more Americans than today, which is many millions more indeed, although not quite the round "hundred million" figure everyone is talking about.

It must be stressed, however, that this is only a projection: it could be high, it could be low. The figure is derived from a series of four alternate projections based on different levels of fertility rates issued by the Census Bureau in 1967. Already the highest two projections—calling for 361 million and 336 million—are out of the question. The third projection called for 308 million and that too now seems high, as it called for a fertility rate of 95 in 1970—about 10 points higher than the 1969 rate. The lowest of the four projections calls for a fertility rate of 84.6 in 1970 (roughly where we are) and yields a population of 283 million in the year 2000.

But even that is not an immutable figure by any means. Just as the first three of the alternate projections quickly proved themselves false, so it may be that Series D may prove high. After all, the Hoover Depression, in an era with far less effective birth control technology, brought fertility rates down to 76. What might a Nixon Recession do in an era of pills, loops, diaphragms, liberalized abortion?

Already the Census Bureau—quite properly—is preparing to revise its projections for the future. The new set of alternate projections—which will bracket the newer, lower, fertility rates—will unquestionably be lower, with a low-end possibility in the general area of 265 million for the year 2000. That too will only be a projection, based on assumptions which may or may not prove valid. But if such a low fertility rate does indeed occur, population

23

in the U.S. would then begin to level off after the year 2000 as the last of the baby-boom babies have completed their own families. The U.S. might then be in an era of near stable population along the lines of many Western European nations.

But even that is sixty million more Americans in just three decades—more than the population of Great Britain today.

Those, then, would seem to be the elementary facts. More Americans, although probably not as many as we may have been led to believe. More Americans, but not necessarily inhabiting a statistically crowded country.

With these facts, we can now turn to the premise set forth by the Explosionists; i.e., more Americans are bad.

Are they? My own judgment is—not necessarily.

There are a number of points made by the Explosionists and they can only be briefly examined here.

Because population growth is currently being linked to environmental problems, we can look there first. The Explosionists say people, and the industry needed to support people, cause pollution. Ergo: fewer people—less pollution.

On the surface, a reasonable enough statement; certainly, population is one of the variables in the pollution problem. Yet, there is something else to be said. People not only cause pollution, but once you have a substantial number of people, it is only people that can solve pollution. Further, the case can be made that *more people* can more easily and more quickly solve pollution problems than can fewer people. For example: let us assume that $60 billion per year is necessary for national defense. The cost of defense will not necessarily be higher for a nation of three hundred million than for a nation of two hundred million. Yet the tax revenues to the government would be immensely higher, freeing vast sums of tax money to be used for the very expensive programs that are necessary for air and water pollution control. Spreading constant defense costs over a large population base provides proportionately greater amounts for nondefense spending. The same sort of equation can be used for the huge, one-time capital costs of research that must go into any effective, long-range antipollution program. The costs are roughly the same for 200 or 300 million people—but easier to pay by 300 million.

Lake Erie, the Hudson River, the Potomac, are ecological slums today. If the U.S. population did not grow by one person over the

24

current 205 million Americans, these bodies of water would *still* be ecological slums. These waters, and any others now threatened, will be decent places only if men are willing to devote resources to the job. That is not a function of population growth, but of national will. It can be done if we, as a nation, decide that we want it done and are willing to pay for it. It is as simple as that and it has relatively little to do with whether the national decision involves 200 or 250 or 300 or 350 million Americans. It should also be remembered that pollution occurs in underpopulated places as well: in Sydney, Australia, today, in medieval Europe, in ancient Rome.

Next, the Explosionists view more people as a crisis because of all the demands they will make upon the society. So many new schools, so many more hospitals, more libraries—services and facilities which we are having difficulty providing right now. Similarly with "new towns." If we are to avoid vast and sprawling megalopolitan swaths, we are told, we must build 100 brand-new towns in thirty years. Unfortunately, we've only been able to construct a few in the last couple of decades—so, alas, what possible chance do we have to make the grade in the years to come?

What this argument ignores, of course, is that it is not governments who really create schools, hospitals, libraries and even new towns. It is *people* who create and build. People pay taxes; the taxes build and staff the schools; the more people, the more need for schools, *and* the more taxes. In an uncanny way it usually works out that every child in America has his own set of parents, and a school to attend. In a nation of a hundred million there were roughly enough schools for the children then present, at two hundred million the same was true and, no doubt, it will hold true at three hundred million. Nor will quality suffer because of numbers; quality suffers if taxpayers aren't willing to pay for quality and it is not harder for 300 million Americans to pay for quality schools for their children than it is for 230 million to buy quality schooling for their offspring.

And those "new towns"? *People* make them too. That's just what's been happening in America in the last few decades. We call them "suburbs," not "new towns," and as the earlier data showed, 32 million Americans opted for this "decentralization" over the past 18 years, long before it became a fashionable, political fad word. People did this because people are not damn fools and when they had a chance to trade a rural shack or an urban tenement for a green quarter acre in suburbia, they did so, even though the faddists then were saying that suburbia was not "decentralized" (which is allegedly good), but "conformist" (which is allegedly bad). What smug town planners like to call urban sprawl, represents uncrowded, gracious living for the former residents of city slums and the quality of such suburban life doesn't necessarily deteriorate if another new suburb rises down the road a mile.

Now, suburbs are not identical to the new town concept. The new towns, in theory, are further away from big cities, they are largely self-contained and they are designed from scratch. But, curiously, as many jobs move from the central cities, suburbs are becoming more and more self-contained; as metropolitan areas get larger, the newer suburbs *are* quite far from central cities; and there are some fascinating new start-from-scratch concepts in planning that are now materializing in suburban areas, particularly in some of the massive all-weather, multitiered, multimalled shopping centers.

All this is not to denigrate new towns or the idea of population decentralization. Far from it. The effort here is only to point out that people often act even faster than their governments in seeking their own best interests. If it is new towns near a babbling brook that Americans feel they want, if the country remains prosperous, some patriot will no doubt step forward and provide same, and even have salesmen in boiler rooms phoning you to sell same. The process is mostly organic, not planned/governmental. It works with 200 or 250 or 300 or 350 million Americans.

There is next the "resources" argument. It comes in two parts. Part one: many of our resources are finite (oil, coal, etc.); more people obviously use more resources; the fewer the people, the less the drain on the resources. Part two: we Americans are rich people; rich people use more resources; therefore, we must cut back population particularly fast, and particularly our rich population.

The resources problem is difficult to assess. A demographer now in his sixties seemed to put it in perspective. "Resources are a serious problem," he said. "We've been running out of oil ever since I was a boy."

The fact is, of course, sooner or later we *will* run out of oil;

26

perhaps in thirty years or fifty years, or a hundred years or two hundred years. So too will we run out of *all* nonrenewable resources—by definition. We will run out of oil even if population growth stops today and we will run out of oil, somewhat sooner, if population growth continues. Whether oil reserves are depleted in 2020 or 2040 or 2140 does not seem to be of critical importance; in any event a substitute fuel must be found—probably nuclear. If no adequate substitute is developed, then we (all us earthmen) will suffer somewhat regardless of numbers.

Part two, that *rich* people are the real menace both resource-wise and pollutionwise , has recently been particularly stressed by Dr. Jean Mayer who advises the President hungerwise but would not seem to be fully up to date demographywise.

For the simple fact is that wealthier people generally have far fewer children than poorer people. With current mortality rates, population stability is maintained if the typical woman has on the average 2.13 children. In a 1964 Census Bureau survey among women who had completed their childbearing years, it was shown that families with incomes of $10,000 and over had 2.21 children, just a trifle over replacement. This compared with 3.53 children for the poorest women. Since 1964, fertility rates have gone down among young women, and it is possible that when these lower rates are ultimately reflected as "completed fertility" we may see that affluent American women of the future just barely replace their own number, if that.

In short, current population patterns show that affluent people do not cause rapid population growth. And if the entire population were entirely affluent, we certainly would not be talking about a population explosion. Further, if the entire population were affluent *and* committed to combatting pollution, we wouldn't be talking about a pollution explosion either.

What then is Dr. Mayer's prescription? Is he against affluent people having babies but not poor people, even though the affluent have relatively few anyway? Or perhaps is it that he is just against the idea of letting any more poor people become affluent people, because they too will then consume too many resources and cause more pollution?

There are two important points that run through most of the above. First is that the simple numbers of people are not in them-

27

selves of great importance in the United States. There is no "optimum" population as such for the U.S., not within population ranges now forecast in any event. Whether we have 250 million people or 350 million people is less important than what the people—however many of them there are—decide to do about their problems. Second, the population problem, at least in the United States, is an extremely long-term proposition, and in a country of this size and wealth, there is more flexibility in solving the potential demographic problems than might be assumed from the current rhetoric of crisis.

To be sure, much of the concern about population growth is sane, valid, and important. Certainly the concept of family planning—which for years had been a political stepchild—is now coming into the mainstream, and properly so. That every family in America should at least have the knowledge and the technology to control the size of its family as it sees fit seems beyond question. This knowledge and this technology, previously available largely to middle-class and affluent Americans, is now being made available to poorer Americans through growing federal programs. Some of the more militant black leaders have called it "genocide," but that is a rather hollow charge when one realizes (a) that the poorest American women now have about 50 percent more children per capita than do middle-class Americans and (b) that more children than can be properly provided for is one of the most classic causes of poverty in America and around the world.

Certainly too, population growth must sooner or later level off. While America could support twice its current population and probably four times its current population—growth can obviously not go on forever and it is wise to understand this fact now rather than a hundred years from now. It is also wise to begin to act upon this knowledge, as indeed we have begun to act upon it. It is, accordingly, difficult to complain about the suggestions for legislation to make conditions easier for women to get and hold decent jobs—the thought being that easier access to employment will slow the birth rate. Our problems in the future probably will be easier to handle with somewhat fewer people than with somewhat greater numbers.

But what is wrong, and dangerous, and foolhardy is to make population a crisis. Doing so will simply allow too many politicians to take their eyes off the ball. When Explosionists say, as they do, that crime, riots, and urban problems are caused by "the population explosion," it is just too easy for politicians to agree and say sure, let's stop having so many babies, instead of saying let's get to work on the real urban problems of this nation. (As a matter of general interest it should be noted that the riot areas, the high-crime areas, the areas of the most acute urban problems *are areas that are typically losing population.* For example, special censuses in Hough and Watts showed population *loss.* Given that kind of data it is hard to accept the Explosionist notion that crowding causes crime.)

When the Explosionists say, as they do, that Yosemite and Yellowstone are crowded and that there is a vanishing wilderness because of too many people—they are wrong again. When visits to national parks have gone up by more than 400 percent in less than two decades, while population growth has gone up by about 30 percent, over the same time, then Yosemite isn't crowded because of population but because of other factors. When you have a nation where a workingman can afford a car, and/or a camper-trailer, when you give him three weeks paid vacation, provide decent roads—there would be something to say for the fact that you have indeed set up the society that Old Liberals, Trade Union Variety, lusted for, and who is to say that is bad? Again, if the population-crisis rhetoric is accepted it becomes too easy to say that the way to an uncrowded Yosemite is to have fewer people, and forget about the hard and far more costly problems of creating more recreation areas, which are needed even if our population does not rise.

When the Explosionists say, as they do, that it's because we have so many people that Lake Erie is polluted, then once again we are invited to take our eye off the tens-of-*billions*-of-dollars ball of environmental safety and we are simultaneously invited to piddle around with 25-*million* dollar programs for birth control, which are nice, but don't solve anything to do with Lake Erie.

Finally, we must take note of the new thrust by the Explosionists: population control. Note the phrase carefully. This is specifically not "family planning," where the family concerned does the planning. This is *control* of population by the government and this is what the apocalyptics are demanding, because, they say, family planning by itself will not reduce us to a zero growth rate. The more popular "soft" position of government control involves what is called "disincentives," that is, a few minor measures like changing the taxation system, the school system and the moral code to see if that won't work before going onto outright baby licensing.

Accordingly, the demographer Judith Blake Davis of the University of California (Berkeley) complained to a House Committee: "We penalize homosexuals of both sexes, we insist that women must bear unwanted children by depriving them of ready access to abortion, *we bind individuals to pay for the education of other people's children, we make people with small families support the schooling of others. . . .*" (Italics mine.)

Now, Dr. Davis is not exactly saying that we should go to a private school system or eliminate the tax exemption for children thereby penalizing the poor but not the rich—but that is the implication. In essence, Senator Packwood recently proposed just that: no tax exemptions for any children beyond the second per family, born after 1972.

The strong position on population control ultimately comes around to some form of governmental permission, or licensing, for babies.

Dr. Garrett Hardin, a professor-biologist at the University of California, Santa Barbara, says, "In the long run, voluntarism is insanity. The result will be continued uncontrolled population growth."

Astro-physicist Donald Aiken says, "The government has to step in and tamper with religious and personal convictions—maybe even impose penalties for every child a family has beyond two."

Dr. Melvin Ketchel, professor of physiology at Tufts Medical School writes in *Medical World News:* "Scientists will discover ways of controlling the fertility of an entire population . . . the compound . . . could be controlled by adjustments in dosage, [and] a government could regulate the growth of its population without depending upon the voluntary action of individual couples . . . such an agent might be added to the water supply."

And Dr. Paul Ehrlich of Stanford: "If we don't do something dramatic about population and environment, and do it immediately, there's just no hope that civilization will persist. . . . The world's most serious population-growth problem is right here in the United States among affluent white Americans. . . ."

What it all adds up to is this: why have a long-range manageable population problem that can be coped with gradually over generations when, with a little extra souped-up scare rhetoric, we can drum up a full-fledged crisis? We certainly need one; it's been months since we've had a crisis. After all, Vietnam, we were told, was "the greatest crisis in a hundred years." Piker. Here's a crisis that's a beauty: the greatest crisis in two billion years: we're about to breed ourselves right into oblivion.

Finally, look at it all from Mr. Nixon's point of view. It's beautiful. You (Mr. Nixon) take office and the major domestic problems, generally acknowledged, are the race situation and the (so-called) crisis of the cities. They are tough problems. They are controversial problems. They are problems that have given way only gradually, painstakingly, expensively, over the years. Your opponents are in a militant mood. They have been co-opted in Vietnam and you fully expect them to hold your feet to the fire on these tough domestic problems.

Apprehensively, you await the onslaught. And what is the slogan? No, it . . . can't be—but yes, it is. It's coming into focus. Read it: "Lower Emission Standards"! And in the next rank is another militant sign; and what does it say? It says, "Our Rivers Stink." . . .

Beautiful. Of course the environment *is* a real problem, an important problem; we knew that from Senator Muskie. Of course your President will respond to it, particularly since almost everyone is for it, particularly if it takes the heat off elsewhere. But even the environment issue is massively expensive—too expensive to do everything now that ought to be done now.

So wait a minute, you say, your opponents have been good to you so far, let's see how really helpful they'll be. And behold, here comes the cavalry.

And what do they say? The problem of pollution is really the problem of too many people. Let the opponents divide among themselves and let the opponents fight among themselves. Let there be a children's allowance, say some of your opponents. Nay, let there not be a children's allowance, it will encourage population growth. Let there be better public schools, say some of your enemies. Nay, let each family pay for their own schooling to discourage population growth. Let us help the poor, say the opponents; nay, let us penalize the poor for having too many children. Let then the Secretary of HEW go forth to the people and say,

"Ask not what your country can do for you, ask what you can do for your country—you shall have two children no more, no less, that is your brave social mission in America."

I imagine there have been luckier Presidents, but I can't think of any.

Population Problems: Myths and Realities*

*Harold J. Barnett***

A great deal is being written today about population growth, its economic and social effects, and the prospects for these. Much of what is written is nonsense. This is unfortunate. Misplaced alarms divert attention from more urgent social questions. From invalid diagnosis, wrong prescriptions are concocted. The serious problems relating to population are obscured by fuzzy thinking and colorful propaganda. The propensity for slogans, lack of objectivity, and absence of scientific analysis is disturbing to social scientists—as Gunnar Myrdal has put it, academicians have a professional peculiarity, "a faith that illusions are dangerous and truth is wholesome."

My design in this paper is to identify several major ideas concerning population problems and to analyze them. Some I find to be valid and some not. For most of the paper I confine discussion to the developed countries. The reason, as I elaborate later, is that I believe the economically underdeveloped nations will develop during the next couple of generations and will then share the population problems of the developed countries.

*Reprinted from *Economic Development and Cultural Change*, Vol. 19, No. 4, July 1971, Copyright 1971 by The University of Chicago, pp. 545-559.

**I am grateful to Professors David Felix, David Glass, and Burton Weisbrod for critical comments, both the ones I accepted and those I did not.

33

The "Law of Diminishing Returns"

Much contemporary and historical writing fears economic impoverishment over the long run due to the "law of diminishing returns." One form of the basic notion, deriving from Malthus, is that agricultural land and other natural resources are scarce. Population growth presses against the limited land, and therefore man's level of living is impoverished from increase in his numbers. A somewhat different concept of natural resources limitation, from Ricardo, is that resources are used in the order of declining quality. As population grows, diminishing returns result from this fact. Both the Malthusian and Ricardian concepts are generally thought to be reinforced by resource exhaustion and ecological damage, thus aggravating the diminishing-returns tendency. For example, in 1863 W. S. Jevons wrote on the dangers of coal depletion and G. P. Marsh on attrition of ecological systems.

Diminishing-returns notions derive from classical economic models. In these, economic output is conceived to depend on the quantities of labor, capital, and useful natural resources. The natural-resource factor is viewed as being fixed or even declining in quantity or quality, while the labor factor increases without end. Ergo, declining product per laborer and per capita.

In the advanced nations, diminishing-returns doctrine is quite erroneous in explanation of long-term economic growth. The errors are pervasive in the assumptions and logic of the classical growth model and in our records of the economic history of these nations over the past 100 years or so. First, birth rates have slowed down as compared with the biological maximum rates which Malthus and Ricardo had contemplated. It cannot be assumed that an increasing population factor will inevitably press harder and harder, endlessly, on limited natural resources. There is no natural law which requires this. Second, the capital stock has increased much faster than population numbers. An increase in capital per worker obviously exerts force contrary to diminishing returns per worker. Third, natural resources have not been fixed in volume as an economic factor, nor have they declined in economic quality. Increased knowledge has greatly improved the availability, access, and usability of natural resources and therefore the products derived from them. The assumption that man will utilize best re-

34

sources first and then lesser ones, thereby descending a quality gradient as population grows, is erroneous in a dynamic world.

Ricardian economic scarcity requires that society be able to array the physically varying natural resources in a declining order of *economic* qualities and that the order remain invariant through time; that it use them in this order; and that the decline in economic quality not be permanently interrupted by access to indefinitely great expanses of unused resources of unchanging marginal economic quality. We consider these propositions:

1. Ordering resources according to economic quality clearly requires relating known and stable physical properties of resources to known and stable sociotechnical parameters in such a way as to arrive at a unique and permanent economic ordering. Yet historically, for example, copper and tin came into use early, iron later, and the light metals last. There is no reason to believe this is an order of declining economic quality. Consider, similarly, the order of use of energy commodities—first dung and wood, then peat, then coal, later oil and gas, now nuclear energy. If we view both knowledge (ignorance) and the stability (instability) of production parameters with hindsight, it would seem that success in translating physical properties into economic qualities should not be viewed as a fact.

2. Even if translation of physical properties into economic qualities were always successful, does society necessarily use resources in this order? For a number of reasons, the answer would seem to be "not always." Impediments are international trade barriers, modern governmental reservations of resources, distances from population centers (recognized by Ricardo as an influence distinct from intrinsic physical properties), and institutional obstacles. But this is not to deny that where economic quality can be determined to be a function of physical properties there is powerful economic motivation to use resources in order of physical properties.

3. Assume now use in declining order of economic quality. Is the decline necessarily an economic continuum? It is relatively so for certain things, particularly if these are defined narrowly, like northeastern cherry wood or high-grade manganese in Virginia. But it is not for others, such as seawater magnesium, taconite, aluminum clays, low-grade manganese ores, lateritic nickel, urani-

35

um in granite, solar energy, etc. Many of our modern mineral resources are quality plateaus of enormous extent.

4. The composition of output has changed greatly. Some newer types of output are less resource intensive. Economic pressure on the more fixed types of resources have moderated or diminished and have shifted to more plentiful resources.

Finally, and in summary, pervasive changes in knowledge, technology, social arrangements, economic institutions, market sizes, and the overall sociophysical environmental context have occurred in the advanced nations. The classical economists omitted sociotechnical change from their economic growth models or underrated its significance and powers.

In Malthus's and Ricardo's time, and to a considerable extent through the nineteenth century, a considerable part of "final" or virtually final output was agricultural goods—foodstuffs, natural fibers, timber, game, etc. To this extent, increase in these outputs could be, and was, viewed as identical with economic growth. Again there was a simple answer as to how these goods would be further processed. They would be *mechanically* shaped from the gifts of nature—the wheat grain would be taken out; the hide separated from the meat; the timber sawed to size; the fibers combed, twisted, and woven; etc. Turning to the derivation of the basic substances from nature, man's role here also was a *mechanical one.* Thus, if a man stood on a square mile of land, or a nation on 3 million, the natural resources relevant for economic activity could be easily identified and measured. They were acres of cropland or pasture, board feet of standing timber, etc.

What has since happened in advanced nations to the meaning of final goods, the methods by which they are produced, and the definition of natural resources is so profound that we find the novelty difficult and seek simplification in possibly archaic analogies. With respect to the meaning of goods, more than 90 percent of the increase in real gross national product in the United States since 1870 has been of nonagricultural origin. As to the method of transforming materials into final goods, this has become far less a purely mechanical one and to a considerable degree a controlled heat or electrochemical process. Finally, the natural resource building blocks have changed radically—they are atoms and molecules. The natural resource input is to a far less degree acres, and to a far greater degree particular atmospheric and other molecules.

This has changed the meaning of "natural resources" for societies which indeed have modern technologies and access to capital. We now look more at contained molecules of iron, magnesium, aluminum, coal, nitrogen, etc., and at their naturally existing chemical combinations, than at acres or board feet. While in a sense the same ultimate world limits still exist, in a more significant sense they do not. How many taconite iron atoms or seawater magnesium atoms and bromine molecules constitute plenitude and how many scarcity? Further, in a significant degree even the ultimate limits are different from Malthus's and Ricardo's. Their natural resources were conceived for a two-dimensional world nourished by acreage. Ours is a three-dimensional one sustained by subsurface resources. Their society could reach natural resources only insignificant distances above and below the acres. We have multiplied our "reach" by a factor of many thousands.

None of the foregoing proves that increases in population numbers are "desirable," or that nonincreases would be undesirable. Rather, our need is to controvert simple-minded diminishing-returns views with logic and facts. The fact is that, in virtually all of the developed or developing nations for which we have long-term economic growth data, increases in economic output per capita have occurred and almost always have accompanied increases in population.

Prospective Children—Their Use of and Contribution to Economic Resources

Visualize prospective children as users of and contributors to economic output. If children are conceived and born, what effect would they have on economic output and incomes per capita in advanced nations?

In such economies the child is a consumer of economic resources for the first 15 to 20 years or so of his life, but he is not a producer. His parents can thus expect to be poorer in their own consumption if they conceive and bear him. The contemporary society in general will also be poorer in consumption per capita; it will have to devote to him public resources (e.g., for schools) which otherwise the adults could have used for themselves. We see that children reduce the level of economic living for the parents and the *contemporary* society which produces and rears them.

But it is not true that the next or later generations are impoverished by births in the current generation. The current generation's children grow into working adults. In the absence of diminishing returns, they at least meet their own needs. More likely, they produce more economic goods than they consume during their working lives. We reach an important conclusion: Only the generation which produces the children experiences adverse economic impact from having these children. Future generations are not adversely affected by the increase in numbers. When grown up, the extra bodies work as well as consume. In the absence of diminishing returns, real output per capita does not decline.

Individual Family Planning

In this section we discuss individual family costs and benefits from children; in the next, society's costs.

We have just seen that the begetting of children reduces the goods and services real income level per capita of the family during the period of childhood and adolescence relative to what it would otherwise have been. Then why do people have children? The reason is that total welfare—economic plus all other aspects of welfare—is likely to have increased for the parents.

We reason thus: The great bulk of adults in the United States and other developed nations is literate, educated, and at least somewhat individualistic. Birth control techniques have been developed very rapidly in efficiency and economic availability in the past several decades. In each case of sexual intercourse, the couple usually has a very clear choice as to whether or not to avoid conception of a child. That is, the couple may be expected to have the will and wit to make a sensible decision and the opportunity to do so. In the great majority of families the number of children does not exceed the number desired. If the couple chooses to expose the woman to pregnancy, this will usually be done deliberately. It will be because, in the great bulk of the cases, the anticipated pleasure of having another child exceeds the anticipated sum of economic and all other costs. The economic costs to the family are rather readily apparent and probably well anticipated. Parents will not choose to have more children than they can economically provide for in their view of economic adequacy. While couples with no children may underestimate the psychic burdens of raising

38

children, couples with one or more children are likely to anticipate these difficulties rather well.

What this leads to for developed nations are these conclusions: (a) couples are likely to make rational benefit and cost decisions as to whether to avoid conception; (b) the means of avoidance are readily available now and are becoming even more universally available; and therefore, (c) the production of children as determined by the parents, at whatever number they choose, is likely to be a rational and appropriate decision for the parents.

In summary to this point, then, we have reasoned that the production and rearing of children can reduce incomes per capita. But it will do so only for the period from children's birth to their entrance into the work force. The advent of children will not reduce income per capita in the future generations. The family decision to have children in an advanced country such as the United States is likely to be a rational one in the sense that there will not be more children in a family than the parents can economically care for on standards which the family views as appropriate.

Social Costs Not Borne by the Parents

The parents' rational, foresighted decision, however, may not be rational for society. The reason is that there are costs for society in the production and rearing of the children which are borne by the contemporary society but not by the specific parents. Such costs are public service expenditures for education, health, recreation, and other public goods.

Visualize a couple with two children and contemplating having a third. In a significant sense they are casting up for the family the accounts for economic and psychic benefits versus economic and psychic costs. If they think the family benefits will exceed their family costs, they decide to have another baby. The difficulty is that they have omitted from consideration a large volume of costs which society will bear for them. Nor will they properly assess these costs against their decision on the grounds that they pay taxes and are members of society. Their tax bill will be no smaller if they refrain from having the child (indeed, if they do beget him their tax bill may be smaller because of tax exemptions and deductions).

It is not my purpose to assess the volume of social costs omitted from the family calculation beyond indicating that they are substantial in size. Society's education cost alone may total $15,000 per child, at current price levels. Society allocates considerable sums in aid to dependent children, public and clinic health services, etc. We have thus identified an important respect in which an advanced society of rational, foresighted, individualistic people will tend to beget too many children. How serious is this dilemma, and is it likely to get better or worse?

The strong trend toward improved social services in advanced countries operates to cause overpopulation, relative to numbers which rational, foresighted families would choose if they individually carried all the costs of their begetting decisions. As society advances and becomes more affluent, it calls for more than proportionate increases in social services—education, health, parks, highways. We desire to buy more of our economic needs communally with tax dollars. The tax assessments tend much more to be levied against income and wealth than against numbers of children.

Each family, rich or poor, experiences, relatively, a smaller cost per child of its own than the costs which the child inflicts on society. That is, the tax bill the family experiences is virtually the same whether *that family* has another child or not. But while the error in calculation occurs in every family, it is of much greater influence for poor families than for rich ones. In the rich family the *economic* elements of the calculation of benefit versus cost in having another child are of smaller importance to family welfare as compared to psychic elements, simply because economic income is very high and marginal dollars of small utility. In the poor family, contrariwise, the availability of public services for children at no cost, particularly education and health, make it possible for them to decide to have children whom otherwise they would not choose to bear and raise. Also, in addition to the stronger incentive from low cost, the children of families of low income are a substitute for pecuniary income and the pleasures money can buy.

In summary,* on the above reasoning, overpopulation may

---

*We have ignored the possibility that there might be social benefits beyond those counted by the specific family. DaVinci, Beethoven, Einstein, and other geniuses have enriched society beyond the pleasures which they provided for themselves and their immediate families.

result, *ceteris paribus* in an individualistic society in which individual families decide how many babies they will have but in which the overall society bears a significant portion of the cost of their rearing.

Obligation to Conserve Natural Resources for Economic Welfare of Future Generations

In this section we concentrate on productivity and economics. In the next, we consider environmental damage.

It is widely believed that natural resources should be physically conserved by all means, for otherwise the future will be economically impoverished. Renewable resources should not be drawn down but should be used at the highest possible level of sustained physical yield. Nonrenewable resources should be used only after renewable resources are fully employed—water power before coal, for example. Physical waste should be reduced wherever it is found. Current production should be constrained to retard the depletion of nonrenewable resources. So far as it is necessary to achieve these objectives, the economic freedom of private property owners, producers, and consumers—specifically freedom to engage in those short-horizon, self-interested behavior patterns which destroy resources or deplete them rapidly under laissez faire—should be restricted in favor of government regulation or ownership.

All of the foregoing is based on the premise that each society should leave the next generation economically as well off as possible and no less well off than it is. But for this objective preservation of specific natural resources is unlikely to be the efficient means. Resource reservation, if not economically meritorious on current calculations, will reduce the economic value of output through time. It may, by curbing research and capital formation, have a perverse effect on future output and welfare.

It is by no means necessary to reduce production today in order to increase production tomorrow. If, instead, current production is maintained and consumption is reduced in favor of research and investment, future production will be increased. Higher production today, if it also means more research and investment today, thus will serve the economic interest of future generations better than reservation of resources and lower current production.

41

The premise that the economic heritage will shrink in value unless natural resources are conserved is wrong for a progressive world. The opposite is true. In the United States, for example, over the period for which data exists the economic magnitude of the estate each generation passes on—the income per capita the next generation enjoys—has been approximately double that which it received. Therefore, resource reservation to protect the economic interest of future generations is unnecessary. There is no need for a future-oriented ethical principle to replace or supplement the economic calculations that lead modern man to accumulate primarily for the benefit of those now living. The reason, of course, is that the legacy of economically valuable assets which each generation passes on consists only in part of the natural environment. The more important components of the inheritance are knowledge, technology, capital instruments, and economic institutions. Far more than natural resources, these are the determinants of real income per capita. Even with respect to natural-resource wealth alone, as Edmund Jones remarked at the White House Conference of Governors which dealt with conservation in 1908, "we shall add far more to our natural resources by developing our ability to increase them than we can ever do by mere processes of saving."

If those now living devote themselves to improving society's productive power and also its capacity to reach decisions concerning the use of that power which will increasingly benefit themselves and their children, the value of the economic heritage will grow continually. To increase current real income, physical capital is accumulated. To satisfy his curiosity, man adds to society's intellectual capital. To enrich its own life, each generation strives to improve the health and education of its children, thereby augmenting society's human capital. And, in consequence of efforts to improve society's functioning as a productive enterprise, economic institutions and standards are rendered more effective. By devoting itself to improving the lot of the living, therefore, each generation, whether recognizing a future-oriented obligation to do so or not, transmits a more productive world to those who follow.

Congestion and Environmental Damage

A more productive world is not necessarily a better world, however. In a progressive society current rational calculations may suffice to serve the purely economic interests of the future as well as the present. But a serious noneconomic problem—environmental damage—has become of major concern, concurrent with man's strong progress in solution of his economic problems. Indeed it is largely because of the economic and technological successes of modern industrial societies and the processes by which they occur that environmental damages have become obtrusive and oppressive.

John Stuart Mill (1848) forsaw this difficulty more than a century ago in the following gentle plea:

> There is room in the world, no doubt, and even in old countries, for a great increase of population, supposing the arts of life to go on improving, and capital to increase. But even if innocuous, I confess I see very little reason for desiring it. . . . A population may be too crowded, though all be amply supplied with food and raiment. It is not good for man to be kept perforce at all times in the presence of his species. A world from which solitude is extirpated, is a very poor ideal. Solitude, in the sense of being often alone, is essential to any depth of meditation or of character; and solitude in the presence of natural beauty and grandeur, is the cradle of thoughts and aspirations which are not only good for the individual, but which society could ill do without. Nor is there much satisfaction in contemplating the world with nothing left to the spontaneous activity of nature; with every rood of land brought into cultivation, which is capable of growing food for human beings; every flowery waste or natural pasture ploughed up, all quadrupeds or birds which are not domesticated for man's use exterminated as his rivals for food, every hedgerow or superfluous tree rooted out, and scarcely a place left where a wild shrub or flower could grow without being eradicated as a weed in the name of improved agriculture.

Alan Paton (1953:3) and Henry Beston (1969) have posed the dilemma for modern industrial societies poetically:

> The grass is rich and matted, you cannot see the soil. It holds the rain and the mist, and they seep into the ground, feeding the streams in every kloof. It is well tended, and not too many fires burn it laying bare the soil. Stand unshod upon it, for the ground is holy being even as it came from the Creator. Keep it, guard it, care for it, for it keeps men, guards men, cares for men. Destroy it and man is destroyed.

> For man is of a quickening spirit and the earth, the strong, incoming tides and rhythms of nature move in his blood and being; he is an emanation of that journeying god the sun, born anew in the pale South and the hollow winter, the slow murmur and the long crying of the seas

are in his veins, the influences of the moon, and the sound of rain beginning. Torn from earth and unaware, without the beauty and the terror, the mystery, and ecstacy so rightfully his, man is a vagrant in space, desperate for the inhuman meaninglessness which has opened about him, and with his every step becoming less than man. Peace with the earth is the first peace.

The essence of the population-environmental damage problem is this. A couple implicitly tallies its prospective benefit-cost accounts in considering whether to have another child. It counts in the cost or disadvantage column the fact that the home will be a bit more crowded, that more clothes will have to be washed, that the plumbing will be worked a bit harder, etc. But it does not take into account in its decision to have a child the fact that the child may make the city more crowded, that a grove of trees will be cut to provide more housing, that more highways will have to be built. Even less will the accounts comprehend that, in order to avoid diminishing returns concurrent with increasing population, society will undertake industrial and technological changes which further increase congestion, the volumes of pollutants, and land disfigurement. These costs will not significantly enter the decision calculus on having a child for two reasons. First, that particular prospective child will contribute only imperceptibly to the city crowding, the increase in pavements, the loss of forests, etc. And second, the burden of even that tiny increase in city congestion will be shared by all the inhabitants of the city, not carried alone by the parents who beget him.

Each family will count no social cost in environmental deterioration in deciding to have another child. But from the aggregate of their decisions will indeed come congestion, pollution, etc., if the parents more than reproduce their own numbers. It is as if each person would stand on tiptoe in a parade so *he* could see better; or throw his candy wrapper in the street because obviously *his* candy wrapper alone would not clutter the landscape; or burn his leaves since obviously his doing so will not pollute the air much.

Some private actions (e.g., leaf burning or littering) which inflict social costs or burdens on society can be prevented by law. Other private actions are impossible or extraordinarily difficult to prevent by law. Begetting children is in the latter category. Laws which deny parents the opportunity to have children are not present in modern societies. The decision is virtually always a private, parental one.

44

However, society, through government actions and private groups, can exert substantial persuasion upon couples to limit their begetting. Indeed, most modern governments, religions, and medical groups, and a number of foundations and other private agencies strongly encourage and assist couples in family planning or planned parenthood. Undoubtedly these efforts do significantly reduce the number of births, and from that the extent of environmental deterioration is somewhat reduced. But family planning has as its purpose encouraging couples to have only the number of children *they* personally desire and they personally can care for. Rational family planning does not treat or solve at all the dilemma in which the environmental damage from a family decision to have a child will be borne by the whole society and not by the family which made the decision.

In summary, *ceteris paribus*, there is a very great likelihood that population growth will not be adequately restrained by the fact of environmental deterioration. There is no reason for the individual family to believe that the damage it experiences in its environment will be less if *it* refrains from having a child. Families will therefore not restrain their begetting children for this reason. This applies even if individual family planning or planned parenthood becomes universal and highly rational. Aside from enacting laws to overcome the population over-pressure on environment, it appears that governments, religions, and foundations have not even recognized that this is a problem which cannot be handled by present concepts of rational family planning or planned parenthood.

Finally, we must note that the problem of population overproduction causing environmental problems has a most troublesome time dimension. If the problem is a serious one at all, then it is serious for future generations as well as present ones and indeed a greater threat to the future than to the present. Each pair of children now born in excess of the number which merely stabilizes population increases congestion by two people during their childhoods. The congestion continues for their whole lives. And then they further increase congestion in their adulthood by the number of children which they in turn beget in excess of the population maintenance rate. In this sense the environmental damage consequence of population growth is a threat which is more harsh than the effects of population growth on output per capita. We noted earlier that society's output per capita was reduced only during the period of childhood, *ceteris paribus*, and was then restored

45

when children became workers. This is not so for environmental congestion and damage, which endures as long as the incremental people do.

Underdeveloped Countries

To this point we have discussed only the advanced nations. But the world's population problem includes the underdeveloped countries as well. Indeed much more than half of the world's population lives there. How should we modify and supplement the foregoing analysis to account for population in underdeveloped countries?

Three attributes of such economies cause us to be greatly concerned about their population increases during the next few generations. These are:

1. The desperate shortage of capital, as a factor of production and carrier of improved technology.
2. The high birthrate.
3. The great increase in population from gains in longevity.

We discuss each attribute in turn:

1. *Capital shortage*

In the advanced countries, increased capital per worker and improved capital devices are major in overcoming diminishing returns when population increases. In the underdeveloped countries, shortage of capital limits the extent to which increased population can be accommodated without significantly retarding gains in worker productivity. If population increases too fast, there is too little gain in capital per worker, and also too much of the scarce capital must be diverted to providing public services. Even as in an advanced economy, children absorb resources during childhood. But in the underdeveloped economy the impact of this diversion on worker productivity, technological change, and improved education is much harsher. There results, if population accretions are large, a much slower rate of gain in output per capita than would otherwise be the case.

2. *High birthrates*

The birthrate in underdeveloped countries are high for a variety

46

of reasons, including less rationality, capacity, and will for family planning. Also children are social insurance for the parents' old age, and they provide psychic income in the families who are poor in economic goods. And there are other reasons, such as a decline in family responsibility when a peasant economy is disrupted by outside contacts. The high birthrates impede capital formation for industry and education, technological advance, and progress toward low birthrates. They also increase more than proportionately the size of the dependent, nonworking population.

3. *Longevity*

The average length of life in underdeveloped countries is now quite low. From worldwide public health measures and medical advances, as well as from the beginnings of economic development, longevity is trending upward. From longevity gains, *ceteris paribus,* we can anticipate very great increases in population in these countries over the next few generations. If life expectancy at birth increased from say, thirty years to fifty or sixty years, it is obvious that the leverage on population numbers is very great. This is so even if the birthrate were to fall to two children per female child ever born, a rate which, in the absence of longevity change, would merely maintain the population at a constant level. However, as just discussed, birthrates in these countries considerably exceed this maintenance level and thus populations will increase from births and longevity. While the longevity gains are favorable in the sense that they provide more workers, they also provide more parents of childbearing age, and there is also needed more capital to maintain and improve productivity.

4. *Summary*

Populations in underdeveloped countries will be subject to considerable increase in the next couple of generations due to large longevity gains, high birthrates, and slow rates of economic progress. Assume that there is no severe thermonuclear war. Assume also that advanced nations will continue to assist the underdeveloped ones in public health and economic aid. Then it is virtually impossible that the population of presently underdeveloped nations would not increase enormously. The increase relative to the populations of the presently advanced countries will be large.

47

Despite the economic development-population increase difficulty, the economic history of the past 100 years tells us that economic advance does occur in the underdeveloped nations. The burst in world population size until each nation achieves a literate, educated, and economically advanced society is likely to be the end of the population explosion. Population may increase thereafter, but it will be at a more deliberate pace and with more deliberation. For with literacy, education, and economic development, and the ready availability of safe and efficient contraceptives, should come the rationality of family planning or planned parenthood, as it has already come to couples in the presently advanced nations. It would seem inevitable that the individual family would come to see advantage in limiting children's births to the number they could economically and psychologically properly care for. This is what has been happening in the presently advanced nations to all races, religions, and colors as contraceptive technology and availability have improved. Why should it not occur in the newer nations as they develop? It may be that population will not stabilize, but if it advances the increase will not be heedless on the part of couples.

The social and political world structures will, however, be much changed from today. Longevity gains are of trivial size, and the birthrates are lower in the advanced countries. The international political, social, economic, and racial consequences of the disparity in rates of growth among nations could be substantial. Far more than now the future world population will be Asiatic and African, yellow or brown or black, ambitious and aggressive in the new nations, experimental in economic systems, and quite divergent from the political philosophy of Bentham, Mill, or Jefferson, and of the United States and Western Europe.

Time Dimensions

It is frequently stated that population growth must be quickly brought under control; that the population bomb which can destroy the world has a short fuse. As compared with my view that populations will eventually level off or rise only slowly, others claim that there is not time.

Let us consider the time problem. We use the present rate of annual world population growth of about 2 percent per year. This gain rate includes both the effects of improved longevity and of birthrates in excess of what would be required merely to replace deaths and hold population constant if there were no changes in length of life. At this rate, population would double in about 35 years. Thus the present world population of almost 3.5 billions would become almost 7 billions in the year 2005. Relatively, more of the increases would occur in the presently undeveloped countries. For example, population in Asia and Africa is increasing at about 2 percent per year and in Latin America at 3 percent per year. At the time that longevity reaches 60 or 70 years in these underdeveloped areas, population gain from increase in length of life will become unimportant, and the rate of population increase will be much lower.

What of birthrates? Each decade more countries climb the development ladder. As they progress, according to the record of economic history, literacy and education improve, knowledge of and access to birth control become available, family incentives to planned parenthood increase, and individual families tend to move toward rationality in family planning. Thus, as we move through time, we also move in development, education, social change, and all other attributes of progressive societies. Increasingly as literacy, education, and access to contraceptives improve, so does rational family planning. More and more does reproduction take on attributes we call "humane and rational," that is, foresight, compassion, and deliberation.

How then can we believe that "there is not time"? How can we believe that in a developed society parents will choose to have children whom they expect to be unable to support, care for, sustain? Increasingly, each child is born out of a specific act of will. If only there be rationality in the intent, future population increase is no greater economic danger than it has been over the past hundred years or so in Europe, the United States, and other advanced societies where the economic standard of living has risen steadily. Growth of population numbers is not, in itself, an evil. It is only if there are, on balance, adverse effects that it merits social concern.

We conclude that an average population growth rate of any size does not march on with independent force all of its own. Malthus and Ricardo thought it did, to the very limit of animal existence. But this was because the great bulk of their society, recently torn and disrupted by the Industrial Revolution, had not yet emerged from its brutal state, from brutish satisfaction of subsistence and sexual hungers, and because there was absence of contraceptive devices, knowledge, or reason. The birthrate in advanced societies will be what people decide it to be, each night, each year, each generation. Intelligent, rational people will determine the statistic; the statistic does not generate the people. In modern societies, the biological and psychological forces toward reproduction are tempered by contraceptives and intelligence. It is not reproduction which should be feared, but inadequate knowledge, lack of reason, and mind-dulling poverty.

If we play out the numbers we began with earlier from a growth rate of 2 percent per year, the 7 billions of year 2005 would, *if the growth rate held constant* (i.e., assumedly overcoming cessation of gains from improved longevity by large increase in birthrate), become almost 14 billions in 2040. This seems like a large figure to me. If I were present (in spirit) and were to be asked, I would advise the grandchildren of my great grandchildren that it seemed to me that there were a lot more people in the world than there were when I was a boy and more than I would have thought desirable.

A major point, however, is that each future generation will choose its own birthrate. It will do so, not mindlessly as a grasshopper horde without regard for available vegetation, but individually, with explicit regard to its own and its children's welfare. As our generation in this rich country has chosen to change the relation of man, society, and nature, so may our descendants in their own fashion change this relation. It is naïve to expect future societies to choose a statistical birthrate according to our preferences. Neither their birthrate nor their environmental management is our decision. We have enough to do in sensibly managing our own birthrates and our own environments without presuming we are or should be making these decisions for future generations. The fear that there is not time because of diminishing returns is not well placed. The difficulty is not diminishing returns.

The difficulty is that the world, states, and even cities are becoming ungovernable, because of pressures which advanced technology and economic power place on political systems and governmental structures conceived in an earlier age. The real problem, I suggest, is that the technologically advanced world which has given us increasing returns has also released problems which so far our societies and governments have not learned to handle. These include, for example, international disorder and holocaust, revolution and civil wars in nations, and violence in cities. They also include environmental congestion and damage related in part to greatly increased population numbers.

Conclusions

For a technologically advanced world there is no reason to believe, because of population growth, that diminishing returns will have set in, that there will be a shortage of natural resources for production of extractive goods, or that income per capita will not be at high levels. The economic future as I see it will have a much larger world population, literate and educated populations in all nations, and incomes per capita ranging from the present levels in western Europe upward.

In summary, I foresee the world with a population problem of the type which presently exists in the advanced countries. The population difficulties will be: (a) that very large availabilities of public and social services for children without explicit cost to the children's specific parents induces a larger birthrate than would otherwise occur; (b) that national societies do not have the governmental capabilities to restrict the birthrate in order to avoid undue environmental congestion and deterioration; and (c) that in the world society composed of sovereign nation states there exist no world governmental capabilities for limiting population growth, just as there are not in the world society effective capabilities for limiting arms, or reliably preventing nuclear war, or avoiding other catastrophes or serious problems.

References

Beston, Henry
    1969   "Herbs and the earth." Quoted by David McCord in Harvard Today.

Mill, John Stuart
    1848   Principals of Political Economy. New York: Colonial Press.

51

Paton, Alan
  1950   Cry, the Beloved Country. New York: Charles
Scribner's Sons.

III.
HOW FULL
IS THE
EARTH?

Introduction

Many advocates of population control argue the Malthusian position that food production has not and cannot keep pace with population growth. Thus in editorializing about Norman Borlaug's 1970 Nobel Peace Prize for his contribution to world food production, the New York Times *noted that his accomplishment only postponed the coming crisis for a few years, and urged that the United Nations launch major population control programs "that might save the world from the catastrophe that a doubled population in the year 2000 would represent." Regardless of new developments in food production, so the gloomy refrain goes, pestilence, famine, or war is just around the corner unless there is massive population control.*

The first article in this section, Philip Low's "Prospects for Abundance: The Food Supply Question," provides extensive documentation for the position that there need be no shortage of food in the foreseeable future even if population growth continues. Professor Low points out that many countries where starvation formerly was a constant specter are now, as a consequence of the Green Revolution, self-sufficient or nearly so with respect to the production of grains. For example, India and Pakistan now raise enough wheat for their own needs; Mexico has been self-sufficient in wheat since the midfifties. Use of new strains of wheat and rice has greatly increased yields, and as other nations develop the technology to use the new grains the battle against hunger should be won.

Nor is there any reason to suppose that the relief afforded by the Green Revolution is merely temporary. Other potential break-throughs in food production discussed by Low include the development of potentially arable soil; development of water resources; irrigation via the use of desalined sea water; utilization of waste heat for soil warming in the colder climates; development of multicropping; development of high-protein foods; farming the seas; and synthesis of food.

Low presents extremely convincing evidence that present or future famines need not be the consequence of the inability to produce sufficient food, even for an increasing population. If such disasters do occur, it will be the result of faulty institutions of distribution, or of failure to develop the tremendous potentialities for increasing food production which scientists have foreshadowed for us. It seems obvious that increased efforts should be directed at dispensing the new technologies of food production to needy nations, and to develop adequate systems of food distribution. But too often the negativism of the neo-Malthusian perspective discourages such efforts to "multiply bread." Instead, "the underlying assumption is that the battle to feed the world's hungry is over. We must therefore simply refuse to accept the challenge" (Neuhaus, 1971:209-210).

Strong concern has been expressed that even if the food supply problem can be solved, the earth is a finite system and the resources, particularly energy resources, are rapidly being depleted. According to this view, eventually man will be left without much of his present material culture because the natural resources to maintain it are not available. Gardner's piece, "Natural Resources and Human Survival" reports that even if the alarmists' population projections are accurate, the world reserves in petroleum, natural gas, coal, water power, and nuclear energy are very large and are adequate to sustain the needs of mankind for centuries.

This does not suggest that we can afford to be wasteful in the utilization of these resources. But neither should people be required to suffer the mental anguish that results from being led to believe that the world is in imminent danger of running out of energy. Studies of energy sources and minerals at Resources for the Future indicate little evidence of increasing scarcity, to say nothing of rapid world depletion. Known reserves seem to keep pace with consumption and in many instances even increase. If reserves of liquid petroleum, natural gas, and solid fossil fuels such as oil shale, tarsands, and coal are aggregated, it is clear that man's energy needs can be met for hundreds of years in the future. Possibilities for development of hydroelectric power and nuclear energy, as well as the potentialities of solar and geothermal energy, extend the period of abundance in energy reserves far into the future.

In addition, concern is often expressed about the depletion of nonrenewable minerals. Reserves of iron, aluminum, and manganese are very large and no shortages are anticipated until well after year 2000 even at extrapolated rates of consumption based on current trends. Reserves of copper, lead, and zinc are not so plentiful, but possibilities exist for substitution for these metals in most production processes and for greater emphasis upon recycling them.

In "Natural Resources, People and the Quality of Life," Behan argues that the equation equating quality of life to limited resources divided by population is invalid. He contends that this simple-minded approach, which he labels "population myopia," retards the search for other solution by focusing only on population size. He rejects the notion that resources are finite and limited, and argues that at present man is utilizing only a very small portion of "spaceship earth." Most of the mass constituting this earth and its atmosphere is labelled neutral stuff, as man at present does not utilize it. Behan suggests that as technology advances we will discover uses of this neutral substance to satisfy man's needs. He reminds the reader that electricity, coal and gas were on this earth with man for a very long time before he discovered how to use them. He suggests that unlimited resources are available; the only limitations are technological. Behan concludes that for all practical purposes resources are not limited or finite but await man's creativity to unlock their potential.

In summary, these three articles are not intended to be exhaustive, but they do offer hope for the future, if we are serious about preventing famines and insuring sufficient resources to maintain or improve the quality of life for all mankind.

Reference

Neuhaus, Richard
    1971   In Defense of People. New York: The Macmillan
               Company.

Prospects for Abundance: The Food-Supply Question

Philip F. Low

In 1798, an English economist and clergyman, Thomas Malthus (1926), wrote a book entitled *Essay on Population*. In it he predicted that, because population increases geometrically (1, 2, 4, 8, 16, 32, etc), whereas, the food supply increases arithmetically (1, 2, 3, 4, 5, 6, etc.), a time would come when there would be famine unless war and pestilence killed people off or unless they exercised "moral restraint," meaning sexual continence. In other words, he predicted that, unless people stopped multiplying, there would not be enough food, regardless of how hard they worked to produce it.

But Malthus's fearful prediction has not yet been fulfilled. Although the world's population has continued to increase at a phenomenal rate (it now approximates 3.5 billion), the overall food supply has kept pace. Fortunately for mankind, in the mid-nineteenth century the experiments of men like Baron von Liebig ushered in the age of scientific agriculture. As illustrated in Figure 1, the yields of crops have been increasing rapidly ever since. Except in localized areas for short periods of time, there has not been famine.

Agricultural Research and Yield Takeoff

In the first half of the present century, agricultural research

59

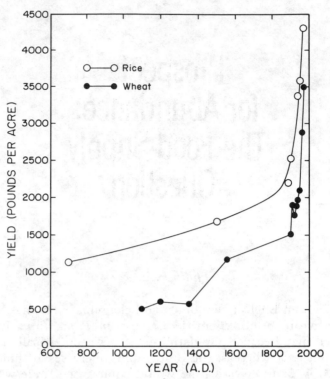

Figure 1.   Rice yields in Japan and wheat yields in Britain since early times (Chandler, 1969; Barrons, 1971, respectively).

gained momentum, especially in the developed countries. By the midthirties, the result was a dramatic yield takeoff, which is illustrated in Figure 2.

As noted by Brown (1965:3-22)

> Once underway, yield takeoffs appear to be irreversible except in time of war or some similar disaster. Thus far, all have continued indefinitely — the rising yield trends have not leveled off or shown any tendency to level off. If anything, the rate of yield increase tends to accelerate as a country becomes more advanced.

Hence, in the developed countries, food production has outstripped population growth and surpluses have developed. In an effort to prevent these surpluses, land has been taken out of production. Figure 3 provides an interesting portrayal of the rela-

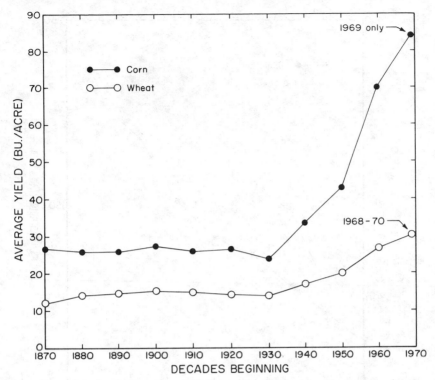

Figure 2.   One hundred years of U.S. corn and wheat production by decades (Barrons, 1971).

tion between population and the amount of land utilized for agriculture in the United States. A recent assessment (Barrons, 1971:33-39) leads to the conclusion that, in this country, for each acre tilled today another acre is available for optional uses because of advances in crop production technology. Had these advances not occurred, nearly 300 million more acres of land would be needed to grow the food now being produced.

The situation has been different in the developing countries. Here the results of agricultural research have not been fully applied. Among the reasons are lack of capital, low educational level, unavailability of fertilizers and pesticides, inadequate transportation, absence of storage facilities, and poor markets. Therefore, yields have changed little from year to year. But the population has continued to increase, especially since the turn of the century. Better sanitation and medical care have reduced the death

61

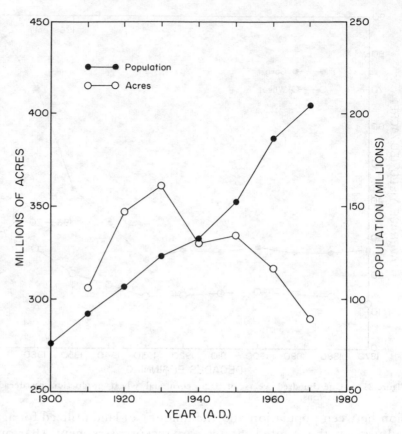

Figure 3. Effect of increased yields on ratio of crop acreage harvested to population; United States, 1910-70 (Barrons, 1971).

rate while the birth rate has remained steady. Consequently, until recently, the food supply did not keep pace with population growth and millions of people lived in constant fear of hunger. Only the assistance of developed countries, especially the United States, has prevented widespread disaster.

The disparity between the rates of increase in food supply and population in large areas of the world has produced a revival of Malthus's theory. There has been much alarm and excitement over the so-called population explosion. Fortunately, however, another yield takeoff has occurred recently, and this time it is occurring in the developing countries. It has been called the Green Revolution.

In 1944 the Rockefeller Foundation sent four young scientists to Mexico to help a hungry country feed itself. In 1970, one of these scientists, Norman Borlaug, received the Nobel Peace Prize for what was accomplished under his leadership. In the intervening years, varieties of wheat were developed which, compared to standard varieties: (1) have shorter, stiffer straw and, hence, can respond to larger applications of fertilizer without lodging (falling over); (2) are adapted to a wider range of climates and day lengths; (3) put forth a greater number of fertile florets per spikelet and tillers per plant, and; (4) are more resistant to diseases and insects (Reitz, 1970:952-955). The net result is that they have a higher yield potential, double or triple that of the standard tall-strawed varieties. Largely because of them, and the necessary applications of fertilizer, water, etc., the average per-acre yield of wheat in Mexico increased nearly fourfold between 1944 and 1967 and total production increased sevenfold. The country became self-sufficient in this grain in 1956 (Borlaug, 1968:1-36), and has remained so ever since.

The impact of the so-called Mexican or double-dwarf wheats has not been limited to Mexico alone. In 1965 they were exported, along with the associated technology, to countries like India and Pakistan. Because of their great adaptability, they flourished there (Borlaug, 1968:1-36). For the first time in history, India and Pakistan are now raising enough wheat for their own needs. Further, it appears that countries such as Turkey, Afghanistan, Nepal, Iran, Tunisia, and Morocco are moving toward the same goal.

New rice varieties, patterned after the dwarf wheats, have recently been developed by the International Rice Research Institute in the Philippines (Chandler, 1969:1007-1010). Their success has been equally spectacular. A conservative estimate is that they are capable of doubling rice yields. Since 1965, when they were introduced, several Asian nations have achieved a sudden significant increase in yields, i.e., a yield takeoff. The Philippines and Pakistan became self-sufficient in rice in 1968. India expects to grow all it needs in 1972 and Burma, Thailand, South Vietnam, Malaysia, Ceylon and Indonesia are not far behind (U.S. News and World Report, 1970:52). Also, populous Japan has changed from

63

importer to a potential exporter but markets are becoming
~~~singly hard to find. Most of Japan's neighbors have enough
~~~eir own, poorly distributed though it may be. A worldwide
surplus is now a distinct possibility (Swegle, 1969:44-48,
Hayward, 1971:9).

What has been done with wheat and rice can and is being done
with other widely used crops like sorghum, millet, soybeans and
maize. As a result, agricultural production is keeping up with the
population and the fight against hunger is being won, even in the
developing countries. This is illustrated by Figure 4. That it will
continue is assured by the fact that, already on the horizon, there
are triple-dwarf varieties of wheat that will outyield the present
double-dwarf varieties by as much as these varieties outyielded
their tall predecessors (Swegle, 1969:44-48, and Patterson, 1972).

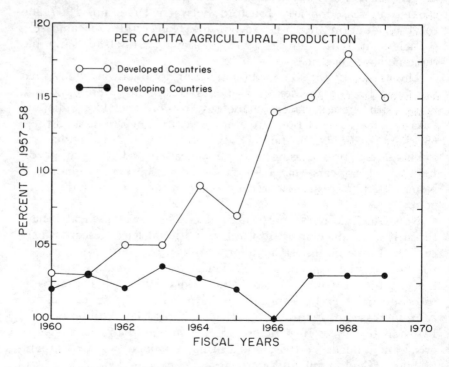

Figure 4.   Per capita agricultural production in the developed and developing
countries (War on Hunger, 1970:14).

Future Developments in Food Production

Is it possible to keep the rate of food production greater than the rate of population growth indefinitely? Has the Green Revolution been only a momentary victory in a war that must inevitably be lost? Many pessimists would say yes. But, in the words of Buckminster Fuller (1967:14-18), they may be "burdened with obsolete knowledge," having their "spontaneous reflexing conditioned only by past experience." In other words, they may be "backing up into the future."

There are valid reasons for optimism. In the first place, the yield takeoffs in the late 1800's, the 1930's and the 1960's were not the result of chance. They were all based solidly on scientific investigation. This kind of investigation has not stopped. There will be additional breakthroughs. Moreover, there are many technical developments that are presently awaiting application and others that are visible on the horizon. These include the development of potentially arable soils and of water resources, soil warming, development of multiple cropping, improvement in per acre yields, changes in land use, development of high protein foods, development of seafood and advances in the synthesis of food. Let us consider each of these briefly.

Development of Potentially Arable Soils

There are about 7.8 billion acres of potentially arable (cultivatable) land in the world, of which more than half, about 4.4 billion acres, are not yet cultivated (President's Science Advisory Committee, 1967:405-469; Kellogg and Orvedal, 1968:14-17). These figures are conservative and *they do not include land that could be brought under cultivation if desalinized sea water or soil-warming systems were available.* Table 1 shows the distribution of cultivated and potentially arable land by continents. Note that Africa and South America are the continents where the greatest increases in cultivated land are possible. Thus, on a worldwide basis, there is no shortage of arable land; nor will there be for some time.

Development of Water Resources

More than any other single factor, the lack of water limits crop

Table 1. Cultivated land compared to potentially arable land by continents.

Continent	Area in billions of acres			Ratio of cultivated to potentially arable land (percent)
	Total	Potentially arable	Cultivated	
Africa	7.46	1.81	0.39	22
Asia	6.76	1.55	1.28	83
Australia & New Zealand	2.03	0.38	0.04	2
Europe	1.18	0.43	0.38	88
North America	5.21	1.15	0.59	51
South America	4.33	1.68	0.19	11
U.S.S.R.	5.52	0.88	0.56	64
Total	32.49	7.88	3.43	44

Source: President's Science Advisory Committee, *The World Food Problem, Report of the Panel on the World Food Supply*, Vol. 2, 1967.

production throughout the world. Yet this need not be the case, especially in the future. There are great reservoirs of untapped fresh water waiting to be used. For example, sloping gently away from the mighty Himalayan mountains, and stretching across the entire Indian subcontinent, the vast alluvial plains of the Indus and Ganges rivers are underlain with water of good quality. This water can be brought to the surface by tube wells for irrigation during the dry season. The difficulty is that there is not enough energy available to operate all the required tube wells. To solve the problem, Dr. Perry Stout of the University of California has designed an agro-industrial complex for the upper Indo-Gangetic plain (Stout, 1968; Young 1969:9-18). In this complex, nuclear power would be used to pump water from the ground to the thirsty fields and to fix nitrogen for fertilizers. Thus, yields could be increased at least fourfold in some areas and tenfold in others. It is estimated that one such complex could add the equivalent of 4.7 million new productive acres and, if the dwarf wheats were planted, provide enough food to feed 44 million people at a cost which is economically feasible. As many as six agro-industrial complexes could be utilized profitably in this region.

66

There are other examples of unused underground water that could be cited but one more will suffice. In Roman times, the Sahara of North Africa was the richest granary in the Empire (McGinnies and Goldman, 1969a:382-397). Now it is a sparsely inhabited desert. But its former productivity could be restored. For beneath its barren surface there is an enormous reservoir of fresh water. In some places the water-bearing sands are 3000 feet thick and they are believed to extend at least 500 miles south of the Atlas mountains (on the northwestern coast of Africa) and eastward into Libya. They contain enough water to irrigate many millions of acres for centuries (Revelle, 1963:93-108; Dregne, 1970). In the vicinity of the oasis of Kufrah, 500 miles south of Tobruk in Libya, it is said that there is as much underground water as the River Nile discharges in 200 years. And it is as close as 300 feet from ground level (Business Week, 1969:168-170). The water beneath the Sahara could turn it into a veritable garden and could double the arable acres presently being cultivated throughout the world.

Arid lands offer great hope for the future in other areas of the world as well. They include as many as 5.2 billion acres within 300 miles and 2.8 billion more within 500 miles of the sea (McGinnies and Goldman, 1969a:382-397). Desalinized sea water could be pumped these distances if it were available—and eventually it will be. Already the U.S. Atomic Energy Commission has plans for a nuclear-powered agro-industrial complex that will be located on a sea coast (Weinberg, 1969:1-14; Aldrich, 1970a:211-227). In it, sea water will be desalinized and pumped to nearby fields, nitrogen fertilizer will be produced and electrical power will be supplied to the associated community, all at an acceptable cost even by today's standards. Enough power could be produced, and facilities provided, for the transportation of water to more remote areas. Two thousand years ago the Romans transported large volumes of water as far as 150 miles in aqueducts. Certainly, we ought to be able to improve on their performance.

Another kind of complex for producing food is now in operation at two coastal sites, one on the Persian Gulf and the other on the Gulf of California (Bazell, 1971:989-990; Hodges and Hodge, 1970:3-5). This latter complex, designed and built by scientists at the University of Arizona's Environmental Research Laboratory, is a series of air-inflated polyethylene greenhouses enclosing vegetables grown in beach sand. The vegetables are irrigated by dis-

67

tilled seawater produced by utilizing the exhaust heat from Diesel engines that are required for power. Dissolved fertilizer is applied with the irrigation water. Only enough water is applied to reach to the bottom of the root zone and transpiration is reduced by keeping the recycled air in the greenhouses at 100 percent relative humidity. Thus, a humid tropical climate prevails despite the arid surroundings. An annual yield of one million pounds of vegetables is expected from a five-acre greenhouse complex at a cost of about 20 cents a pound. Since there are approximately 20,000 miles of desert coasts on earth, the importance of this development is evident.

Irrigation, the principal consumer of water, takes less than four percent of the total flow of the earth's rivers (Revelle, 1963:93-108). More of their flow could be utilized. The Russians plan to dam the Arctic-bound Ob and Yenisei rivers and create a lake nearly the size of Italy. The impounded water would irrigate over 100 million acres. Equally impressive plans have been designed for the North American continent (Revelle, 1963:93-108; McGinnies and Goldman, 1969a:382-397, 1969b:341-352, 1969c:363-374). These plans, and others like them, will materialize if the demand is great enough.

Rainmaking is still in its infancy. But, as Gale Young (McGinnies and Goldman, 1969a:382-397) asserts, "it has passed beyond the rain dance and early experimental phases." The most commonly used method is to seed clouds with condensation nuclei such as silver iodide. At the present time, there is a pilot rainmaking project on the upper Colorado River basin which is expected to increase the precipitation in the target area by 16 percent (Hammond, 1971:548-549). Another such project is underway in Montana. Although the likelihood that rain can be made to fall on deserts is remote (the air above them contains too little water vapor), it can be made to fall on neighboring mountains where it can be stored. Then it can be conveyed to where it is needed.

About half the water reserved for irrigation is lost in transportation. And half of what is left drains or evaporates from the fields without being used by plants (Revelle, 1963:93-108). There are many ways of increasing the efficiency of water use and thereby extending the supplies that are available (Aldrich, 1970b:255-303). But space will not permit them to be considered here. What has

68

been presented should demonstrate that much of the arid land of the world, covering a third of its surface, can be supplied with water and made productive.

Soil Warming

As time passes, an increasing amount of our energy will be derived from nuclear power plants. In the United States at the present time, these plants account for only about 0.3 percent of our energy; but by the year 2000 they are expected to provide about 23 percent of it (U.S. News and World Report, 1971:62-64). The trend is the same elsewhere in the developed world.

One of the problems with such plants is that they produce large amounts of heat which must be dissipated in some way. This problem can be turned to an advantage in cool temperate or arctic climates. For the waste heat can be used in another kind of agro-indust .ial complex. In cool temperate regions, water heated by it can be circulated through buried pipes to warm the soil in open fields. Evidence obtained by Dr. Larry Boersma (1970) indicates that, even in the mild climate of Oregon, the yields of such crops as corn, tomatoes and beans can be increased as much as 35 to 75 percent by this technique. In colder climates, the growing season can be lengthened in a like manner. And in arctic climates, the heated water can be used to warm greenhouses and the soil beneath them. This is currently being done in Scandanavia. Thus the soil climate can be tempered to enhance crop production. The same agro-industrial complex could include heated animal shelters and fish ponds. Interest in the beneficial use of waste heat is high. For example, symposia on the subject have been held recently by the U.S. Atomic Energy Commission and the American Society of Agronomy.

Development of Multiple Cropping

Reference to Table 1 shows that the greatest areas of *unused* arable land are in Africa and South America. These areas have tropical or subtropical climates with a yearlong growing season. They could be planted to as many as four consecutive crops a year. Further, there is convincing evidence that, with the necessary

69

investments in research and technology, they are capable of producing the high yields that are characteristic of the temperate zones (Kellogg and Orvedal, 1968; Aldrich, 1970c:229-242). Hence, they have four times the productive capacity of an equivalent area there.

Large parts of Asia also have tropical and subtropical climates. Where only a single crop per year is harvested now, three or four could be harvested. This is true, for example, in the Philippines where land that traditionally produced one rice crop a year of one ton per acre now yields up to eight tons from successive crops of rice, sweet potatoes, sorghum and corn (Aldrich, 1970c:229-242). It is also true in India where a sequence of rice, wheat, potatoes and pumpkins has proved to be successful (Stout, 1968). Crops like soy and mung beans can be substituted in the sequence. Thus, multiple cropping could greatly augment the food supply.

Improvement in Per-Acre Yields

Every day, step by step, and sometimes by great strides, agricultural scientists are adding to the store of knowledge about food production. New ideas on plant breeding, fertilizer use, water application, plant spacing, chemical growth regulators, weed killers, pesticides, tillage, planting, harvesting, storage, etc., are constantly being generated and tried (Aldrich, 1970d:72-121). But not all of our present knowhow is being applied. To illustrate this fact, a comparison is made in Table 2 between average yields and the maximum yields that *have been* obtained. Note that the latter are not the maximum yields that *may be* obtained. The theoretical limit of photosynthetic production of carbohydrates is approximately a hundred thousand pounds per acre per year (Aldrich, 1970e:191-210). This is equivalent to about 1800 bushels of corn, 1600 bushels of wheat and 2200 bushels of rice, respectively.

Changes in Land Use

In the United States, wheat produces twice as many calories per acre as rye, whereas, potatoes, rice, corn and carrots produce twice as many calories per acre as wheat (Hardin, 1969:41-87). These ratios will vary with the climate and soil. However, they show that some crops are relatively high yielders and could be planted in preference to others to enhance the food supply.

70

Table 2. Some average and record yields of crops and other foodstuffs.

Plant or animal foodstuff	Average yield	Record yield
Corn - bu./acre	80 (USA)	304
Wheat - bu./acre	29 (USA)	209
Rice - bu./acre	24 (World)	266
Oats - bu./acre	53 (USA)	297
Sorghum - bu./acre	56 (USA)	347
Soybeans - bu./acre	27 (USA)	95
Potatoes - bu./acre	350 (USA)	1,400
Sugarcane - tons sugar/acre/year	2 (World)	5.5
Cow - lbs. of milk/year	8,800 (USA)	45,000
Chicken - eggs/year	230 (USA)	365

Source: Wittwer, S. H., "Research and Technology on the United States Food Supply," in Daniel G. Aldrich, ed., *Research for the World Food Crisis 92*, Washington, D.C.: American Association for the Advancement of Science, 1970. © by the American Association for the Advancement of Science. Reprinted by permission.

Man-made fibers are replacing cotton and wool, releasing acreage for food production. In addition, tractors are replacing animal power with the same effect. Replacements of this kind have been going on for some time in the developed countries. They have yet to make their full impact in the developing countries.

In the United States and other developed countries, much of the land under cultivation is used to produce grains that are fed to livestock. Then the livestock are used for meat. This is a highly inefficient way to produce food. For instance, one acre of land will produce approximately 43 pounds of animal protein. The same acre, planted in soybeans, will produce about 450 pounds of protein. The relative costs of net utilizable protein are 31¢ per pound for soybean flour and $3.26 for beef (Worthington Foods, Inc.). In general, about seven times as much food can be produced per acre if plants are grown instead of animals (Daly, 1969:87-92; Brooks, 1970:10-14, 33). Consequently, conversion to a plant agriculture could increase the productivity of land in the developed countries tremendously. It would have far less effect in the developing countries because theirs is already largely a plant agriculture. Nevertheless, it is estimated that, if all crops were consumed directly as food, total world food tonnage would be increased by 20 percent, protein by 28 percent and calories by 33 percent (Rasmussen, 1969:654-672).

Development of High-Protein Foods

There is a difference between being undernourished and malnourished. A malnourished person may have enough food insofar as calories are concerned, but not enough proteins, vitamins, minerals, etc., to maintain good health. Many diets in the world are deficient in proteins. Hence, there are many malnourished people.

Much effort is being expended to produce high-protein foods. The results to date are most encouraging. Recently, scientists at Purdue University found that a gene called *opaque-2* was responsible for high amounts of two essential amino acids, lysine and tryptophan, in corn protein (Mertz, et al., 1964:279-280; Hankins, 1967:77-79). Corn containing this gene was called high-lysine corn. When high-lysine corn was fed to animals, their growth rates were 50-100 percent better than when ordinary corn was fed to them. Even more important, when children in advanced stages of protein starvation in Colombia were fed this kind of corn, they recovered in a few weeks' time (U.S. House of Representatives, 1971). Had they remained on a diet of ordinary corn, they would have died. It now appears that by combining other genes with the *opaque-2* gene, modified corns with even better protein quality and kernel characteristics may be obtained (Glover, 1972). These discoveries have far-reaching consequences. Next to wheat and rice, corn is eaten by more people than any other grain.

The content and quality of proteins in wheat, rice and other grains are receiving their share of attention. A search is now underway for genes that will do for these crops what *opaque-2* did for corn. Also, attempts are being made to produce new artificial plant species having high yields and protein contents.

Soybeans are an excellent source of high quality protein. New processes are becoming available for processing them to obtain this protein in a concentrated and edible form. It is already being used as soy flour and in meat analogs (Worthington Foods, Inc). Also, it can be spray-dried and then reconstituted with water to prepare an infant beverage (Mustakas, et al., 1971:534-540).

Another excellent and as yet undeveloped source of protein is fish protein concentrate. Many species of fish are either unutilized or underutilized. For example, along the Atlantic coast of the United States alone, about 420 million pounds of fish of various species are available annually, over and above the present catch (Pariser, 1971:1162-1174). And the sea along the 4,600-mile coast of Brazil is virtually untapped (Crisan, 1970:1132-1138). In order to avoid the problems of distributing and storing fresh fish, the fish protein can be extracted by the use of a solvent for the removal of fats and lipids. Then it can be dried and ground to a powder (Crisan, 1970b:1132-1138; Sidwell, et al., 1970:876-882). Present processes provide a 5:1 weight reduction coupled with a more than fourfold increase in protein content. The product, fish protein concentrate, contains at least 70-80 percent protein. It is not intended to serve as the sole source of protein in the diet but rather as a protein supplement. It can be incorporated into such things as bread, pasta (macaroni), crackers and cookies (Sidwell, et al., 1970:876-882). Since even fodder or trash fish can be used for fish protein concentrate, it offers great possibilities in meeting the protein needs of people everywhere.

Microorganisms such as yeast, fungi, bacteria and algae constitute an even more unique source of protein (Tannenbaum, 1971:962-967; Jarl, 1969:1009-1012; Dabbah, 1970:659-664). To illustrate their potential, it is instructive to compare their productivity with that of beef cattle or grain. In one day, a 1000-pound steer produces about one pound of protein, whereas, 1000 pounds of bacteria produce about a trillion pounds of protein (Tannenbaum, 1971:962-967; Jarl, 1969:1009 1012; Dabbah, 1970:659-664). A crop of corn or wheat yields only 150 grams of protein per square meter per year; a culture of algae will produce about 7000 grams of protein on the same area (Tannenbaum, 1971:962-967; Jarl, 1969:1009-1012; Dabbah, 1970:659-664). In addition to their high yield of protein, microorganisms can be grown economically. They use such substances as waste starch, rejected potatoes, petroleum, waste paper, wood pulp, etc., as substrates. At the present time, the cost of their proteins is about $0.35 per pound as compared to $0.41 for skim milk protein.

From what has been said, it is obvious that the protein needs of the world can be met now and for many years to come. The problem is not so much to produce foods containing proteins of high quality as it is to make these foods acceptable to people.

Dietary patterns are difficult to change, especially where people have had traditional diets for centuries (Downey and Eiserle, 1970:1226-1229).

Development of Seafood

A nonagricultural food that offers great promise for the future is fish. With proper methods of marine and lake "farming," the catch of fish can be increased enormously. In small areas of Japan's Inland Sea, oysters cultured by special methods yield as many as 46,000 pounds of meat per acre annually. Studies in Rhode Island indicate that comparable yields can be expected along the eastern seaboard of the United States. Other studies at the Woods Hole Oceanographic Institute show that much larger yields of mussel meat are possible (Pinchot, 1970:15-21).

In places like the Philippines and Taiwan, milkfish are harvested in fertilized ponds. Yields average as high as 4,000 pounds per acre. The United Nations Food and Agricultural Organization has calculated that more than 140,000 square miles of land in southern and eastern Asia could be added to the area already devoted to milkfish husbandry. If this were done, the resulting yield of milkfish would be more than today's total catch from all the world's oceans.

There are certain places where deep, cold ocean waters laden with mineral nutrients well up to the surface. It has been observed that these are the places where fishing is best. In fact, areas of natural upwelling comprise only 0.1 percent of the ocean's surface but supply almost half of the total fish catch. This observation motivated scientists at the Lamont-Doherty Geological Observatory of Columbia University to sink long, plastic tubes into the deep water off St. Croix in the Virgin Islands and pump it into ponds on the shore (Pinchot, 1970:15-21; Lafayette Journal and Courier, 1971). They found that selected plant life grew 27 times faster in this water than in surface water and sustained a much greater growth of oysters and clams. Since there are many ocean depths that lie near land, their procedure could lead to a much greater production of seafood.

Synthesis of Food

The recent exploits of man in space have given impetus to the

74

synthesis of foods that he might use in space capsules or on other planets. As a result, many exciting possibilities have come into focus. It now appears to be possible to synthesize carbohydrate-like compounds such as formose sugars and glycerol from carbon dioxide and water (Shapira, 1970:992-996), or edible fatty acids and lipids from metabolic wastes (Frankenfield, 1968). Undoubtedly, additional research will open up other possibilities.

Discussion

A common statement is that the world is or will soon be over-populated. In considering this statement, it is legitimate to ask the questions: overpopulated with reference to what, and according to whose values or ethics? The Malthusian reply to the first question is that it is or soon will be overpopulated with reference to the food supply. The relative rates of increase of population and food supply are supposed to be as depicted in Figure 5. But this figure

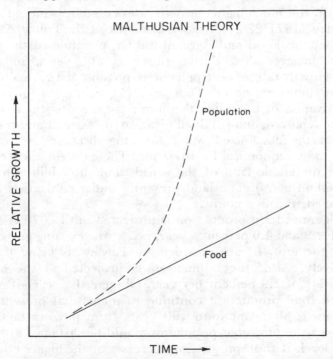

Figure 5.   Relative growth rates of population and food according to the Malthusian Theory.

75

does not represent historical fact. As shown in Figures 1 and 2, the food supply has increased at a rate that is more nearly geometric than arithmetic. And it should increase at an even faster rate in the future. This is because the underlying technology is expanding rapidly.

Both scientists and the knowledge that they discover are increasing faster than the population. The rate of increase of scientists in the United States has been 6.6 percent per year since 1900; the rate of increase of the world's scientific journals, the repositories of scientific knowledge, has been 4.6 percent per year since 1750 (Hubbert, 1963:365-378). On the other hand, the rate of increase of the world's population is 1.9 percent per year (Statistical Abstract of the U.S., 1970).

During the last fifteen years, the food supply in 75 developing countries has been growing at a rate of 2.9 percent a year (Ceres, 1971:9). Growth rates in the developed countries have been comparable (Hardin, 1969:41-87; U.S. Dept. of Agriculture 1971:10). But much higher growth rates could be achieved. Walter H. Pawley (1971:22-27), who is Director of the Policy Advisory Bureau in the Food and Agricultural Organization of the United Nations, believes that, during the next 100 years, an average annual growth rate of 4.0 percent is possible if two major technical developments occur. They are: (1) techniques for continuous cultivation of the soil in the humid tropics after the tree cover has been removed, and (2) desalinization of seawater and transportation of the desalinized water for long distances at costs low enough to be economical for irrigation. These developments would increase the arable land of the world to about 7 billion hectares (17.3 billion acres). The land presently under cultivation is only about one-fifth this amount.

In Figure 6, food production is projected until 2070 at growth rates of 2.9 and 4.0 percent a year, i.e., at the existing growth rate and at the growth rate regarded by Pawley as being possible, respectively. Also, the population is projected at the existing growth rate of 1.9 percent per year. Observe that, even if population and food production continue to increase at present rates, there can be abundant food 100 years from now. In fact, more than twice the *projected* population could be sustained at today's dietary level. If food production increases at the higher rate, then about eight times the *projected* population could be sustained at

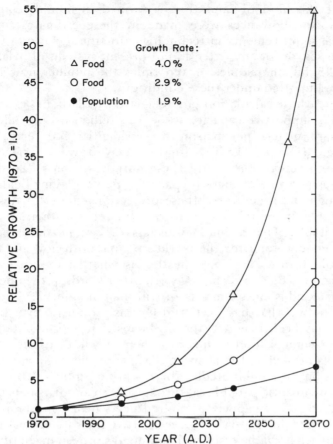

Figure 6.   Projections of food production at growth rates of 2.9 and 4.0 percent and of population at a growth rate of 1.9 percent for the next 100 years (1970=1.0).

this level. Or fewer people could be sustained at a much higher dietary level.

The foregoing projections are in keeping with others that have been made. Dr. Colin Clark (1970), the eminent British economist, estimates that it takes about 2763 square meters (0.68 acres) to supply one person with food and fiber at the standard enjoyed in the United States. He further estimates that, if agricultural methods already practiced in the developed nations were universally employed, the productive capacity of the world's arable lands would be *equivalent* to 9.73 billion hectares (24 billion

77

acres) of the kind of land that is farmed in humid temperate climates. No allowances were made in these estimates for any additional improvements in technology, for the inclusion of food from the sea, or for any extension of present systems of irrigation. Hence, 35 billion people, or ten times the number now living, could be supported under these conditions.

De Wit, whose calculations are reviewed by Clark, has estimated the earth's supportive capacity to be 146 billion people, allowing 750 square meters per person for residential and recreational purposes (Clark, 1970). In the new towns designed in England, the area reserved for these purposes is only 220 square meters per person and there is space for parks, playing fields, etc.

Although the accuracy of these projections and estimates may be debatable, it should be evident that famine is neither imminent nor inevitable. The technology exists or can be developed to produce enough food for the world's people both now and in the foreseeable future. The real question is whether or not we will take advantage of this technology. In other words, providing food for all mankind is more a matter of will than of ability.

Admittedly, what has been said here is optimistic. No specific mention has been made of the problems that will be entailed in producing enough food to meet the demand, in distributing it to where it is needed and in assuring that people have the purchasing power to buy it. Undoubtedly, there will be problems. But there will also be unanticipated breakthroughs. We cannot visualize with certainty what will happen a hundred years hence any more than Malthus could in his day. However, two things give reason for optimism: what *can* be discerned, and man's proven ingenuity.

References

Aldrich, Daniel G. (ed.)

1970a   "Nuclear power in agro-industrial development by R. Phillip Hammond in Research for the World Food Crisis 92. Washington D.C.: American Association for the Advancement of Science.

1970b   "Water management," by Robert M. Hagan in Research for the World Food Crisis 92. Washington D.C.: American Association for the Advancement of Science.

1970c   "Increasing food production in the tropics by multiple cropping," by Richard Bradfield in Research for the World Food Crisis 92. Washington D.C.: American Association for the Advancement of Science.

1970d   "Research and technology on the United States food supply," by S. H. Wittwer in Research for the World Food Crisis 92. Washington D.C.: American Association for the Advancement of Science.

1970e   "Nitrogen and future food requirements," by C.C. Delwiche in Research for the World Food Crisis 92. Washington D.C.: American Association for the Advancement of Science.

Barrons, Keith C.
1971   "Environmental benefits of intensive crop production." Agricultural Science Review 9: 33-39.

Bazell, Robert J.
1971   "Arid land agriculture: shaikh [sic.] up in Arizona research." Science 171 (March 12):989-990.

Boersma, Larry
1970   Talk at the Conference on Beneficial Uses of Thermal Discharge, sponsored by New York State Department of Environmental Conservation. Albany, New York (September 17-18).

Borlaug, Norman E.
1968   Proceedings 3rd International Wheat Genetics Symposium. Canberra, Australia, pp. 1-36.

Brooks, Robert
1970   "People versus food." Saturday Review 53 (September 5):10-14,33.

Brown, Lester R.
1965   "Population growth, food needs and production problems." American Society of Agronomy Special Publication 6 (February):3-22.

Business Week
1969   "Libya adds water to its riches." Business Week 2060 (February 22):168-170.

Ceres
1971   Ceres (F A O Report)4:9.

Chandler, Robert F. Jr.
1969   "Improving the rice plant and its culture." Nature 221 (March 15):1007-1010.

                "Maximum yield potentialities for rice." General Contribution No. 916. University of Philippines Publication Series A.

Clark, Colin
1970   Starvation or Plenty? New York: Taplinger Publishing Co.

Crisan, Eli V.
1970   "The fish protein concentrate story. Part II. A demonstration program in Brazil." Food Technology 24 (October):1132-1138.

Dabbah, Roger
1970   "Protein from microorganisms." Food Technology 24 (June):659-664.

Daly, Rex F.
1969   "Food enough for the U.S.? a crystal ball look
                ahead." U.S. Department of Agriculture Year-
                book:87-92.

Downey, W. J. and E. J. Eiserle
1970   "Problems in the flavoring of fabricated foods."
                Food Technology 24 (November):1226-1229.

Dregne, Harold E. (ed.)
1970   "Water in the deserts," by Dean F. Peterson in
                Arid Lands in Transition. Washington D.C.:
                American Association for the Advancement of
                Science.

Frankenfield, John W.
1968   NASA Contractor Report 1104 (July).

Fuller, Buckminster
1967   "Man with a Chronofile." Saturday Review
                (April 1):14-18.

Glover, Dr. David V.
1972   Private Communication, Agronomy Department
                Purdue University.

Hammond, Allen L.
1971   "Weather modifications: a technology coming of
                age." Science 172 (May 7):548-549.

Hankins, B. J.
1967   "A New Corn," Grain (June):77-79.

Hardin, Clifford M. (ed.)
1969   "Food for more people and better nutrition,"
                by Don Paarlberg in Overcoming World Hunger.
                New Jersey: Prentice Hall Inc. for Columbia
                University.

Hayward, Henry S.
    1971   "Rice revolution rolls on—greening of Asia."
                    Christian Science Monitor (March 9) 2nd section.

Hodges, C.N., and C.O. Hodge
    1970   "Man-made oases/power + water = food." War
                    on Hunger 4 (February):3-5.

Hubbert, M. King
    1963   "Are we retrogressing in science." Geological
                    Society of America Bulletin 74 (April):365-378.

Jarl, Kurt
    1969   "Symba yeast products." Food Technology 23
                    (August):1009-1012.

Kellogg, Charles E., and Arnold C. Orvedal
    1968   "World potential for arable soils." War on
                    Hunger 2 (September):14-17.

Layfayette, Journal and Courier
    1971   Lafayette, Indiana Journal and Courier. (June
                    17).

Malthus, Thomas
    1926   Essay on the Principles of Population as It
                    Affects the Future Improvement of Society.
                    (First edition, reprinted for the Royal Economics
                    Society) London: The Macmillan Co.

Mc Ginnies, William G., and Bram J. Goldman (eds.)
    1969a   "Import alternatives," by Gale Young in Arid
                    Lands in Perspective. American Association for
                    the Advancement of Science. Tucson: University
                    of Arizona Press.

    1969b   "Historical background and philosophical basis
                    of regional water transfer," by C. C. Warnick in
                    Arid Lands in Perspective. American Association
                    for the Advancement of Science. Tucson: Uni-
                    versity of Arizona Press.

1969c   "Social and ecological implications of water importations into arid lands," by Gerald W. Thomas and Thadis W. Box in Arid Lands in Perspective. American Association for the Advancement of Science. Tucson: University of Arizona Press.

Mertz, Edwin T., Lynn S. Bates, and Oliver E. Nelson
1964   "Mutant gene that changes protein composition and increases lysine content of maize endosperm." Science 145 (July 17):279-280.

Mustakas, G. C., W. J. Albrecht, G. N. Bookwalter, V. E. Sohns, and E. L. Griffin Jr.
1971   "New process for low cost, high protein beverage base." Food Technology 25 (May):534-540.

Pawley, W. H.
1971   Ceres (FAO Review) 4:22-27.

Pariser, E. R.
1971   "The potential, the problems and the status of using proteins of aquatic orgin as human food." Food Technology 25 (November):1162-1174.

Patterson, Fred
1972   Private communication. Agronomy Department Purdue University.

Pinchot, Gifford B.
1970   "Marine Farming," Scientific American 223 (December):15-21.

President's Science Advisory Committee
1967   The World Food Problem. Report of the Panel on the World Food Supply. Vol. 2:405-469.

Rasmussen, Clyde L.
1969   "Man and his food: 2000 A.D." Food Technology 23 (May):654-672.

83

Reitz, Louis P.
    1970   "New wheats and social progress." Science 169
                    (September):952-955.

Revelle, Roger
    1963   "Water." Scientific American 209 (September):93-108.

Shapira, Jacob
    1970   "Physiochemical methods for the synthesis of
                    potential foods," Agricultural and Food Chemistry 18 (November-December):992-996.

Sidwell, V. D., D. R. Stillings, and G. M. Knobl Jr.
    1970   "The fish protein concentrate story. Part 10.
                    U.S. Bureau of Commercial Fisheries FPC's:
                    nutritional quality and use in foods." Food
                    Technology 24 (August):876-882.

Statistical Abstract of the United States
    1970

Stout, Perry R.
    1968   Potential Agricultural Production from Nuclear-
                    Powered Agro-Industrial Complexes Designed
                    for the Upper Indo-Gangetic Plain, Oak Ridge
                    National Laboratory-4292, UC-80, Reactor
                    Technology.

Swegle, Wayne E.
    1969   "New world food problem—abundance." Successful Farming 67 (September):44-48.

Tannenbaum, Steven R.
    1971   "Single-cell protein, food of the future," Food
                    Technology 25 (September):962-967.

U.S. Department of Agriculture
    1971   War on Hunger 5:10.

U.S. House of Representatives
1971   The Population Explosion and the Green Revo-
                lution. Hearings before a subcommittee of the
                Committee on Appropriations. U.S. House of
                Representatives, 92 Congress, first session.

U.S. News and World Report
1970   "Whatever happened to the—promised miracle in
                Asia's rice field," U.S. News and World Report
                69 (August 31):52.

U.S. News and World Report
1971   "The search for pollution—free fuel," U.S. News
                and World Report (July 5):62-64.

War on Hunger
1970   Vol. 4, No. 5 (May):14.

Weinberg, A.M.
1969   Research with a Mission. American Society of
                Agronomy, Special Publication No. 14:1-14.

Young, Gale
1969   "Apollo over the Ganges, an agro-industrial
                complex for increasing food production in
                India." IEEE Transactions on Nuclear Science
                16 (February):9-18.

Natural Resources
and
Human Survival

B. Delworth Gardner

It is an "article of faith" of most proponents of population control that the world is rapidly running out of nonrenewable natural resources: energy fuels, minerals, arable land, water and air. The earth has been likened to a spaceship (Jarrett, 1966:3-14), completely dependent on its own resources except for the energy received from the sun. Since in a physical sense the resources of the earth are indisputably finite, any positive rate of net consumption of nonrenewable resources will ultimately deplete these resources and end human life as we know it on this planet.

This conclusion is not an hypothesis, it is a tautology. It is true by definition. The interesting question, however, is not *whether* mankind will run out of natural resources given positive rates of consumption, but *when*. A favorite game these days is to extrapolate present trends of population and economic growth and thereby project resource requirements in the years ahead. Requirements are then compared with known reserves and the arithmetic dictates the date of impending doom.

The latest, and perhaps the most prestigious, group to play this game is "The Club of Rome" (Meadows, 1972). Utilizing sophisticated modeling techniques and computer programming, these revamped Malthusians reached the following conclusions, "If the present growth trends in world population, industrialization, pollution, food production, and resource depletion continue unchanged, the limits to growth on this planet will be reached sometime within the next one hundred years. The most probable result will be a rather sudden and uncontrollable decline in both population and industrial capacity" (Meadows, 1972:23).

The pure logic of this conclusion is unassailable if the assumption of continuing trends is granted. When population, pollution, and utilization of resources are programmed to increase at a fixed geometric rate, the computer calculates very large magnitudes in a relatively short number of future years. Such is the inevitable result of any geometric progression such as 1, 2, 4, 16, 32, 64, etc. With their differential equations of geometric growth, the Club of Rome imitates exactly the reasoning method of T. R. Malthus. And just as the experience of the past 150 years has shown Malthus to be wrong, the conclusions of the Club of Rome are also not likely to come to pass.

Why? Because the postulated continuing rates of geometric growth do not, in fact, persist (Gardner, 1968).*Man, individually and collectively, reacts to his changing condition. He is not driven relentlessly and inexorably to his doom by immutable laws of nature, although sometimes change is slow and difficult. Man is a thinking creature who can and often does change his course when threatened. There are few valid reasons why present trends can be expected to continue. The intense activities of groups such as the Club of Rome are themselves designed to prevent the bleak future implied by continuing trends.

Newsweek columnist, Henry C. Wallich (1972), has stated a similar view, "Their (Club of Rome's) principal assumptions are, broadly, that natural resources cannot be expanded very much by new technology, that pollution cannot be very effectively controlled, and above all that people show so little foresight that they always overshoot the equilibrium point and land in disaster. In each instance, the opposite assumptions seem to me more plausible, leading to the opposite results."

Let us turn specifically to some of the propaganda about impending natural shortages.

One of Paul Ehrlich's statements (1970:188) is typical:

---

*For further discussion of this point, see the referenced works by B. Delworth Gardner.

Even though we have only 6 percent of the world's population in the country (U.S.), we consume over 35 percent of the world's natural resources. . . . Twenty years from now (1990), we'll be even a smaller percentage of the population, but it would take about 75 percent of the world's natural resources just to maintain our projected insane level of consumption and our wasteful economy.

Others make the same point, using different and even more extreme figures (Fisher, 1965). "If present trends continue, the U.S. within 15 years will have about 9½ percent of the world's population. At this time, this 9 percent will be consuming some 83 percent of all the raw materials and resources produced in the entire world."

Authors of a recent book argue (Reinow and Reinow, 1970):

This nation is consuming the world's reserves of minerals and fuels at an almost terrifying rate. How far are the advanced countries, including the United States, morally justified in using their present economic leadership and power to strip their own and other countries of vital, non-renewable resources at rates that may create alarming shortages and some economic difficulties within the lifetime of people already born?

It is my opinion that the foregoing view of what is likely to happen in the next half-century is too pessimistic in light of the best scientific evidence. At the least, it is certainly not the view of the entire scientific community. Nearly everyone agrees that wasteful use of resources should be stopped. Indeed, mankind would be well served by stronger efforts to conserve natural resources through careful use, recycling, and technological advance. But advocating caution in the use of natural resources is not the same thing as predicting disaster because man has practically run out of available supplies.

As a practical matter, the availability of natural resources for man's use is related to four factors: (1) the physical amount of resources contained in the earth, (2) the technology of resource use, (3) the quality of the environment (the absence of resource pollution and despoliation), and (4) the number of people consuming resources. In this essay, I shall deal explicitly with the first factor and tacitly with the second, and focus primarily on energy fuels and minerals.

In my judgment, the most knowledgeable collection of scientists in the world who specialize in natural resource problems is the group called "Resources for the Future (RFF)." RFF consists of about twenty-five scholars who represent a wide variety of academic disciplines. In one sense, this paper is a brief report of their work, a digest of the summaries and conclusions of a number of books written under the auspices and support of this organization.

As pointed out earlier, I have no quarrel with the conclusion that the earth must ultimately be depleted of resources so long as a positive rate of nonreplaceable consumption exists, unless some way can be found to augment existing supplies. The real issue is whether the best scientific evidence actually indicates that exhaustion will occur in the next hundred years, even at present rates of utilization.

Energy Fuels

Since the consumption trends relative to reserves of energy fuels, especially fossil fuels, seem to be most alarming, these resources shall be discussed first. On the "alarmist" side, Paul and Anne Ehrlich (1970:60) have presented figures that suggest that the United States' reserves of crude oil will be depleted by about 1975 and those of the world before year 2000.

Dr. M. A. Adelman in his article (Clawson, 1963), "The World Oil Outlook," sees the situation quite differently. Professor Adelman agrees that there is a popular consensus that by 1975 the non-Soviet world demand will be around 15 billion barrels of crude petroleum annually, which is about twice the 1964 level. On the face of it, present world reserves of 284 billion barrels seem to be hardly more than comfortable (Clawson, 1963:98-99). To Adelman, however, there are great hazards in looking at the problem in this way. Because of technological advance and better knowledge over time, the estimates of reserves contained in a given petroleum field are almost continuously revised upwards. For example, Professor Adelman points out that the National Petroleum Council estimated that proved reserves discovered in new fields and pools in the United States in 1937-44 were 3.9 billion barrels. By 1944, the original reserves in those same fields were already being estimated at 10.6 billion barrels and by 1959 at 17.6 billion. When the 1945 estimates of all U.S. reserves are compared with the 1960 estimates of reserves in these same fields, the latter are 50 percent higher than the former (Clawson, 1963:99).

If an increase factor of one third is applied to the U.S. and one half to the rest of the non-Soviet world (as suggested by Adelman; Clawson, 1963:100), reserves in deposits already discovered at the end of 1962 are around 421 billion barrels. If the 142 billion barrels that are cited as anticipated consumption through 1975 are subtracted, the difference is 279 billion barrels or a 19-year supply of the estimated 1965 annual consumption.

In addition, not only are the reserves in already proved fields being continuously adjusted upwards because of technological advances and better knowledge, but significant new discoveries are being made every year. In the past three years, large pools have been discovered on the North Coast of Alaska and off the coast of Indochina. It is, of course, economic waste to expend scarce resources in exploration activities to provide reserves that are not needed. The one salutary effect of exploration is to assure the world's people that energy resources in the earth are much greater than presently known. Thus, oil reserves grow when the boards of directors of the oil companies decide that it is in their interests for them to grow (Clawson, 1963:21). Even though it would be comforting for most of us to understand with some certainity how much crude oil exists in some kind of an absolute sense on this planet, such knowledge might well be deleterious in keeping the price of oil at or near present levels. For this reason, the oil companies cannot be expected to reveal information on "excess" reserves even if they had it. The important point is that published statements of known reserves are not reliable data for predicting future depletion dates.

Professor Adelman goes on (Clawson, 1963:103): "It is already obvious to any student of the petroleum industry that even with present knowledge of reserves and world demand that the world oil market has and will continue to have great excess capacity." In fact, many kinds of artificial supply controls have been erected in the United States and elsewhere in order to keep the price of oil far above the costs of production. Conservation regulations that limit the amount of oil that can be pumped from each well monthly and the spacing of wells do much to restrict the short-run supply (Lovejoy, 1967). In this way, the price is propped up, even though the result may be more oil being ultimately pumped from

91

the ground in the very long run. Tariffs and quotas on oil imports keep American prices above world production costs. The purpose obviously is to protect a domestic industry which has per barrel production costs considerably above those in South America and the Middle East, the other primary supply sources for the Western World. Of course, fortunately if one is worried about running out of oil, the effect of these supply controls is to conserve oil by reducing current consumption.

Dr. Adelman (Clawson, 1963:28) gives three basic reasons for the oversupply in the market. The first is the incredibly rich fields in the Middle East which changed the whole petroleum picture in the world when they came into production. Secondly, through regulation of the industry, prices have not been allowed to fall far enough to eliminate some of the higher cost sources of petroleum to remove the excess capacity over time. And thirdly, the new and most productive areas have been largely shut off from the consuming market in the world (the United States) by trade barriers. Professor Adelman is skeptical whether any of these three factors will be allowed to change much in the near future. He expects, therefore, continuing oversupply in the oil industry in the foreseeable future. So do his colleagues, Lovejoy and Homan (1967:112), at Resources for the Future, according to their independent study. In other words, whatever the available supply is, its consumption will be stretched farther into the future by these trade and regulative policies. This is hardly indicative of an industry where critical shortages on a world scale are expected in the next few years as the alarmists contend.

One rather significant recent development has occurred since the publication of Adelman's work that almost certainly will increase world petroleum prices, and thus, reduce the rate of consumption. Many of the nationalistic Arab states, the world's largest suppliers of oil, have been demanding and getting significantly higher royalties on oil exported to markets in Western Europe, Japan, and the United States.

Of course, petroleum is only part of the total energy picture, albeit an important part. There are many other energy fuels which can substitute for petroleum if the need should arise. Professor Adelman points out (Clawson, 1963:101):

A second reason for thinking petroleum resources are greater than

92

the estimated 421 billion barrels is the existence of natural gas, particularly nonassociated gas. It has been intensively sought only in Canada, the U. S., and the U.S.S.R. In the first two countries certainly, and in the last possibly, its reserves exceed oil in heat content. It is not altogether wreckless, I think, to expect it at least to come near equality in other areas where it has not yet been looked for.

Natural gas is of peculiar importance because often it is a joint product with crude oil. Therefore, the more gas that is found, the more oil that is potentially available at a low cost (Clawson, 1963:102). Alternatively, since oil is overpriced, exploration is enhanced and new natural gas fields are discovered in the process of looking for oil.

Despite the encouraging long-run outlook for increasing supplies of natural gas, some serious short-run problems of meeting demands are anticipated. Better delivery systems have made this popular fuel available to greatly expanded numbers of consumers, and natural gas prices are at all-time highs in some localities. One observer (Schanz, 1972:3) has called it "our most limited fossil fuel in a total resource sense."

Another important factor on the energy scene is the truly enormous reserve of solid energy fuels just in case we need them. The United States seems on the brink and has been for many years, of developing a source of supply of oil from oil shale. Deposits of oil shales in the United States, principally in the Green River Formation extending over large areas of northwestern Colorado, east-central Utah, and southwestern Wyoming amount to the equivalent of over three trillion barrels of crude petroleum. One and one-half trillion barrels of oil are held in commercial-quality shale that assays at least 15 gallons per ton (Gardner, 1967:169-196). This reservoir of energy fuel is extremely large even in view of the 1975 non-Soviet world expected demand of around 15 billion barrels annually. The tarsand deposits in Canada are also of great magnitude and are already producing commercial oil on a limited scale.

Studies indicate that the costs of producing oil from shale in the U.S. are approximately the same as the current cost of producing oil from crude petroleum if exploration and finding costs are added to production costs (Gardner, 1967:171-172). A crucial factor in the development of an oil shale industry is whether or not the Federal government will permit the richest deposits, which are found on Federal lands, to be commercially developed. Some parcels have recently been released for development on an experimental basis.

Much of the oil shale lies near enough to the surface to be strip-mined. Processing the shale to remove the oil substance called Kerogen leaves large quantities of spent ash that must be disposed of. Both mining and processing create delicate problems in maintaining environmental quality. Processing the shale also requires large quantities of water. These questions have been studied (Gardner, 1968:569-586), and it appears that solutions exist, although admittedly the conflicts between developers and environmental groups are deep and intense.

Nearly everyone agrees that the reserves of coal in the world are very large. The Ehrlichs themselves admitted that coal and lignite reserves would last until the year 3000. Projected demands for coal for the United States for 1980 and 2000 are 630 and 718 million tons annually (Landsbery, et al., 1963:290). Reserves have been estimated at 1.9 trillion tons (Schurr and Netschert, 1960:306). Even if the U.S. had to depend on its own reserves, and assuming the projected year 2000 consumption levels, the reserves would last from 250-300 years.

The United States is a very heavy consumer of electricity. The primary sources of electricity are conversion of coal and oil, hydropower, and soon, nuclear energy. In 1959, the Federal Power Commission estimated the capacity of developed and installed hydroelectric power resources as 30.2 million kilowatts. The estimate of potential undeveloped capacity was 91.9 million kilowatts (Schurr and Netschert, 1960:447), for approximately three times 1959 capacity.

Nuclear power is likely to become a very significant factor in the world energy picture. During 1966, 60 percent of all new power capacity contracted for in the United States was nuclear. Some plants have now been completed. Obviously, the development of atomic energy need not wait until the fossil fuels are used up. The uranium potential of the United States alone for atomic energy production is a figure of energy equivalents much greater than a combined total of the world's known resources of recoverable coal and potential resources for oil and natural gas (Schurr, 1963). Some people are now talking seriously of atomic power costs of the order of 1.5 mills per kilowatt hour (California Insti-

94

tute of Technology, 1967), although other authorities are skeptical of such a low figure. In comparison, the average cost of producing electricity from hydropower sources is about one order of magnitude greater.

Nuclear power plants are now being utilized and planned employing a process known as nuclear fission. Looking far into the future, it is indeed conceivable that fusion, where light atoms such as heavy hydrogen are fused into heavier atoms to produce power, is a distinct possibility. The technology has not yet been developed, and it appears that it may not be for many years. But if and when it is, and providing the process is economically feasible, a revolution will occur in the whole energy picture. There is an almost unlimited supply of heavy hydrogen in the oceans of the world.

Another long-run possibility for producing electric power is the harnessing of steam from the earth's hot springs and geysers to drive the power generators. Geothermal power plants presently exist in California, New Zealand, and Italy.

In assessing the total energy situation, it is significant that energy sources are readily convertible into one another; e.g., coal can be converted into electricity and even into fuel for internal combustion engines. Thus, it is the sum of energy resources which is most relevant for the long run. Prices will largely dictate the specific output of resource use and even the rate of technical advance in making conversions between output classes.

In summary, while it is true that the energy resources of the world are finite, it would also seem to be true that the world reserves, when considered as a whole, are very large indeed and that the projected needs of mankind can be served far beyond one century. This does not suggest that mankind can afford to be wasteful in the utilization of these resources. But neither can drastic population policies be justified solely on the basis of a fear that the world is in imminent danger of running out of the energy sources.

Minerals

High levels of consumption of manufactured products in the American economy have also necessitated the utilization of huge quantities of metallic and nonmetallic minerals. Increases in purchasing power from expected rising per capita incomes will probably significantly increase demands for minerals over the foreseeable future. The question is whether or not the earth can continue to yield what is demanded.

Barnett and Morse (1963) tried to define an answer in a Resources for the Future book. They contended that any estimates are inherently risky as our information is so limited.

> Very little was known about the physical properties of most resources in the United States of 1850. Today (1963) information on the properties and quantities of agricultural lands, forest, and surface waters is quite good; on underground water and ultimate coal deposits is less good; on ultimate oil and gas pools, fair to poor; and on ultimate metallic and non-metallic mineral deposits, poor to very poor (p.142).

Since it is impossible to know the physical properties of available mineral reserves with great reliability, Barnett and Morse propose another way of assessing scarcity. They developed a "scarcity model" from which implications can be drawn and tested that would reveal whether mineral resources are becoming more or less scarce through time. The model assumes that the most economic mineral reserves can be expected to be exploited first in our profit-oriented economic system. As reserves are used up, production is shifted to lower yielding ores, inevitably raising production costs and with them an increase in mineral *prices*. If the price does not rise, there is no increase in the effective scarcity of mineral deposits.

> From 1890 onward, costs per unit of net mineral output, measured in either labor or labor and capital, have declined rapidly and persistently . . . Again, increases in productivity were more rapid in the latter half of the period than in the early half . . . In summary, instead of increasing unit costs in the mineral industry, as called for by the scarcity hypothesis, a declining trend of cost was experienced (Barnett and Morse, 1963:170).

More specifically, Barnett and Morse point out that

> New domestic reserves of minerals have been found, or have become economically accessible, more rapidly than old ones have been used up. This generalization has a few exceptions—zinc, lead, and bauxite—among the major commodities with the United States. But for oil and gas, coal, iron, copper, sulfur, and other major commodities, known and usable U.S. reserves have increased, and this has facilitated the rapid decline in unit costs of extractive products (Barnett and Morse, 1963:196).

Barnett and Morse conclude (1963:247-248):

> The conservationists' premise that the economic heritage will shrink in value unless natural resources are "conserved" is wrong, for a progressive world. The opposite is true. In the United States, for example, the economic magnitude of the estate each generation passes on—the income per capita the next generation enjoys—has been approximately double that which he received, over the period for which data exist. . . . The more important components of the inheritance are knowledge, technology, capital investments, economic institutions. These, far more than natural resources, are the determinants of real income per capita.

Another Resources for the Future study by Fisher and Potter (1964) assesses consumption trends and supply projections to the year 2000. A generally optimistic pattern emerges with a few exceptions.

> . . . for iron, aluminum and manganese, the known and inferred reserves are large enough, worldwide, to supply projected demands for the next forty years without significant increase in cost. Doubts about the existence of unknown or inferred reserves may be moderated by noting that in recent years major new sources of iron ore, for example, have been discovered in Venezuela, Canada, Liberia, Brazil, and Australia, as well as other places. Techniques for beneficiating lower grade ores have also been improved (p. 60).

Fisher and Potter are less sanguine when it comes to copper, lead and zinc, however (Fisher and Potter, 1964:60-61).

> The demands which we have projected are expected to exhaust presently known and inferred reserves by the year 2000. Either large new discoveries of ore bodies or considerable advances in technology will be necessary to take care of the increased demands which will be experienced if anything like the 1950-60 rate of growth continues. It should be kept in mind, however, that there are satisfactory substitutes for these metals in most uses, and that substitution, technology, and probably discovery will proceed at an accelerated pace if costs and prices rise.

My conclusion is that the best scientific evidence reveals no impending natural resource (either energy or minerals) shortages that will critically curtail economic growth, let alone threaten man's existence.

The effective supplies of "fixed" natural resources are related to many variables, including the total known stock of reserves; the technology of extraction, processing, and delivery; and prices. Technological advances, discoveries of new stocks, and/or the finding of substitutes lower the relative prices and thus increase the effective supplies. The exhaustion of higher grade supplies or large increases in demand relative to supply will increase the price. Thus, the market is a remarkable instrument for allocating resources to various uses and users and over time. It is an immutable law of the market that rising prices signal resource scarcity, and for most natural resources, relative prices are not rising over time. If they were, we have much confidence in the intelligence, innovative abilities, and adaptive capacities of man himself. Man's history in the use of natural resources is one of continuous adaptation to new condition, most of which he has generated. When properly motivated, people are likely to invent ways to stretch scarce resources. No reasons come to mind to suggest that people will be less ingenious, enterprising, and innovative in the future than in the past.

References

Barnett, Harold J., and Chandler Morse
1963   Scarcity and Growth, the Economics of Natural Resources Availability. Resources for the Future. Baltimore: Johns Hopkins Press.

California Institute of Technology
1967   The Next Ninety Years. Pasadena: California Institute of Technology.

Clawson, Marion (ed.)
1963   "The world oil outlook," by M. A. Adelman in Natural Resources and International Developments. Baltimore: Johns Hopkins Press.

Ehrlich, Paul R.
1970   "Ecological destruction is a condition of American life." Mademoiselle 70 (April).

Ehrlich, Paul R., and Anne Ehrlich
1970   Population; Resources; Environment. San Francisco: W. H. Freeman and Company.

Fisher, Hugo
    1965   "Esthetics and economics." Sierra Club Bulletin
                    (September).

Fisher, Joseph L., and Neal Potter
    1964   World Prospects for Natural Resources. Re-
                    sources for the Future. Baltimore: Johns Hop-
                    kins Press.

Gardner, B. Delworth
    1968   Protein and the Pill: A Pivotal Partnership,
                    Faculty Honor Lecture, Utah State University,
                    Logan (April).

Gardner, B. Delworth, and Allen D. LeBaron
    1968   "Some neighborhood effects of oil shale devel-
                    opment." Natural Resources Journal Vol. 8 No.
                    4 (October):569-586.

Jarrett, Henry (ed.)
    1966   "The economics of the coming spaceship earth,"
                    by Kenneth E. Boulding in Environmental
                    Quality in a Growing Economy. Resources in
                    the Future. Baltimore: Johns Hopkins Press.

Landsbery, Hans H., Leonard L. Fischman, and Joseph L. Fisher
    1963   Resources in America's Future. Resources for
                    the Future. Baltimore: Johns Hopkins Press.

Lovejoy, Wallace F., and Paul T. Homan
    1967   "Economic aspects of oil conservation regula-
                    tion." Resources for the Future. Baltimore:
                    Johns Hopkins Press.

Meadows, Donell H., Dennis L. Meadows, Jorgen Randers, and
William W. Behrens III
    1972   The Limits to Growth, A Potomac Associates
                    Book. New York: Universal Books.

Rienow, R., and Leona T. Rienow
    1970   Moment in the Sun. New York: The Dial Press.

Schanz, John J.
1972   "Economic aspects of the development of energy resources." Proceedings, Intermountain Universities' Conference on Policy Formulation in the Development of Energy Resources. Salt Lake City (May).

Schurr, Sam H.
1963   "Energy." Scientific American 209 (September).

Schurr, Sam H., and Bruce C. Netschert
1960   Energy in the American Economy 1850-1975. Resources for the Future. Baltimore: Johns Hopkins Press.

Wallich, Henry C.,
1972   "More on growth." Newsweek (March 13).

Natural Resources, People, and the Quality of Life*

By R. W. Behan

Man and Resources

Natural resources, we have come to understand after three generations of rhetoric, are the substances and the forces that make human life possible.

The substances provide us with the consumer goods that each of us needs. Timber resources provide us with housing, the forest products industry is quick to tell us. The forage resource is translated, through the digestive tracts of domestic animals, into beef, shoes, and wool shirts; and we are frequently reminded of that by the livestock industry. So much for the substances.

The forces component of natural resources are the sources of energy we use to move substances to the people who want them or people to the substances they need. Or perhaps we use energy sources just to move people hither and yon with not much reason at all, but with great benefits to their spiritual and psychic well-being. In a particular case this is called "driving for pleasure," and it constitutes one of the most popular forms of outdoor recreation in the United States today. This fact must provide a great

*Reprinted by permission from *Ecology-Economics-Environment,* edited by R. W. Behan and Richard M. Weddle, Montana Forest and Conservation Experiment Station, University of Montana School of Forestry, Missoula.

sense of satisfaction and fulfillment to the petroleum industry, perhaps sufficient to assuage any lingering guilt about the Santa Barbara Channel.

Since the great conservation crusade of three generations ago the importance of natural resources to human existence has been axiomatic in our pleas to treat the good earth sensibly. We can grow only so much timber, so we mustn't overcut; we can grow only so much forage, so we mustn't overgraze. And there is just so much petroleum—and we can't grow any more of that at all—so we must use it wisely, avoid waste, etc.

The earth and its resources are fixed and finite, we have come to believe. In the current issue of the journal, *Environmental Education,* Professor Durward L. Allen (1969:36) puts it this way: "... we are dealing with a strictly limited quantity, the finite earth, its space, and raw materials." When the earth is used up and polluted, there won't be any more.

This was the rationale for the Conservation Movement, and it is the rationale today for the concern with the physical environment: our water courses, air masses, and landscapes can stand only so much pollution. . . .

The earth—"Spaceship Earth," we are increasingly fond of calling it—is 25,000 miles in circumference. It has a finite mass and atmosphere, a finite ecosystem, to use a more precise and certainly more voguish term; and within that fixed ecosystem man must fashion his "lifescape."

Population Myopia

What we see is man fashioning men—more and more and more of them. People. Populations. Humanity. Masses. Maggots. We read the population statistics, the growth rates of the human species all over the world, and we become alarmed. Recently an advertisement has been appearing in a number of national magazines; a headline in the ad says, "Whatever your cause, it's a lost cause unless we control population." Let me quote from the ad:

> At last an American President has acknowledged that it is his Administration's "clear responsibility to provide essential leadership" to control the flood of humanity that threatens to engulf the earth. . . .
>
> "Today the world population is three and a half billion persons," the

President told Congress. "It took many thousands of years to produce the first billion people; the next billion took a century; the third billion came after 30 years; the fourth will be produced in just 15.... Over the next 30 years ... the world's population could double! ... With birth rates remaining high and with death rates dropping sharply, many countries of Latin America, Asia and Africa now grow 10 times as fast as they did a century ago."

There will be a hundred million more people in *our own country* in another 30 years or so. Whatever your present cause, it is a lost cause unless we check the population explosion. Good causes ... will inevitably be swamped by too many people . . . (Time, 1969:11).

Some very important and impressive people lent their names to this ad, which was sponsored by an organization called "the Hugh Moore Fund." Robert McNamara, David Lilienthal, Eugene Black, Philip N. Hauser, and a number of other influential folks are conspicuously concerned about the population explosion.

They are concerned because we have structured the environmental problem in such a way that any intelligent person has to be concerned. We have perceived a fixed earth and a growing population. The consequence of this structure is clear and it is alarming: each of us gets less of what the earth has to offer. As the family gets larger, the pie has to be cut in smaller and smaller pieces.

I don't mean to accuse Messrs. McNamara, Lilienthal, Black, and Hauser of behaving like greedy kids at pie-time, for certainly our standard of living or our quality of life has a great many other components that are affected by too many people, too: crowded public facilities, traffic jams, overloaded schools, and waiting in line are all consequences of increasing numbers of people bearing down on fixed quantities.

We can write a very simple equation that expresses the relationship between natural resources, people, and the quality of life, and it looks like this:

$$\frac{\text{Resources}}{\text{People}} = \text{Quality of Life}$$

This is how we have structured the environmental problem today, I think; and in this form it has some very important consequences. One consequence of imposing a growing population on

103

a fixed resource base is obvious; and we hear it expressed in all sorts of "gangbusters" terms today: "catastrophe," "disaster," "crisis," "the population bomb keeps ticking," and "good causes . . . will inevitably be swamped by too many people." This "doomsday" consequence is apparent when we structure the problem this way, but there is another consequence, less apparent than the first but far more important. It is an operational consequence.

When the relationship of resources, people, and the quality of life is structured in the above fashion, we have only one decisionable variable. We have only one avenue of escape from doomsday; and that is to control population: resources are fixed, and the quality of life is a dependent variable beyond our control. Thus, we must focus on population: "Whatever your cause it's a lost cause unless we control population," the ad reads. We can do nothing else.

I call this single-minded approach "population myopia," and I think it is the unfortunate consequence of structuring the problem the way that we have. But let me make a clear distinction here: population myopia is a consequence not of the environmental problem, but of the way we have structured or perceived the problem. And I think it is an unfortunate consequence because it keeps us from inspecting some other avenues of escaping doomsday. Thus, we are led to formulate what I call "blockbuster" policy. In other words, a single-minded perception of the problem produces simpleminded solutions to it. We fail to look at other solutions, other combinations of solutions, when we suffer population myopia, and it could just be that we need all the help we can get.

So let us consider how we have structured the problem to see if we have done so accurately, precisely, and completely.

Resources, Neutral Stuff, and Technology

First, the numerator of the equation, the fixed resource base: is that an accurate representation of reality?

Certainly the mass of the earth is fixed and finite, and so is the biosphere, the ecosystem. But Spaceship Earth is carrying an immense amount of excess baggage.

We subsist in a very shallow stratum of Spaceship Earth. That stratum extends from perhaps a mile beneath the surface to several miles above it, and within it we find all the resources we need. The

104

rest of the mass must have a name—"excess baggage" is not very descriptive—and I am drawn to a term used by geographer Norton Ginsburg. He would call the rest of the earth's mass "neutral stuff." It comprises the substances and the forces that have no existing or reasonably foreseeable human utility, and its quantity is truly immense in comparison to that skinny little stratum in which we live.

Now, by turning my terms inside out, we come up with a reasonable definition of what a natural resource is: a substance or force that does fulfill an existing or reasonably foreseeable human need. My definition of natural resource is altogether man-centered. Whether we should be man-centered in our thinking is a question I will leave to others. It is obvious to me that we do think in man-centered terms, and I see no particular immorality in doing so. We save the whooping crane for our own satisfaction, it seems to me, not for his; and I find it defensible—and fortunate for the whooping cranes—to define natural resources in this way. For it is not so much man's being at the center as what man does at the center that should really concern us.

What do I mean by "reasonably foreseeable"? Well, I do not think it is reasonably foreseeable that man will need all the neutral stuff contained in Spaceship Earth. Long before we need to tap the metallic ore bodies in the molten core of the earth, we will have invented less costly schemes of recycling on the surface; we can't really throw anything away after all. And, long before we need to tap that same core for a source of thermal energy, we will have invented less costly ways of using solar energy. Now the sun will expire, as I recall, in about four billion years; and by "reasonably foreseeable" I mean foreseeable substantially sooner than that. In fact, I would say that a reasonably foreseeable human need is one that might be expected to arise within the next 50 years.

All our natural resources then—substances and forces with existing or foreseeable human utility—are found in that small, skinny stratum of Spaceship Earth. But not everything in this stratum is a natural resource: there is lots of neutral stuff in the rocks and sands, and lots of useless energy in the tides. The listing could go on and on, but the conclusion is clear enough: The ratio of neutral stuff to natural resources is great. We don't need, want, or use very much of Spaceship Earth.

I am implying strongly here that we need to be concerned only with those things which have human utility. I suspect many will find this offensive, but consider this: if we care about something— say the whooping crane or clean air or pretty landscapes—we are simply saying that it does have human utility, and so we become concerned about it. This is not sophistry, incidentally; it is history.

For mankind has been appraising his environment for many years, and he has found a succession of utilities in it. First he found flowers and fruits and nuts, and he wandered around gathering his subsistence. (There are some who suggest we should go back to this "happy primate" stage. I disagree.) Then man discovered a sharp stone and some seeds, and the agricultural revolution was underway. Then he found that bronze would make better tools than would stones and that animals could augment his own physical energy. Then he appraised the possibilities offered for a better life by iron and coal, and the Industrial Revolution was underway. And then steel and petroleum were seen to be superior in many ways, and here we are. The automobile, in spite of its ostentatious chromium, nonsensical dimensions, and subliminal sexuality, and in spite of its generating some 60 percent of the nation's air pollution, is a magnificent symbol of contemporary substance and energy resources. Built of steel and propelled by petroleum, it is the current expression of a long history of environmental appraisals and discovered utilities. (It may also be the first expression of discovered disutility.)

Notice the replacements we have made. In substance resources bronze replaced stone, iron replaced bronze, and steel replaced iron. In energy resources the animal replaced the human back, coal (to· produce steam) replaced the animal, and petroleum products replaced coal. In each case man invented new ways of using his environment, but note this: the substances and energies had always been in the environment; we had only to discover or invent ways of using them. . . . The physical environment, in other words, has been relatively constant; but the ways of using it have changed dramatically and sometimes very quickly.*

---

*There is a major weakness in my generalization here, of course: the physical environment changes as a consequence of using it. Energy in particular is used up or consumed, and substance resources are moved around to a greater or lesser degree. But these impacts are of less and less consequence, for I see quantum jumps in the evolution of technologies. First, both our substances and energies were utilized as they occurred physically in nature:

The ways of using the environment have changed as better appraisals have been made. On the one hand, we appraise the environment better and discover better ways of doing things. As a consequence, petroleum products replace coal as an energy source because pumping is easier than digging and pipe-lining is easier than bulk hauling. On the other hand, we make better appraisals of our wants and needs and discover something else. Instead of discovering a better way of doing things, we discover some better things to do. National parks, wilderness areas, and outdoor recreation in general, and efforts to maintain clear air, clean water, and attractive landscapes are the results of such introspection; they are better things to do.

As a result of better appraisals we discover better ways of doing things or better things to do or both; and, as a result of that, we change our ways of using the environment.

In short, we change our technologies.

This technology is a funny business. We think of it in terms of white laboratory coats, test tubes and computers, and esoteric buildings having lots of plumbing and gauges and meters. We think of it preeminently as something that either will or will not, depending on our disposition, save mankind from one or another of several dozen potential disasters. "Technology," the word, has come to have a reality all of its own. Black magic, I suppose, has been replaced by white magic; and, typically, either we believe in it with sanguine, often industrial conviction, or we doubt it and damn it with wild-eyed frenzy.

Let us inspect a small and particular way we use the environ-

---

rocks, seeds, and human (later animal) energy. With the discovery and adoption of fire, man made his first quantum jump; now he was operating at a chemical level, though his substance technology remained largely physical. With the discovery of how to make polyethylene and other materials with petrochemical processes, we seem now to have made the quantum jump in substance resources; both energies and substances now rely on chemical as well as physical processes. And, of course, we have made another quantum jump lately to atomic sources of energy. In the case of breeder reactors we are relying on atomic processes to produce substances as well. In a sense we have progressed from cellular technologies through molecular technologies to atomic technologies. I suspect particle technologies are not inconceivable; but I wonder, at the same time, what might happen to the world monetary system if we chose to realize the alchemist's dream. It seems to me the transformation of lead to gold is well within the realm of atomic technology.

ment, the technology of wilderness use. First we build a system of trails. Then we import a strange, nonnative ungulate called the horse and equip him with a Decker packsaddle, perhaps. We ride on saddles, too, and stick our feet into stirrups, a piece of technology we borrow from early European warfare. Without the trails, the horses, and the saddles, the wilderness user would be in desperate straits indeed; and only a red-necked backpacker can say that with such relish and enthusiasm.

But of course I have a technology of wilderness, too; it includes a high-riding aluminum pack frame and Vibram soles on my hiking boots; and I would be in as much trouble without my technology as my horseback friends without theirs.

Recall now, please, the concept of neutral stuff—the substances and forces that do not have human utility—and the concept of natural resources—the substances and forces that do. *Technology is the engine of transformation.* We make better appraisals of our environment and our needs; we change our way of using the environment; and neutral stuff becomes natural resources. We have been doing this since the stone age, through the bronze age, through the iron age, and into the present. With horses and pack frames we make the neutral stuff of the wilderness into a pleasant, or exciting, and satisfying experience, a "recreation resource." We have been doing this for thousands of years, and I expect, without being terribly bold, that we can keep at it. Technology, then, is not magic, a disembodied spirit; in any culture technology is intrinsic.

Please notice a peculiar but very important property of technological progress suggested by my argument here. We don't accumulate technologies so much as we supplant technologies. Latex paints doomed the turpentine industry, and when was the last time milady slipped into a pair of silk stockings? My point is simply this: the engine of transformation runs in both directions— some neutral stuff becomes natural resources, and also, as a consequence of a supplanting technology, certain natural resources become neutral stuff.

We have already seen that the ratio of neutral stuff to natural resources, at any given time on Spaceship Earth, is enormous; the excess baggage far, far outweighs those substances and forces that do have current utility. And through time we shift particular substances and forces from the category of neutral stuff to the category of natural resources and vice versa.

108

The conclusion of this analysis is inescapable, I think: *the resource numerator of our equation, through time, is neither fixed nor finite.** It is defined and determined by our technology, our way of using the environment. These things have changed throughout man's history, and, again without being terribly bold, I expect they will continue to change.

But the important thing to keep in mind here is this: the changes have come about as results of deliberate human decisions. Let me be very explicit here: We have changed the resource base by making decisions about technology, by deciding on new ways of using the environment so that neutral stuff becomes natural resources.

We can express this relationship with another neat equation:

$$\text{Resources} = f(N,T)$$

Resources are functions of neutral stuff and technologies. At a slight cost in mathematical rigor, but with a great gain in understanding, we can also write the relationship this way:

$$\text{Resources} = N \times T$$

Resources are the products of neutral stuff and technologies.

And now the temptation is simply irresistible to go back to our original relationship and substitute some terms. Now that we know that resources are the products of neutral stuff and technologies, we can write the equation this way:

$$\frac{\text{Neutral Stuff} \times \text{Technologies}}{\text{People}} = \text{Quality of Life}$$

Suddenly, or at least apparently, we have one more decisionable variable in our equation. There is another escape from doomsday, and it has to do with the decisions we make about the resource numerator. The escape is dependent on our making decisions about the resource numerator, however, and if our case of population myopia is severe, we are predestined to failure. We cannot make decisions that we do not see.

---

*It is fixed at any one instant, according to the particular pattern of technology at that instant.

109

I will discuss shortly some of the resource-numerator decisions I think should be made. For now, let us simply mark it as a decisionable variable, not a fixed and given quantity, and consider the third term in our equation, the "quality of life."

Quality of Life: An Independent Variable

We often perceive the quality of life as a *dependent* variable—it just falls out the bottom, strictly determined by the relationship of resources to people.

I propose that in particular countries the quality of life, can be and should be an independent variable. As a matter of fact, I contend that in some countries, and certainly in the United States, it is an independent variable.

In general terms, what I mean is this: our first, independent decision specifies the quality of life we want, and the other terms in the equation, resources and population, are conditioned or determined by that choice.

Let me explain in specific terms: Each of us chooses a specific quality of life, and then we spend our incomes and our leisure in order to attain it. The sum of all these decisions, incidentally, is a very important determinant of the quality of the physical environment; but let us look first at the individual choices.

One of the foremost decisions we make as individuals—typically in a bilateral conversation—has to do with the size of our family. American couples are clearly choosing smaller families these days; between 1957 and 1966 the birth rate dropped from 25.0 to 19.4 births per thousand people. It is still dropping, and when it hits 14 per thousand, our population will stabilize (assuming a 70-year life expectancy). This happened, I suspect, because we began defining a high quality life as one including, among other things, fewer kids; at any rate, the decline wasn't caused by any scarcity of resources.

If you will permit me a quick simplification, I have just described how quality of life decisions condition or determine the population denominator in our equation. Population is a dependent variable, then.

But what about the resources numerator? This is determined by our income and leisure decisions. Income and leisure are probably direct, zero-sum tradeoffs, i.e., we gain income at the expense of

110

leisure and vice versa. The hippie opts for one extreme, I guess, and the corporation executive working a 70-hour week opts for the other.

In this initial income-leisure decision we exert a strong influence on the resources numerator: the hippie needs a few beads, a little brown rice, and some sandals—perhaps several hundred pounds of stuff, if you include his books on Zen Buddhism. The corporation executive, by contrast, needs tons and tons of stuff: his Chrysler for commuting, his Thunderbird for the country club, his Land Rover for fishing trips, *et cetera ad infinitum*.

Having chosen a particular magnitude of income, we face another series of quality of life choices in how to spend it. Generally, we have three options: we buy private goods, we buy public goods, or we save or invest.

Shall we look first at private goods?

An adult human being can subsist for a year on 791 pounds of wheat flour, cabbage, spinach, and navy beans, and 57 cans of evaporated milk (Stigler, 1952:2). At current prices this would cost about $145. Assuming a like amount for clothing and perhaps twice that for shelter, we can live on about $580; I guess everything above that is spent for luxuries.

I neither advocate being nor claim to be quite that spartan; but nevertheless, we call for more resources than we really need, particularly in the private goods sector.

John Galbraith, of course, took us all to task for redundant consumerism in his book, *The Affluent Society*, but he spoke in the hard-goods-and-logical-world language of the economist.

Benton MacKaye (1962:217) invented a nontechnical word, "decreation" that described the "degenerate element of play." MacKaye then depicted a scene of "decreation" at a cocktail party:

> We focus on some tea table about 5 p.m. in some ornate tomb on the twenty-ninth floor of the latest apartment house where innately good, if over polished, people gather to discourse assiduously on the relative merits of their bathroom sets, their window curtains, their motor oils, and their other intricate means, within the sign-decked and encumbered limits of their horizon, for dressing up and going nowhere.

And Japhy Ryder, the hero in Jack Kerouac's (1958:77-78) great novel, had a vision of a better day—or a better way:

111

... the whole thing is a world full of ruck sack wanderers, Dharma Bums refusing to subscribe to the general demand that they consume production and therefore have to work for the privilege of consuming, all that crap they didn't really want anyway such as refrigerators, TV sets, cars, at least new fancy cars, certain hair oils and deodorants and general junk you finally always see a week later in the garbage anyway, all of them imprisoned in a system of work, produce, consume, work, produce, consume, I see a vision of a great ruck sack revolution; thousand or even millions of young Americans wandering around with ruck sacks, going up to mountains to pray, making children laugh and old men glad, making young girls happy and old girls happier. . . .

Somewhere in all this allegory, I think Galbraith's message is clear: we spend too much on consumer goods and place an inordinate burden on natural resources. In the language of economics, for example, most of us face negative marginal returns in our consumption of food; we would be better off if we ate less.

In the public goods sector perhaps we are near the poverty level. I share Professor Galbraith's sense of amazement at the contrast between expensive and sophisticated private automobiles on one hand and our shoddy patchwork of public streets on the other, between $10,000 pickup campers and crowded campgrounds, and between air-conditioned houses and a fouled atmosphere outdoors. And, certainly, many of the amenities of life that make both work and leisure more meaningful are classed as public goods: libraries, parks, museums, and so on. I might also mention here such things as sewage treatment plants and solid waste disposal systems. Both bear on the quality of the physical environment, and both could at least tolerate large doses of public funds. The decisions we make—or fail to make—in spending for public goods also influence quite heavily the natural resource numerator.

But in a particular way, perhaps it is the savings and investment sector that is the most significant. For it is here that direct investment is made in research and development activities—precisely the point at which technologies are developed. New ways of using the environment are discovered; neutral stuff becomes natural resources and vice versa as a direct result of research and development activities.

I hope I have built a convincing case that in the United States the quality of life is an independent variable. We decide on that first, and then both resources and population follow as dependent variables. A country at a bare subsistence level, on the other hand,

112

faces the conventional pattern: resources and population are the independent variables, and the quality of life does depend on their relationship. But in our country we have reversed the dependencies because we can afford to: our economy produces enough to satisfy our wants and still add to its stock of capital, its research and development, its technologies, and consequently its resources. The Secretary-General of the United Nations, Mr. U Thant, described this situation not long ago:

> The truth, the central stupendous truth, about developed countries today is that they can have—in anything but the shortest run—the kind and scale of resources they decide to have. . . . It is no longer resources that limit decisions. It is the decision that makes the resources. This is the fundamental revolutionary change—perhaps the most revolutionary mankind has ever known (Kaiser Aluminum News, 1966:30).

There are two major implications here that bear on our quest for a high quality of life, which includes a pleasant, agreeable physical environment. One is the absolute indispensability of a prosperous economy so that we can keep quality of life as an independent variable, so we can make some choices, so we can invest in research and development, so neutral stuff can become natural resources, and so we can pay the cost of cleaning up our air, water, and landscapes. The alternative to economic prosperity is clearly retrogression; and if anyone cares to live the happy-go-lucky life of a flower-picking primate let him go do his thing and leave me in the twentieth century problems and all.

Population Control vs. Development

The other implication is this: it is not population *alone* that distinguishes the prosperous nations from the less fortunate ones.

I propose that, worldwide, the problem is not exclusively, nor perhaps even primarily, one of population. It has to do with development. If U Thant is right, if developed countries make resources through decisions, and if in so doing they escape doomsday, then we need desperately to foster the development of the world's backward countries, and not suffer population myopia once again. But I have heard it proposed recently, although I hope facetiously, that the United States should develop birth-control chemicals and add them secretly to the water supplies of Asian

113

cities. That kind of thinking is insane. I can think of no more expeditious means to trigger a race war against the United States, and a justified one, than a damnfool stunt like that.

The image of populations, particularly Asian populations, characterized by uncontrolled animal breeding is popular, frightening, and wrong. A modern version of the Yellow Peril is presented to us here, it seems to me, with elements of racism, ethnocentric vanity, and fears of property loss all inherent in the image. Let me quote from a new book, *Resources and Man,* recently published by the National Academy of Sciences—National Research Council. In an essay entitled "United States and World Population," Professor Nathan Keyfitz says:

> If the future of North American populations depends ... on the changing sentiments of parents ... the future of the underdeveloped world depends on quite different circumstances—whether parents will adopt birth-control measures and what proportion of parents will use it effectively ... only when such measures finally result in real population control can mankind relax the effort to relieve the population pressures on the already over-crowded "Spaceship Earth". . . . Attention is drawn especially to the increase in the proportion of the total world population expected in the underdeveloped regions—from 68.5 to 76.5 percent. *This will inevitably place severe pressures on the developed regions* (italics added) (NAS-NRC, 1969:51, 56).

The way to keep the Barbarians away from the gates, apparently, is to slip 'em the Pill.

If there is racism here, and if there is self-righteousness here, I find the image repugnant on these grounds alone. But the image is repugnant to intellectual grounds as well.

The institution of the family is universal among men, and it comprehends a concern for the welfare of offspring. Indeed, as Desmond Morris (1969:43-85) tells us, "pair bonding" and the care of helpless young are ancient and powerful biological urges. If North American families are adept at changing their sentiments, and hence determining North American populations, why do we assume that Asian families cannot and do not do the same thing?

I think it is more likely that families everywhere assess their environments just as we do—with the knowledge and values their cultures provide—and voluntarily adjust their family size accordingly. There are errors in both assessment and adjustment, true;

114

and Malthusian checks are always waiting in the wings, the checks of disease and misery and starvation. But where on earth is a human population growing anywhere near its biological capacity? If marriage to menopause is, say twenty-five years, why aren't family sizes on the order of twenty to twenty-five children? Allowing for miscarriage, chance infertility, and the like, one child per year or a little less is a reasonable biological maximum. But family sizes don't average that anywhere in the world, and infant mortality doesn't account for this population phenomenon either.

In my view, Professor Colin Clark (Agarwala and Singh, 1963:33) makes a great deal of sense:

> . . . most Malthusian propagandists give an extraordinary illustration of their unawareness of facts. They believe that if they can have the latest European and American contraceptives sufficiently advertised and cheaply distributed throughout the Oriental countries, the number of children born in the Orient would immediately and permanently fall. Nothing seems more improbable. Children are born in the Orient, as they were among our ancestors, and as most children are born in the Christian world today, because of their parents wishes and consciences and religious beliefs; not because their parents wished to prevent them from being born but are unable to obtain contraceptives.

If my reasoning, and Professor Clark's, is sensible, a clear conclusion emerges: the world population is not wildly out of control, "exploding" beyond human will and comprehension at all; the population of the world is *decision-determined* right now while we talk about it. The population problem, then, is that the decisions of others simply don't agree with our own. There is a great difference in value judgments, in other words, about how many people is too many people. But when judgments take on the appearance of divine and absolute truth, we have the preconditions for holy wars. Then the infidels are slain for their own redemption; cities are destroyed to save them; and we superciliously pass out the Pills to the Barbarians. Let us be more sophisticated than that; let us indeed be magnanimous.

Let us share our contraceptive techniques with those who share our population attitudes and objectives and respect those who don't. Let us not aim exclusively at the population "denominator" of other societies, but help them to expand the resources "numerator." Let us share our tools and avoid imposing our values. This may be what Professor Keyfitz had in mind at the end of his

115

uneven essay when he finally said, *"The only escape . . . is through the economic development of the countries of Asia, Africa, and Latin America"* (NAS-NRC, 1969:62).

Largely by historical accident, and with a great deal of attendant human misery, the Western cultures have stumbled onto three major components of high and growing productivity: specialized labor, pools of accumulated capital, and mass production. These are some of the components of our status as a developed country, and some of the reasons why our standard of living is an independent variable. Perhaps, in our humanitarian efforts to aid the underdeveloped areas of the world, we might concentrate on these ideas instead of violating the local culture's ideas about children and family size. In so doing, we might pull off one of the greatest trades in the history of mankind. If the Western cultures can show the Eastern cultures how to produce more, perhaps they can teach us the wisdom of wanting less.

Toward a Higher Quality of Life

Well, obviously I have injected a great deal of my personal judgment into the paper so far. I want always to reserve the right, incidentally, to change my mind, for it is only by changing our minds that we learn anything at all.

But to continue, we need not be in perfect agreement on everything I've said so far. Can we agree that we, as a society, can make some decisions that affect the resource numerator, that we can make some decisions that affect the people denominator, and that we can make some decisions about our quality of life? This is all the agreement we need: that all three variables are decisionable. If they are decisionable, they will be decided by the dialogue of civilized cultures. I would like to add to that dialogue by expressing my opinion about things we should do.

First, let us consider the resource numerator, or the "neutral stuff X technology" term. If we can leave anything of value at all for future generations, I think a wide range of options must rank near the top. I have heard it suggested that we freeze technology, that we take a "technological holiday." Since technology "causes" our environmental problems, it is argued, we should have some sort of moratorium in technological development. This is nonsense, for such a moratorium would burden future generations with the problems of today which are usually perceived to be physical problems of air, water, and landscape pollution. It would leave all the problems and prohibit the seeking of solutions. But more than that, it would saddle future generations with only today's ways of using the environment. Freezing technology obviously would impose severe restrictions on the choices that future generations would have for it would also freeze the resource numerator. A broad array of technological options and the consequently broad array of resources would be a far more valuable legacy.

I suggest, therefore, that research and development expenditures be substantial and permanent in both the public and private sectors (cutting off the creation of knowledge is a blockbuster means of deciding what to do). We don't know yet, for example, how to control the fusion reaction of deuterium, a heavy isotope of hydrogen. If we deliberately avoided finding out, we would commit one of mankind's greatest blunders; for the fusion reaction produces enormous amounts of energy, and deuterium is plentiful in sea water. Let me quote once again from the NAS (1969:230) study to illustrate the magnitude of this potential:

> Should enough deuterium be withdrawn to reduce the initial concentration (in sea water) by 1 percent, the energy released by fusion would amount to about 500,000 times that of the world's initial supply of fossil fuels.

This is a little difficult to grasp, so I made some simple calculations. Assume that we began using fossil fuels in 1800 and that we will exhaust the world's supply in A.D. 2000. That means fossil fuels will have lasted 200 years. At this rate of consumption one percent of the deuterium in sea water will furnish mankind's energy, after fossil fuels are exhausted, for 100 million years. After that, I suppose, we can begin using the 99 percent of the deuterium still remaining in the oceans. And when all that is used up, our sun will have been dead for six billion years.

No, I am not suggesting that we should exploit this potential resource. I am suggesting it would be nice, comfortable, and secure simply to know how. For it is not what we know but what we do that generates problems in our physical environment.

Nor should we overlook the particular technologies that have to do with feeding people. I am not, incidentally, proposing that

117

technology will save the world, nor even that technology should. For I am not prepared to say that technology—in the conventional sense of the word—has to save the world. I am saying that we should develop feeding techniques to support any population that we choose to produce. And we might begin by exploiting the technologies we have at hand. Hybrid grains seem to be doing well, but what have the Western developed countries done with freeze-drying, for example, except to adapt it to our recreation cookery and lately to our instant coffee? If we add storage technologies to the transportation and distribution technologies we already have on hand, the effective resource numerator, on a global scale, becomes much larger indeed.

In short, relative to the numerator of our equation, I propose a deliberate and vigorous effort to generate, disseminate, and use a broad spectrum of technologies; let man unlock his ingenuity and struggle with the real freedoms it can provide. (Judging from the freedom enjoyed by contemporary artists in all the media, and from the struggles they are having, we should anticipate some lively scraps.)

Now what about the population denominator? Dr. Paul Ehrlich, in 198 pages of florid prose, imagines a "population bomb," a situation in which global population is outstripping the global capacity to produce food. He says, with endearing metaphor:

> I wish I could offer you some sugarcoated solutions, but I'm afraid the time for them is long gone. A cancer is an uncontrolled multiplication of cells; the population explosion is an uncontrolled multiplication of people (1968:166).

Dr. Ehrlich sees massive famines within the next decade or so and, with a great deal of cowardice—or intelligence—he stops just short of advocating compulsory birth control.

This same problem of population versus food supply was discussed in 1798 with nearly identical assumptions—and with far greater elegance and clarity—by the Reverend Thomas Robert Malthus (Arbor, 1964), an English minister and erstwhile economist. Fortunately for mankind, but unfortunately for Dr. Ehrlich's argument, 172 years of history have demonstrated the ability of man's brain to keep ahead of his stomach; he has learned to be productive far beyond the imagination of Parson Malthus, and he has improved immensely his means for voluntarily ad-

118

justing his family size (NSA-NRC, 1969:46).* A simultaneous failure of all man's technologies, of his institutions, of his social structures, and of the beliefs and urgings that have sustained him so far is just barely short of inconceivable.

Professor Ehrlich (1968:18) refers, but very selectively, to an article by a British physicist, J. H. Fremlin. Ehrlich fails to mention that Fremlin, in his article, sees virtually no technical problems in feeding colossal populations. Fremlin does see an absolute limitation on human population, however, but it is not food. It is the capacity of the earth's ecosystem to dissipate the heat that a global population might generate. We will reach this thermal saturation, however, only when the global population is about 17 million times the present world population. Obviously, the world, under those conditions, would be almost literally a hell of a place to live; and, indeed, Fremlin must rely on feeding technologies that are, at best, speculative. The National Academy of Sciences, however, in simply extending existing technologies, and rather timidly at that, suggests that we can feed 30 billion people, about nine times the present population. Whatever figure is appealing, I think there is an obvious inference to be drawn: we have a great deal of time to make some decisions before doomsday.

I suggested a while ago that we should develop technologies for sustaining any population we care to produce. (Short of that "heat limit," of course.) I am saying, in other words, that resources and population should remain dependent variables: they should follow from the *a priori* decision, the fundamental decision we make about the quality of life we want.

The idea of Spaceship Earth I find very appealing, and it makes sense to be concerned with our craft's structure. It also makes sense to be concerned with our fellow passengers.

Marshall McLuhan's idea of a "global village" is appealing, too. I think we might spend some time and money and effort—and spend them very well—seeing to it that all of the village's inhabitants face the same kinds of decisions that we do. In our country and state and county and city the independent decision-variable is quality of life. This state of affairs is a worthy global objective. But that will

---

*See Keyfitz' account of population control among the peasants in post-revolution France, NAS-NRC:46. The method was coitus interruptus—far less certain, say, than the IUCD, but apparently it was effective.

take us into a long hortatory exercise about defense budgets that are astronomical and foreign aid budgets that are minuscule and involve a lot of academic, ivory-tower prattling about the welfare and the brotherhood of man.

Our real interest in the environment, of course, has more to do with our favorite trout stream facing a threat of pollution or a pulpmill stench that intrudes into our patio cocktail parties or a logged-over hillside that compromises the sales commission of a real estate agent.

I am a little cynical here, all right, because too often we define "environment" or "quality of life" exclusively in terms of pure air, sparkling water, and beautiful, uncluttered landscapes. We don't really overlook decent housing, nutritious diets, and the public services of protection, health, and education: we simply take them for granted, in the United States, in defining "quality of life." Then we go on to raise hell about water pollution, air pollution, and landscape pollution.

The National Wildlife Federation recently found that 85 percent of the public is concerned with the physical environment—I don't mean to doubt the problem—and that three out of four people are willing to increase their taxes to improve it. But some other findings of the survey are extremely important, too. Let me quote from a recent report:

> High majorities (some topping 80 percent) of the college educated, the suburbanites, the people with higher incomes, and those under 30 years of age were in favor of more federal money going into conservation. The *least support for spending on conservation was seen among the blacks, the uneducated, and those with low incomes* (italics added) (National Outlook, 1969:854).

We seem to have a white, wealthy, educated, upper class issue here, largely because, I suspect, those of us who are white, wealthy, and educated already enjoy a fantastic material life. Perhaps we suffer another kind of myopia. Perhaps we assume that a good material life is universal and see only the physical environment of pure air, sparkling water, and beautiful, uncluttered landscapes.

A recent, well written, and widely read example of this attitude is a book called *Moment in the Sun,* (Rienow and Rienow, 1967) *A Report on the Deteriorating Quality of the American Environ-*

120

ment. Its authors, Robert and Leona Rienow, have chronicled very well our capacity to litter our air, waterways, and landscapes with gaseous, liquid, and solid garbage. But they have defined environment exclusively as physical environment. Extending the implications of such a definition, we come to an absurd conclusion: the highest quality environment is populated by flower-picking primates; the Garden of Eden has no human inhabitants at all; the contriving mind and the cunning hand of man are absent. It is a harmless pastime to wish for it, but we can't really go back.

Difficulties of the Environmental Dialogue

One criticizes *The Population Bomb* and *Moment in the Sun* at no small peril, of course. The "conventional wisdom" contained therein is quoted by Presidents, Secretaries of the Interior, and others whose intellectual reputations are well-known. And so I must apologize for my impudence by getting some tangents off my chest. The environmental dialogue today is burdened with at least three major difficulties, and I have a tangent about each one.

Tangent No. 1—The Comfort of the Polar Position

This has to do with the well-known and often-invoked fallacy of excluding the middle. Gifford Pinchot, the father of American forestry, once said, "He who is not for forestry is against it."

Pinchot did a grave injustice to a great many Americans who were comfortably, and legitimately, indifferent to forestry.

A colleague lately provided us with another example when he said, "Anyone who fights for these (lenient pollution) standards is on the wrong side and is a . . . company man (The Daily Missoulian, 1969:1).

These polar positions are truly comfortable because they are well defined and rich in oratory. They place no burden on us to think with sophistication, discrimination, or, indeed, with much intelligence about very complex problems. It is the business, again, of single-minded thinking producing simpleminded, blockbuster solutions. Polar positions leave precious little room, if any at all, for criticism; and the real trouble comes when our criticisms are made public: if we fail to heartily endorse one pole, our audience frequently assumes an endorsement for the other. Indeed, an

121

audience may take it upon itself to drive us to the other pole. I am pleased to avoid both poles. Categorically, I dislike categories, but right now I would like to offer a major testimonial: I support, endorse, and warmly advocate an environment fit for man's survival. When the argument is put in those terms, I am unequivocally for it.

Tangent No. 2—The Debate of Great Principles

When arguments are posed in terms of great principles, they often lead directly to deadlocks. Wilderness preservation and timber cutting are absolutely irreconcilable in principle. In practice, in the real world, we can escape this deadlock by separating wilderness areas and cutting areas in space, in time, or in both. So let's argue situations not principles.

The great principles of the environmental issue are many and trite. We hear questions like this often posed: "What right does industry have to pollute public water courses and air masses?" And the great principle is easily formulated: "Industry has no right to pollute public properties."

I maintain that debating in terms of great principles is pointless because agreement on them is universal in the first place. Industry does not "pollute public properties," you see: it disposes of wastes in an economical manner in order to keep prices low, and it does so in the best interests of the public. This argument has an altogether familiar tone—and there is a grain of truth in it. For nobody seeks pollution, nobody wants dirty streams or air masses. They are consequences, not goals; they are consequences of our past unwillingness or inability to meet the dollar costs of keeping our environment clean. Industry today is merely one of the agents of pollution; we are all, collectively, the cause of a dirty physical environment.

We can all be, collectively, the cause of a cleaner physical environment. In a few minutes I will suggest some means of going about it, for I think the condition of our physical environment can be anything we choose and anything we are willing to pay for.

But why do we have to pay for it? Don't we have a right to a pure environment? There is a great principle here that I don't care to debate; let us instead look at the situation. We need to pay for a clean environment because we have a dirty one now. To debate our right to something that doesn't exist seems fairly futile to me.

122

So what do we want? An environment absolutely pristine? We can get that by stopping the industrial mechanism and going back to picking fruit and flowers like happy primates—but again, I'll stick to the twentieth century, problems and all.

Or do we want a sane, sensible, dignified and noble, man-inhabited environment with improved air, water, and landscapes (none of them "perfect" but all of them fulfilling our needs for a pleasant environment)?

We can design such an environment and determine the costs of achieving it. Having done that, we can then determine how to pay for it, and this is what most great principle debates are really all about. Perhaps we would do better to stay with this format in the first place—objectives, costs, and who bears the costs—and leave the great principles to the philosophers.

Tangent No. 3—The Problem of Circles

This has to do with another well-known difficulty in formal logic, the problem of dealing with generalizations. We can have a generally good situation within a big circle. But within the big circle there may be smaller circles containing generally bad situations. And within those there may be even smaller circles again containing generally good situations. We need to know what "circle" we are talking about.

Let me summarize and illustrate this tangent with some propositions about human welfare: 1) In the global circle the level of human welfare, in per-capita consumption of goods and services, is bad. 2) In the United States circle the level of human welfare is good. 3) In the State of Montana circle the level of human welfare is not-so-good. 4) In the Missoula County circle the level is not-so-bad.

There is an interesting relationship between human welfare and another property of the same circles. Pollution of the physical environment, in the world circle, is not bad, but it is in the United States circle. Statewide, air pollution is not bad in Montana, but in Missoula County it is.

In short, as the consumption of goods and services has risen, so have pollution levels; and this, of course, is precisely what *Moment in the Sun* is all about. The correlation, historically, has been positive; but I do not think that the relationship is immutable or fixed or rigid or that it is the consequence of some

123

inexorable law. Water pollution, air pollution, and cluttered land-scapes have resulted from increasing consumption of goods and services, but they need not continue. And in any given circle welfare can rise without pollution for pollution is primarily a matter of waste disposal; that is a technical problem, not the result of immutable law. As an eminent ecologist, Barry Commoner (1966:126), says, "The problems of industrial and agricultural pollution, while exceedingly large and complex, are nevertheless capable of correction by the proper technological means."

But let's keep in mind a broad definition of "quality environment." It must include air-water-landscape things at a level at least fit for human biological survival. For most of mankind's history, this level has been maintained. (A spectacular exception, now something of a classic, was the tragic killer smog in London in 1952.) But a quality environment must also contain goods-and-services things, too.

If money is scarce, and if our goods-and-services component is at or near subsistence, we simply can't afford much in the way of air-water-landscape things. If, on the other hand, our goods-and-services component is supersaturated, then it makes a great deal of sense to buy fewer goods and services and more air-water-land-scape things. This is just a simple case of what economists call "equating at the margin": our total satisfaction is greater if we shift some expenditures around. But the important thing to keep in mind is the variation between circles and within circles: a rational allocation of expenditures in one circle is not automati-cally rational in all circles.

In any given circle we have to keep our priorities straight. Man does need bread, after all, before it becomes the thing that he cannot live alone by. If you'll pardon the awkward syntax, that means the provision of a good material life must come first (and it would be nice if it were universal). It includes a sizeable chunk of public services—public health and public education can do a lot, incidentally, to influence population levels—and it may have to include pollution of the physical environment. Providing this good material life, in other words, may necessitate using the least expensive methods of waste disposal, and, when it does, we should know it and choose deliberately to use them. Now it is self-evident that we need to maintain the safe minimum standard for biological survival, and, if history is reliable, that really is not very difficult.

124

Happily enough, there are few, if any, circles within the United States where the absolutely least expensive methods of waste disposal are essential.

Once we have the bread, in other words, we can make some air-water-landscape choices above the safe minimum standard level; and the United States certainly has the bread, both literally in terms of subsistence and figuratively in terms of money. Some of our less well-endowed circles can be easily subsidized to acquire air-water-landscape things: Congress recently appropriated $800 million to help communities build sewage treatment plants, an exceptionally wise thing to do I think. This is one way of buying air-water-landscape things: through politics and the expenditure of public funds. Another way works indirectly through the market system.

It is called "internalizing the costs," and it works like this: first we declare what we want, again politically, through air pollution laws, laws requiring the fencing of junkyards, etc. Then the polluters comply with the laws, typically taking as long as they can; for initially they face the entire cost of doing so. But soon they raise their prices, and we as consumers are then, and only then, presented with the bill. This process is a little bit risky in that we are, in a sense, buying something without knowing the price; but it is also devilishly effective and equitable in that products come to us with price tags that cover all the costs. And yet it isn't quite as simple as that, either, because now the price tag really represents two things: the goods-and-services component and the air-water-landscape component. If we want either one, we are forced to buy both. And, of course, under those circumstances, we may decide we don't want the package at all, in which case we drive some producers out of business. Such is the sovereignty—and the tyranny—of the consumer, and I would have it no other way.

Assertions, Facts, and Value Judgments

There is a great deal of verbalizing today that the air-water-landscape component of our quality of life is descending to the safe minimum standard level of biological survival. It is asserted that we have from ten to forty years left to live. This is an assertion, and I choose to treat it as I choose to treat most assertions—

skeptically. Certainly I haven't much more evidence, if indeed any more, that the assertions are false than the asserters do that they are true. And, just as certainly, there is little to be gained in the type of argument that assertions and counter-assertions generate: "It is." "It is not." "It is too." "It is not." I am simply unconvinced that doomsday is a decade or so away. (But, again, I reserve the right to change my mind.)

But perhaps we miss the point arguing about doomsday. Do we simply want cleaner air and waterways and more attractive landscapes in the United States? If the answer is yes—and my answer is yes—then we ask the next question. Can we afford to clean things up? Again my answer is yes. In the United States we certainly can: our goods-and-services component is characterized by obesity diets and more toys than we have time to play with. Our air-water-landscape component, by contrast, is characterized by trash and foul smells. If we want a better physical environment and we can afford to pay for it, then we face the very difficult and complex questions of how, in real world, operational terms, to get it. Single-minded thinking and simpleminded blockbuster solutions are spectacular and fun and appealing and newsworthy and useless. For there is, I think, an institutional ecology of laws and social structures and procedures and financial arrangements and many other objectives of public policy that is every bit as complex as biological ecology; and we need to recognize the web of interrelationships within it. I have argued in another paper (Behan, n.d.), for example, that the institutional ecology in Montana today is rather perverse: we buy a higher quality physical environment in our state largely at the cost of improved public services for low income groups. In effect, those who can least afford to will subsidize the rest of us in buying cleaner air and water unless we change some of the other strands in the web as well. (In this particular case we need to alter our tax structure.)

We need to consider this institutional ecology as well as natural ecology as we seek to improve our quality of life. We need to avoid the comfort of the polar positions—a position somewhere between them need not be at dead center in any case. We need to avoid arguing great principles. And we need to know what "circle" we are talking about and something of the smaller circles it contains. The problems are enormously complex and sophisticated: our thinking must be, too. If we have blasted natural

126

ecology with DDT, let us avoid the parallel mistake of blasting our institutional ecology with blockbuster policy.

We will need a great deal of validated information.

The universe of information has been divided rather neatly by a scholar named Herbert A. Simon (1965). He differentiates very clearly between factual propositions on the one hand and value propositions on the other. Factual propositions, Simon says, are statements about the observable world and the way in which it operates. Value propositions assert "oughts" rather than facts: they have "should be" or "ought to be" implications that factual propositions do not. Simon further discusses how each type of statement is validated; factual propositions can be wrong, after all, and values are always open for discussion. Factual propositions are validated simply by their agreement with the facts of the observable world. Value propositions are validated, in Simon's words, by fiat, by decree. They are validated by saying so and then by seeking a consensus through social institutions such as the market and the political process. (This is why I am skeptical of the doomsayers, incidentally: they are attempting to validate factual propositions by fiat, by saying so.)

We can get factual information from scientists—in the case of our current concern, from the ecologist and the economist. But we must be wary of them both. Again, let me quote Dr. Barry Commoner in his book, *Science and Survival* (Commoner, 1966:108-109).

> . . . the scientist, as the custodian of knowledge, has a profound duty to impart as much of it as he can to his fellow citizens. But in doing so, he must guard against false pretensions and avoid claiming for science that which belongs to the conscience. . . . Despite their origin in scientific and technological achievements, the issues created by the advance of science can only be resolved by moral judgment and political processes. In these processes, the scientist has one vote, and no claim to leadership. . . .

The natural scientist, then, can tell us that Y will happen if we do X, for that is a factual proposition. But he cannot tell us that Y is either good or bad, for that is a value proposition. The social scientist, the economist, can tell us that Y will cost Z dollars, but he cannot tell us it is worth it.

For only all of us, acting collectively, can validate the "should be's" of natural resources, people, and the quality of life.

127

References

Agarwala and Singh
    1963   "Population growth and living standards," by Colin Clark reprinted in The Economics of Underdevelopment. New York: Oxford University Press.

Allen, Durward L.
    1969   "Needed: citizen conservationists," in Environmental Education 1 (Winter).

Behan, R. W.
    n.d.   Economic Development and Environmental Quality. Missoula: School of Forestry. University of Montana. 11 pages mimeo.

Commoner, Barry
    1966   Science and Survival. New York: The Viking Press.

Daily Missoulian, Missoula, Montana
    1969   A story headlined Economic Development Consideration Urged (November 20).

Ehrlich, Paul R.
    1968   The Population Bomb. New York: Ballantine Books.

Kaiser Aluminum News
    1966   Vol. 24 No. 1:30.

Kerouac, Jack
    1958   The Dharma Bums. New York: New American Library.

MacKaye, Benton
    1962   The New Exploration. Urbana: University of Illinois Press.

Malthus, Thomas Robert
    1964   "Populations: the first essay." Ann Arbor: University of Michigan Press.

Morris, Desmond
    1969   The Naked Ape. New York: Dell Publishing Company.

NAS and NRC (National Academy of Sciences and National Research Council)
    1969   Resources and Man. San Francisco: W. H. Freeman and Company.

National Outlook
    1969   Journal of Forestry 67 (December).

Rienow, Robert and Leona Rienow
    1967   Moment in the Sun. New York: Ballantine Books.

Simon, Herbert A.
    1965   Administrative Behavior. New York: The Free Press.

Stigler, George J.
    1952   The Theory of Price. New York: The Macmillan Company.

Time
    1969   (November 21):11.

IV.
WHAT EVERYONE KNOWS:
THE "DISADVANTAGES"
OF LARGE FAMILIES
AND HIGH DENSITY

Introduction

Most children the world over are born and reared in families, and any discussion of population, resources, and the future will sooner or later (usually sooner) focus on issues central to marriage and family. Thus concern for population growth or changes in demographic rates ultimately boils down to concern about families and how they function. Apparently Malthus was well aware of this point. Interestingly enough, Malthus' proposed solution to the population problem was not an emphasis on birth control which he opposed, but rather the "postponement of marriage until the individual had the prospects of supporting a family, even if this meant remaining permanently single" (Kodel, 1972:40-41). At least one nation (Germany) was sufficiently impressed with the Malthusian thesis to enact legislation to accomplish just that—the postponement of marriage. The consequence of this massive legislation was not that which had been anticipated. True, marriage rates for younger aged adults dropped, but illegitimate birth rates increased, and the overall reduction in population growth seems to have been very slight. One author concludes that "the added burden to society created by the additional illegitimate births may well have offset whatever gains had been achieved" (Kodel, 1972:45). When solutions to "population problems" do not take into account the complexities of family life and the relationships

133

between family structure and process and the other institutions of society, unintended consequences are likely to occur.

Such is the caution presented in the first paper in this section by Thomas, who maintains that the most crucial challenge facing social scientists working in the area of family size is to identify the important causal variables. It does not follow that because "studies show that children from small families tend to be healthier, more emotionally stable, happier, more creative, and more independent" (ZPG, 1972:3), reduction in family size will produce *those characteristics in children. Family size is probably not the critical causal variable. In a comparative analysis of data from three different cultures, Thomas finds that when there are adequate controls for religion and socioeconomic level, family size is not a good predictor of the children's characteristics. He does find, however, that the quality of interaction between parent and child (the level of emotional support or warmth) does predict the child's characteristics in each of the three different cultures. Similarly, Kunz reports that when researchers control for the relevant social class variables, family size manifests little relation to academic performance. These authors maintain that the burden of proof that family size is an important causal variable lies with those who extol the virtues of the small family.*

Traditional exponents of Malthusian perspectives on population have maintained that "population growth intensifies social and urban problems. It increases the frequency with which they occur, it increases their magnitude, and it drains away resources that might be used in solving them" (ZPG, 1972:4). In a thoughtful and thorough review of the literature on density and its relationship to health, deviant behavior, and the quality of life, Chadwick calls into question such facile interpretations. An examination of the evidence provided by animal studies, urban-rural comparisons, conditions before and after urbanization, and of crowded institutions such as military training camps raises serious questions about the validity of the supposed causal relationship between disease, death, and human density. There is even some evidence that suggests that positive effects may derive from high density living, in that it may facilitate sanitation and the providing of preventive and corrective medical care. With respect to the link between density and social disorganization, animal studies, census data, and social surveys produce limited and inconsistent support for the

134

widely accepted generalization. The oft-cited animal studies are not as convincing as is generally supposed. There is a great deal of interspecies variation, and the effects of drastic changes in density (either increasing or decreasing) are usually not distinguished from the effects of stable levels of density. Among humans the relationship between density and social disorganization tends to disappear when the effects of social class are controlled.

Taken together these three papers underscore the need for more research and the tenuousness of many of the widely accepted notions about the impact of family size and high density on human welfare. The important causal variables remain to be identified; an understanding on how these variables interact is essential to the solution of the negative conditions now alleged to be "population problems." Solutions based on inadequate identification of the critical variables are likely to be no more successful than Germany's attempt to solve social problems by legislating the postponement of marriage.

References

Kodel, John
1972   "Malthus amiss: marriage restrictions in 19th century Germany." Social Science (Winter).

Zero Population Growth
1972   Information distributed in the mails to tell purposes and goals of ZPG.

Family Size and Children's Characteristics

Darwin L. Thomas *

Difficulty of Identifying Causal Relations

That variations in family size correlate with various character-istics of the child such as health (both physical and mental), intel-ligence, achievement, verbal ability, personal adjustment, etc., is known among social scientists. However, what is not known or agreed upon is the nature of the causal model underlying the research data which demonstrate that as family size changes, var-ious attitudinal and behavioral dimensions change.

Perhaps the most urgent task for social scientists working with family size is that of unravelling the causal connections among the myriad of variables which are known to be associated with each other. As an illustration of some of the problems, consider what is known and not known about the nature of the relationship between intelligence and family size. Evidence from research is available which shows that as family size increases, the average intelligence scores of children reared in those families decreases. Likewise, there is considerable evidence demonstrating that as the socioeconomic level increases, intelligence scores increase (Wray, 1971:403-431; Waller, 1971:122-136). The research also shows

*Appreciation is expressed to John Thompson for his assistance in the prep-aration of this report.

that as socioeconomic level increases, family size decreases (Smith and Zopf, 1970:342-350).

What is not known is how these variables combine with others to cause the various associations which have been demonstrated in research. In short, what is lacking is the development of some theoretical formulations which will prove useful in explaining and giving meaning to the findings. Does variation in socioeconomic status *produce* the differences in both family size and intelligence? Or another way of asking a similar question is: is it only the larger families in the lower socioeconomic levels which produce the children who have markedly lower intelligence scores?

The failure to be able to identify accurately causal relations creates a critical problem growing out of the present concern over population problems and solutions. In the face of demands for action over population problems, solutions are being sought not only by the man in the street, but by state and national legislatures as well. Some are willing to point to the empirically demonstrated relationship between family size and "negative" consequences such as health and intelligence and then propose that family size be reduced in order to reduce problems of personal well-being (Lieberman, 1970:87-92). It would be unfortunate indeed if such proposals rested upon the available evidence. How can intervention programs be proposed if causal relationships are not understood? Would a reduction in family size enhance personal well-being or cause other unintended consequences? Such questions as the foregoing cannot be answered until social scientists bent on developing and formulating explanations about family interaction approach the study of family size in a serious and multifaceted nature.

Family Size, Intelligence, and Socioeconomic Level

By more carefully analyzing the relationship between intelligence, family size, and socioeconomic level, one can further illustrate some of the problems that must be answered before satisfying answers can be given. Wray (1971:424-430), in one of the more complete reviews of the literature on the effects of family size, documents the negative consequences for the development of intelligence as family size increases. Wray reproduces four tables from previously reported research showing the decline in intelligence scores as family size increases.

138

The problem of determining what the data say and then carefully and accurately reporting it can be illustrated by analyzing the intelligence scores of children in Minnesota (Reed and Reed, 1965). There is virtually no difference in mean I.Q. scores in children coming from families of five or less children (an interpretation from an inspection of the means in Table 1). In families of six or more the average I.Q. score drops as family size increases. However, it should be noted that there are very few families in these categories. With such small numbers of families having such a great amount of variation in I.Q. scores (notice the size of the ± figures in Table 1) one cannot draw conclusions about the nature of the

Table 1. Mean I.Q. of children, by family size, Minnesota, USA, 1910-1960.

Family size	Number of families	Number of children tested	Mean I.Q. of children
1	141	141	106.37 ± 1.39
2	370	583	109.56 ± 0.53
3	287	606	106.75 ± 0.58
4	122	320	108.95 ± 0.73
5	57	191	105.72 ± 1.15
6	21	82	99.16 ± 2.17
7	7	39	93.00 ± 3.34
8	4	25	83.80 ± 4.13
9	5	37	89.89 ± 2.94
10	2	15	62.00 ± 7.55

Source: Reed, Elizabeth W., and Sheldon C. Reed, *Mental Retardation: A Family Study*, Philadelphia: W. B. Saunders Co., 1965. Cited in Wray, Joe D., "Population Pressure on Families: Family Size and Child Spacing," *Rapid Population Growth: Consequences and Policy Implications*, prepared by a Study Committee of the Office of the Foreign Secretary, National Academy of Sciences, Johns Hopkins Press, 1971, p. 427. © W. B. Saunders Co. Reprinted by permission.

relationship between family size and intelligence with any degree of confidence. These aspects of the data are not discussed by Wray. In fact he presents the evidence in such a way as to *assume* that the data demonstrate that as family size increases intelligence decreases. After presenting the data in Table 1, the author (Wray, 1971:426) states that "the figures require no comment." The point is that the figures do require comment because there is no consistent difference in families up to the size of five children. Why it should drop *after* that point requires comment, especially if the researcher is using the data to demonstrate (1) that large families have negative consequences and (2) that by reducing family size population pressure will be reduced and that personal well-being of individual family members will be enhanced.

The problem of accurate interpretation of research findings can be illustrated further by considering the variable of socioeconomic level in Wray's report. Three out of the four tables showing the relationship between family size and intelligence have no information about the socioeconomic level. Thus one does not know how socioeconomic level might be influencing the results. However, one table (see Table 2) presented by Wray contains average I.Q. scores by both socioeconomic level and by family size. This data deserves considerable analysis, especially in view of the author's conclusions based upon the data. One conclusion Wray (1971:425) gives is that the effect of family size on intelligence was "not ameliorated by social class." The author (Wray, 1971:455) also concludes that reducing family size would likely reduce the negative consequences of larger families because "those studies in which social class as well as family size were examined, the lower-class mothers who had only one or two children seem to have provided as well for their children as the upper class mothers." The data presented on intelligence do not support either conclusion.

The effects of family size on intelligence are "ameliorated" by social class in the data presented by Wray (See Table 2). The mean I.Q. of the only child in the *upper middle class* is 114.3 while that of the child from the sibship size of 7 or greater is 106.2. The mean I.Q. of the only child from the *lower working class* is 101.4 while the child in that same social class from a family of 7 or more children has an I.Q. of 88.0. The average difference in I.Q. scores between children in the sibship of one compared to seven for the upper middle class is 8.1 while the average difference is 12.5 for lower working class children. This finding of the relatively greater effect of family size difference on intelligence in the lower social classes agrees with other research cited by Wray but *not* emphasized. Of this other research he notes that "the negative correlation between intelligence and family size *varied* (emphasis added)

140

Table 2. Average intelligence test scores[a] by completed family size and social
class, Great Britain 1954-1957.

		Completed family size							
Social class	Age at test	1	2	3	4	5	6	7 or more	Un-known
Upper middle	11	59.87	57.31	55.80	56.49	55.65	54.45	54.00	55.00
	8	59.20	56.82	55.44	56.79	54.60	52.14	54.33	63.50
Lower middle	11	54.60	55.27	53.20	52.02	51.81	50.11	47.81	59.00
	8	53.88	54.26	52.64	50.20	50.03	51.43	47.95	58.00
Upper manual working	11	52.74	52.19	49.90	48.61	47.40	45.80	50.54	47.50
	8	52.27	51.64	49.93	48.65	47.31	48.53	42.49	44.00
Lower manual working	11	50.93	48.71	48.16	46.64	45.78	44.86	42.19	44.73
	8	51.54	49.64	48.38	47.44	45.27	45.51	42.44	45.09
All social classes	11	52.96	52.16	50.41	48.57	47.51	46.04	42.49	47.17
	8	52.86	52.09	50.36	48.74	46.87	47.07	43.06	47.00
Social class held constant	11	52.87	51.63	50.27	49.06	48.26	46.97	43.98	49.31
	8	52.83	51.69	50.23	49.07	47.53	48.03	44.61	49.14

[a]These are "T" scores which were designed so that the average score for all children
in the population is fifty and the standard deviation 10. . . . To convert T scores into
I.Q.'s the following formula may be used:

$$I.Q. = 25 + 1.5 \text{ (T score)}$$

Source: Douglas, J. W. B., J. M. Ross, and H. R. Simpson, *All Our Future*, London:
Peter Davies, 1968, cited in Wray, Joe D., "Population Pressure on Families:
Family Size and Child Spacing," *Rapid Population Growth: Consequences
and Policy Implications* prepared by a Study Committee of the Office of the
Foreign Secretary, National Academy of Sciences, Johns Hopkins Press.
1971, p. 427. © Peter Davies Ltd. Reprinted by permission.

among the classes. It was 'clearly apparent' in children of farmers,
manual laborers, and clerical workers, 'negligible' in children from
the managerial classes, and 'barely discernible' among those from
the professional class." The nature of the variation in the negative
correlation is apparent from the above description; i.e., the
strength of the relationship between family size and intelligence
decreases as socioeconomic level *increases*.

The conclusion that Wray reaches that those from families of
one or two children in the lower classes are as well provided for as
children from upper class families cannot be supported from the

data he presents on intelligence levels. In his data the difference in means is greater on the average across the social classes than it is across family size variations. In the figures in Table 2 the average difference in scores across family size is 8.08 while it is 8.97 across social class. The average I.Q. score of *only* and *two child* families is 100.3 while the average I.Q. level of children from sibships of seven or more in the upper middle class is 106.2. Furthermore, it can be seen that the difference in I.Q. scores for the eleven-year-olds across social classes is greater than it is for eight-year-olds. This is important since it would seem to imply that as the child gets older social class will have a greater negative effect, whereas the effects of family size do not change.

Conclusions *other* than those given by the author can be generated from the data in Table 2. For example: It is better to be reared in a family of seven or more children in the upper middle class than to be reared as an only child in the lower working class (higher I.Q. level). Furthermore, if you are an eight-year-old it is better to be reared in a family of seven or more in the upper middle class than it is to be an only child in the lower middle class (Note that this is only one step lower on the class breakdown used). It is even better to be born into a family of six children in the lower middle class than to be one of two children in a lower working class family. The above is enough to clearly demonstrate the importance of socioeconomic class upon average I.Q. scores and question any research on family size which does not take socioeconomic variation into account.

On the basis of the available evidence, the social scientist concerned about family size does not know whether it would be better to marshal forces to reduce family size in an effort to better the personal well-being of family members or to reduce socioeconomic discrepancies. Or, must the social scientist advocate that both dimensions be changed in order to effectively improve the family members' conditions? The data cannot at present provide satisfying answers.

Before answers to the above questions are forthcoming, social scientists will have to do considerably more research and include more variables in the analysis. Family size and socioeconomic level are not the only forces present in families which have an impact upon children. To overlook how children are treated by their parents would be a gross oversight in any attempt to identify

142

the relationship between family size, socioeconomic level, and children's attitudes and behavior. One would have a hard time making the case that it would be better for a child to grow up in a family where he was the only member and was despised and rejected by his parents than it would be to grow up in a family of ten children where the parents loved him, taught him, and gave him responsibility.

Family Size, Resources, and Parental Support

The foregoing has identified a need for social scientists interested in the functioning of families, to enter the arena of family size research and show how family size, socioeconomic resources and parent-child interaction could theoretically be related to produce different attitudinal and behavioral characteristics of the child. How should the above variables be conceptualized in order to generate researchable hypotheses about the effect of family size on the child's characteristics? Firm answers cannot be given but some preliminary suggestions can be offered leading to research to attempt to verify or modify the original formulations. That which follows is offered as a beginning.

If socioeconomic level is conceptualized as an indication of the amount and types of resources that any set of parents has at their disposal in the rearing of their children, then it becomes possible to begin to offer some insight into how socioeconomic level might or might not interact with family size to produce specific outcomes in children's attitudes and behavior. Adams (Adams and Meidam, 1968:230-239) has used this basic theoretical approach in interpreting the results of the variations in college attendance by family size. His basic position can be stated as: the greater the number of children the lower the probability of college attendance due to a reduction in resources for any one child. It is interesting to note in Adams' data (Adams and Meidam, 1968:230-239) for white collar males there is essentially no difference in college attendance for families of one to four children with the drop in college attendance occurring in families of five or more children. This trend is similar to that noted earlier in I.Q. level (See Table 1 in this report). This could be interpreted to mean that even the larger white collar families begin to experience limited resources since college education is expensive. Adams shows that the female

143

child from the *blue collar level*, who has male siblings is especially · vulnerable to being left out of the running for family resources which can be used for college education. In a family of two with no male siblings she has a 45 percent chance of getting some college education whereas if she has one brother her chances drop to 18 percent. The use of the resource explanation coupled with the desire to give male children an education before female children is offered by Adams as possible explanations for this finding.

Other interpretations could be given for Adams' findings. For example, Adams has no measures of the degree to which parents give their children emotional support and encouragement. Support is here defined as that quality of interaction between parent and child which is perceived by the child as establishing a positive *affective* relationship between him and the parent. This emotional dimension has been shown (Heilbrun, 1969:605-612; Heilbrun et al., 1967:29-40; Heilbrun and Waters, 1968:913-927) to be related to motivational and cognitive dimensions of children and could thus be related to college attendance.

A considerable amount of evidence has been produced by various researchers demonstrating that the emotional dimension (parental warmth) is one of the most important variables in parent-child interaction (Thomas and Weigert, 1971:835-847; Maccoby, 1961:357-371). The social scientist studying family size would need to take this variable into account. By including the emotional dimension along with the socioeconomic variable, a central question can be formulated: what kinds and types of effects will variations in family size have upon children if (1) parents have adequate resources to provide for their children, and (2) if those parents through interaction with their children can give *sufficient* emotional support and warmth *necessary for* their development?

Data are available which allow for these questions to be investigated in three specific attitudinal and behavioral areas: (1) the degree of the child's religiosity, (2) the tendency to conform to the expectations of others, and (3) the level of self-esteem. While one cannot point to past research findings for hypotheses in each of these areas, some evidence is available which can be combined with knowledge of how groups of different size function in order to suggest some working hypotheses.

As group size increases more formal procedures are instituted for decision making and less reliance is given to informal commu-

144

nication nets. In the family this means that parents in larger families are more likely to interact with children in an autocratic fashion (Bowerman and Elder, 1964:551-567; Hoffman and Hoffman, 1966:1-53). This reasoning would lead one to hypothesize that irrespective of socioeconomic level *children in larger families will be socialized more toward patterns of conformity than children from smaller families* (hypothesis 1).

However, when interaction between parent and child on the emotional dimension is also included an alternative hypothesis is suggested. Some earlier research on family size shows that as family size increases the emotional level between parent and child decreases (Bossard and Boll, 1955:71-78). In addition, considerable research shows that as the degree of emotional support and warmth *increase* between parent and child, the child's level of conformity and religiosity *increase* (Thomas and Weigert, 1971:835-847, Weigert and Thomas, 1970:29-36). By combining these research findings, it seems logical to *hypothesize* that the *degree of conformity and religiosity will decrease as family size increases* (hypothesis 2) since the emotional level between parents and children in larger families is hypothesized to be lower than in smaller families. The analysis to follow should aid in determining which of the alternative explanations best fits the relationship between family size and conformity and religiosity.

With respect to self-esteem and its relationship to family size, one hypothesis suggests itself from past research and theorizing. If larger families are characterized by lower emotional support from parents, then one would *hypothesize* that *as family size increases self-concept should decrease* (hypothesis 3). This is expected since considerable research (Gecas et al., 1970:317-324; Gecas, 1971:446-482) has shown the degree of emotional support from parents to be positively related to the child's level of self-esteem. This hypothesized relationship between family size, parental support, and self-esteem will also be investigated in the analysis to follow. In addition, the data will allow for a test of these hypotheses in three different cultural contexts: U.S., Puerto Rico, and Merida, Yucatan.

Methodology

Sample data were collected from Catholic adolescents attending parochial schools in each of four cities: St. Paul, Minnesota; New

145

York City; San Juan, Puerto Rico; and Merida, Yucatan (Thomas and Weigert, 1971:835-847). A boys' school and girls' school were selected in each city such that the respondents came from middle and upper middle class families. Across the eight schools, an average of 85 percent of the respondents came from families where the father's occupation was either technical-professional, proprietor-official, or of another white-collar occupation. The respondents' parents were nearly all Catholics (95.6 percent). Thus the sample can be described as upper middle-class Catholic adolescents attending parochial schools.

Measurement

A questionnaire was filled out by the respondents in a classroom setting measuring conformity, religiosity, and adolescent's self-concept and parental support. The religiosity measures followed the work of Glock and Stark (1965; Weigert and Thomas, 1970:29-36) in measuring different dimensions of religiosity: religious practice, knowledge, belief, and experience. Scores from a number of questions on each of these dimensions were summed into a total religiosity measure.

The conformity measure was designed to test the adolescent's tendency to conform to the expectations of significant others: father, mother, priest, and best friend (Thomas and Weigert, 1971:835-847). Three questions were asked for each of the four significant others and the responses to these four questions were summed to yield a total conformity score.

Two different measures for the self-concept were used. The first was the Twenty Statements Test where the respondent was asked to write twenty statements answering the question "Who am I?" Each statement was then coded for self-esteeming content and self-derogating content on a scale from 1 to 3. These were then summed across all statements to form the self-esteem and self-derogation scores. A second measure of self-esteem was created from the semantic differential consisting of ten adjective pairs such as good-bad, happy-sad, just-unjust, etc. The respondent rated himself on a scale of 1 to 5 on each adjective pair. These ratings were then summed to yield the semantic differential self-esteem score.

Support was measured by four questions (repeated for each

146

parent) that the respondent filled out about how his parents treated him. This measure is the short form of the Cornell Parent Behavior Description which has been used in considerable research (Weigert and Thomas, 1970:305-326). Examples of these questions are If I have any kind of problem I can count on her (him) to help me out. She (he) makes me feel she is there if I need her (him). The response categories for the support questions were very often, fairly often, sometimes, hardly ever, never. The answers to these questions were summed across both parents to create the parental support score (Thomas and Weigert, 1971:835-847).

Data Analysis

Analysis of variance is used as the basic technique for testing the working hypotheses. This particular method allows the researcher to ask whether family size is a significant source of variation in conformity, religiosity, and self-esteem scores. (If it is, then a significant F ratio for family size will appear in the data.) Another way of saying this is that the researcher can determine whether the average self-esteem scores, for example, in a family of two children differ significantly from the average self-esteem scores in a family of seven. Likewise the researcher can determine if children on the average who receive a high amount of parental support differ significantly on self-esteem from children who receive a low amount of parental support. In addition, the researcher can ask a further question: namely, if family size and parental support combined together produce effects on self-esteem scores different in kind from either family size or parental support taken alone. If this happens then the researcher would find a significant F ratio for the interaction of family size by parental support.

Findings

The data do not confirm either of the first two working hypotheses linking family size with the adolescent's level of religiosity. This is due to the failure of family size to be related to adolescent religiosity. The different dimensions of religiosity (practice, belief, knowledge, and experience) were not significantly influenced by variations in family size. Table 3 presents the F ratios for the total

147

religiosity score, none of which are significant. It will be noted, however, that the level of parental support is a significant source

Table 3. Analysis of variance F ratios and significance levels for family size and support across dimensions of conformity.

	New York	St. Paul	San Juan	Merida
Total Conformity				
Family size	1.3	2.4*	0.8	1.1
Support	10.5**	19.7**	5.4*	14.8**
Family size X support	1.6	1.4	0.8	0.7
Total Religiosity				
Family size	0.6	1.6	0.7	1.3
Support	19.5**	25.0**	12.1**	0.1
Family size X support	2.1*	0.5	1.9	0.3

* $p < .05$
** $p < .001$

of variation in the religiosity scores in three out of the four cities (the exception is Merida, Yucatan). The meaning of the data in Tables 3 and 5 is that if a child receives a relatively high amount of support from his parents he will tend to be high on religiosity. In separate analysis of each of the four dimensions of religiosity, religious knowledge is the one dimension that is not affected by the degree of parental support; all others are. The data also indicate that parental support and family size, when combined, do not produce unusual effects upon religiosity. Another way of saying this is that variations in parental support will produce variations in religiosity in children from larger families as well as small families. The F ratios for family size times support are not significant. This same relationship can be seen in the ranking of the religiosity cell means in Table 5 where those adolescents receiving high parental support tend to have a higher ranking on religiosity in each of the different family size categories across the four cities.

As with religiosity, neither of the first two working hypotheses linking family size with conformity receive any consistent verification in the data. Conformity to the expectation of significant

148

others (father, mother, priest, and best friend) is not related to the size of family that the adolescent comes from. One F ratio for family size is significant for the St. Paul sample on the total conformity scale. Under closer analysis of the different dimensions of conformity it was clear that conformity to father and mother were weakly related (relatively small F ratio) to family size, but the meaning of this relationship was not apparent in the data. That is to say, it was not apparent which size of family was tending to produce more or less conformity to father or mother. Furthermore the patterns of conformity to father across the different size families were not the same as to mother so the meaning of this one significant F ratio remains unclear. It could be a chance occur-

Table 4. Analysis of variance F ratios and significance levels for family size and support across self-esteem and self-derogation measures.

	New York	St. Paul	San Juan	Merida
Self-derogation (TST)				
Family size	2.0	0.9	1.4	0.5
Support	10.9**	4.4*	5.7*	2.9
Family size X support	0.8	0.9	0.6	0.9
Self-esteem (TST)				
Family size	0.2	1.1	0.5	1.6
Support	16.5**	6.4*	8.2*	10.4**
Family size X support	1.7	0.4	0.6	0.2
Semantic differential self-esteem				
Family size	1.6	0.8	1.4	0.8
Support	45.3**	38.2**	26.1**	21.7**
Family size X support	2.3*	0.2	0.1	1.1
Happy-sad				
Family size	1.8	0.3	1.0	0.2
Support	40.0**	37.3**	49.5**	25.5**
Family size X support	1.3	0.7	0.9	0.4

* $p < .05$
** $p < .001$

149

rence since it appears in only one city. The relationship of parental support to conformity is similar to that of religiosity in that children who receive a relatively low amount of parental support tend to score lowest on the conformity measures (note the cell rankings in Table 5). This finding tends to hold across families of different sizes. Furthermore parental support and family size do not combine to produce unusual results (no significant F ratios for family size times support).

The third hypothesis predicting that as family size increased adolescent self-concept would decrease is not supported by the data (See Table 4). As with religiosity and conformity, the reason is because family size is not significantly related to the level of self-concept. Knowing that a child comes from a family of seven does not tell one anything about the level of that child's self-concept. However, if it is known that the child comes from a home where the level of parental support is high, then it is known that the child will have a relatively high level of self-esteem and a relatively low level of self-derogation (see cell ranking in Table 5). The data also indicate that this will tend to be true for children from families of different size (parental support tends to predict the level of self-esteem and self-derogation for various family sizes).

In addition there is one important trend in the data when only-children are considered in the one sample (New York, in Table 5) where there are enough to make meaningful comparisons. Only-children, reared in a home where parents are high on the amount of emotional support given the child, tend to rank lowest on self-derogation and highest on self-esteem, religiosity, and conformity to expectations of significant others. However, only children reared in homes where parents are low on emotional support tend to rank *highest* on self-derogation, lowest on self-esteem, religiosity, and conformity. This finding apparently signifies that children reared without sibling relationships are more dependent upon the *quality* of parent-child relationship for adequate development of self-concept. If the parents provide sufficient emotional support and warmth to the only child, he develops a strong positive self-concept, but if the parental support is lacking he develops negative feelings about self and will tend to reject parental values (score lower on religious dimensions and be more inclined to *not conform* to the expectations of significant others).

150

Table 5. Ranking of cell means by sipship size and level of parental support for self-derogation, self-esteem, conformity, and religiosity.

	Parental support level	New York Sibship size							St. Paul Sibship size							San Juan, Puerto Rico Sibship size							Merida, Yucatan Sibship size						
		1	2	3	4	5	6	7	1	2	3	4	5	6	7	1	2	3	4	5	6	7	1	2	3	4	5	6	7
Self-derogation (TST)	High	14	10	8	13	12	7	9	1	11	12	8	7	13	6	13	14	11	10	12	8	1	1	3	9	13	12	7	10
	Low	6	2	4	11	5	1	3	14	9	5	10	4	2	3	7	3	4	5	9	6	2	14	4	8	5	6	2	11
Self-esteem (TST)	High	2	3	4	8	5	6	1	12	2	6	8	4	1	3	4	2	6	3	9	1	5	1	2	10	4	5	7	8
	Low	11	12	9	7	13	10	14	14	11	13	9	10	7	5	11	12	8	7	13	14	12	3	6	13	9	11	12	14
Self-esteem (semantic differential)	High	1	2	6	3	5	11	4	2	7	4	3	8	5	6	3	2	5	4	6	1	8	14	5	7	4	2	6	3
	Low	12	13	9	8	7	10	14	1	13	10	9	14	11	12	13	10	11	9	12	7	14	1	12	10	11	9	13	8
Total conformity	High	2	8	7	5	4	6	3	11	5	9	8	2	6	1	1	7	3	2	8	10	5	6	2	7	8	3	5	4
	Low	14	9	12	10	11	13	1	4	7	12	14	13	3	10	13	9	6	12	14	4	11	1	13	9	12	10	11	14
Total religiosity	High	1	3	5	6	7	4	9	1	6	4	9	5	7	3	8	5	6	1	7	14	3	13	12	7	9	2	4	3
	Low	14	11	12	10	2	13	8	2	8	13	14	10	11	12	4	10	12	9	13	2	11	14	5	10	8	6	11	1
N=	High	16	38	41	33	25	13	13	2	26	35	29	51	22	56	8	42	44	33	15	4	14	1	11	31	28	34	32	30
	Low	12	38	52	34	15	14	20	3	17	36	45	42	31	50	6	41	34	31	12	7	12	3	14	24	42	30	20	43

Aside from the analysis reported in this research, family size was also correlated with a considerable number of other variables, including achievement motivation, in an effort to discover other child characteristics associated with family size. The only variables consistently related to family size were parents' religiosity, parents' educational level, and father's occupational level. For these Catholic samples the greater the parents' religiosity (practice and belief) the more children they tended to have. For the Anglo Catholic samples the general trends in the data are that the greater the father's education level and occupational level the larger the family (average correlations across the samples .16 and .11 respectively). These findings are consistent with past research (Hoffman and Hoffman, 1966:12-13). The correlations are low probably because of the lack of variation in occupation and education in the samples; most respondents are upper middle class.

Discussion and Conclusions

The most important finding in this research is a nonfinding: the failure of family size to be significantly related to any of the adolescent attitudinal and/or behavioral dimensions in any of the samples from the three different cultural settings. The cross-cultural data allow for a more general test that can be done in just one culture. It was assumed that family size might mean different

151

things in the Latin culture than in the Anglo settings and thus might produce different effects. This assumption is not supported by the data.

The second most important finding is the ubiquitous nature of the effects associated with different levels of parental support. Past research had shown that parental support was an important predictor of adolescent conformity, self-concept, and religiosity even under different levels of parental control (Thomas and Weigert, 1971:835-847; Gecas, 1971:446-482; Weigert and Thomas, 1970:29-36) as well as in families having either syncratic, autonomic, mother-dominant, or father-dominant conjugal power structures (other unreported analyses of these data are currently in progress). In addition, the analysis reported here clearly shows that the effects of parental support also hold for families of different sizes.

Why were the expected relationships between conformity, religiosity, self-esteem and family size not found in this research? A number of reasons appear plausible. Both religion and socio-economic level are important variables in any proposed explanation. In the general population when educational and occupational levels rise family size tends to decrease, while in the Catholic population the relationship tends to reverse with family size (Hoffman and Hoffman, 1966:12-13). Thus if relationships between family size and some child characteristic do not hold for Catholic populations, the critical causal variable is probably not family size but could likely be some variable associated with socio-economic status. Past research has already shown that school performance and achievement motivation are more affected by variations in family size for protestants than for Catholics (Hoffman and Hoffman, 1966:12-13). These differences need to be further analyzed through research.

There is some evidence accumulating that since 1940 in the western world the relationship between family size and socio-economic level is reversing so that the old adage "the poor get children" may no longer be true (Clark, 1967:183-252). If this trend continues such that the higher social classes, since they can "afford" children, have the larger families, then the social scientist could likely expect to find higher I.Q., self-concept, etc., in larger families unless he controls for social class. The differences between Catholics and other segments of the population may likewise change considerably.

Another reason for the failure to find the expected relationships between conformity, religiosity, self-esteem, and family size was likely due to some false assumptions generated from past research. It was assumed that parental control would be greater in larger families and the amount of emotional support would decrease as family size increased. On the basis of these assumptions, it was hypothesized that as family size increased conformity and religiosity would increase whereas self-esteem would decrease. These hypothesized relationships did not hold for Catholic samples from the upper middle class. Further research is needed to determine if they might hold for other populations. In these data the amount of parental control and punishment of children is not related significantly to family size. Neither is the amount of emotional support given to children related to family size. The correlations between family size and these dimensions of parental behavior are consistently low. Since the basic assumptions upon which the hypotheses were based do not appear in the data, one would hardly expect family size to be associated with the various dimensions of child behavior.

In sum, what can be said about the effect of family size upon various dimensions of the child's attitudinal and behavioral characteristics? The failure of family size to be related to anything* but parents' religiosity, educational level, and to father's occupation points to the need in future research on family size to control carefully for social class differences. The fact that there are slowly accumulating enough research findings indicating that family size does not produce similar results for Catholics and other populations should sensitize researchers to the need to get some measure of the meaning that children have in the lives of parents. Researchers studying family size should likewise be aware of the importance of the emotional dimension of support that parents

---

*Aside from the analysis reported in the tables in this research, the family size variable was dichotomized into large and small families in an effort to see if this analysis would produce any significant relationships since the N's in some of the family sizes categories are rather small. Contingency tables and coefficients of associations were prepared for large and small families and each of the dependent variables, i.e., conformity, religiosity, and self-esteem. This analysis produced no significant relationships except for parents' religiosity, educational level and father's occupation. The higher categories on each of these variables had a disproportionately high number of large families. This finding is similar to the correlational analysis as well as the analysis of variance findings.

give to their children. If the number of children in a family differs markedly from the number that parents would like to have (a case of value behavior discrepancy [Christensen, 1968:283-289]) then one might conclude that parents may not be as supportive of their children, which in turn could produce a variety of negative consequences.

The central message of this research can be summarized in words approaching those used by Clausen (Hoffman and Hoffman, 1966:14) when he summarized the available research by saying "Family size, then does appear to make a difference in the way children are reared and in the attributes they develop, *but the effects are small and depend upon a number of circumstances*" (emphasis added). The evidence of this research would further specify what some of those "circumstances" are by maintaining that the effects of family size will be neglible if (1) parents are of a sufficiently high socioeconomic level thus possessing adequate resources to provide for their children, and (2) parents possess the ability to give their children needed emotional support. Conversely, family size will have greatest effect upon the child when parents lack resources and are unwilling and/or unable to give the necessary emotional support to their children. The data seem to say that how the parents interact with their children on the emotionally supportive dimension is far more critical in determining the child's characteristics than the number of children in the family. The fact that this seems to hold in at least three different cultural contexts is impressive evidence.

The evidence from this research cannot be said to be conclusive, but it strongly suggests the need for more and better research upon the effects of family size. The fact that variation in family size is not related to the various child characteristics measured in this research when respondents are equated on religion and socioeconomic levels raises the caution flag, especially to those willing to make sweeping generalizations about the negative consequences of large families and who advocate corrective measures in the form of reduction of family size. Hopefully, the social scientists will seriously consider the challenge confronting those who would *explain why family size should have an effect on children's characteristics*. Clearly the burden of proof lies with those who maintain that family size is *the causal* variable with respect to some child characteristic.

154

References

Adams, Bert N., and Miles T. Meidam
1968   "Economics, family structure, and college atten-
                 dance." The American Journal of Sociology 74
                 (November):230-239.

Bossard, James H.S., and Eleanor Stoker Boll
1955   "Personality roles in the large family." Child
                 Development 26 (March):71-78.

1956   The Large Family System. Philadelphia: Uni-
                 versity of Pennsylvania Press.

Bowerman, Charles, and Glen H. Elder, Jr.
1964   "Variations in adolescent perception of family
                 power structure." American Sociological Review
                 29 (August):551-567.

Clark, Colin
1967   Population Growth and Land Use. New
                 York: Macmillan.

Christensen, Harold T.
1968   "Children in the family: relationship of number
                 and spacing to marital success." Journal of Mar-
                 riage and the Family 30 (May):283-289.

Gecas, Viktor
1971   "Parental behavior and dimensions of adolescent
                 self-evaluation." Sociometry 34 (Decem-
                 ber):446-482.

Gecas, Viktor, Darwin L. Thomas, and Andrew J. Weigert
1970   "Perceived parent-child interaction and boys'
                 self-esteem in two cultural contexts." Inter-
                 national Journal of Comparative Sociology 11
                 (December):317-324.

Glock, C.Y., and R. Stark
1965   Religion and Society in Tension. Chicago: Rand
                McNally.

Heilbrun, Alfred B., Jr.
1969   "Perceived maternal child rearing and effect of
                delayed reinforcement upon concept acquisi-
                tion." Developmental Psychology Vol. 1 No.
                5:605-612.

Heilbrun, Alfred B., Jr., Samuel N. Harrell and Betty Jo Gillard
1967   "Perceived child-rearing attitudes of fathers and
                cognitive control in daughters." Journal of Ge-
                netic Psychology 111:29-40.

Heilbrun, Alfred B., Jr., and David B. Waters
1968   "Underachievement as related to perceived
                maternal child rearing and academic conditions
                of reinforcement." Child Development 39 (Sep-
                tember):913-927.

Hoffman, L.W., and M. L. Hoffman (eds.)
1966   "Family structure, socialization, and personal-
                ity," by John A. Clausen in Review of Child
                Development Research, II. New York: Russell
                Sage Foundation.

Kunz, Phillip R.
1965   "The relation of income and fertility." Journal
                of Marriage and the Family 27 (Novem-
                ber):509-513.

Lieberman, James E.
1970   "Reserving the womb: the case for the small
                family." American Journal of Public Health 60
                (January):87-92.

Maccoby, Eleanor E.
1961   "The choice of variables in the study of social-
                ization." Sociometry 24:357-371.

156

Reed, Elizabeth W., and Sheldon C. Reed
1965   Mental Retardation: A Family Study. Philadelphia: W. B. Saunders Co.

Smith, T. Lynn, and P. E. Zopf, Jr.
1970   Demography: Principles and Methods. Philadelphia: F. A. Davis Co. For contrary views see Kunz, 1965:509-513; and Hoffman and Hoffman, 1966:1-53.

Thomas, Darwin L., and Andrew J. Weigert
1971   "Socialization and adolescent conformity to significant others: a cross-national analysis." American Sociological Review 36 (October):835-847.

Waller, Jerome H.
1971   "Differential reproduction: its relations to I.Q. test scores, education, and occupation." Social Biology 18 (June):122-136.

Weigert, Andrew J., and Darwin L. Thomas
1970   "Secularization: a cross-national study of Catholic male adolescents." Social Forces 49 (September):29-36.

Weigert, Andrew J. and Darwin L. Thomas
1970   "Socialization and religiosity: a cross-national analysis of Catholic adolescents." Sociometry 33 (September):305-326.

Wray, Joe D.
1971   "Population pressure on families: family size and child spacing," in Rapid Population Growth: Consequences and Policy Implications. Prepared by a study committee of the Office of the Foreign Secretary, National Academy of Sciences. Baltimore: Johns Hopkins Press.

Family Size
and
Academic Achievement

Phillip R. Kunz and Evan T. Peterson*

That variations in family size correlate with various dimensions of personal well-being is an apparently well-established fact. Yet social scientists do not agree about the nature of the causal model underlying the empirically demonstrated relationship between family size and various attitudinal and behavioral dimensions.** It is the purpose of this paper to consider family size and its relevancy to specific behavioral dimensions. This will be accomplished by (1) analyzing the evidence presented in support of a small family as being most desirable for the well-being of its members (the primary focus will be upon a paper written by Dr. E. James Lieberman (1970) entitled, "Reserving the Womb: Case for the Small Family"), and (2) reporting research results focusing on unanswered questions about the relationship of family size to academic achievement.

The Case for the Small Family: A Review

The "Case for the Small Family" is illustrative of material that

*Appreciation is expressed to Lynn W. Davis for his help in preparing this material.
**See the article by Darwin L. Thomas in this book for a discussion of the problems of identifying causal relations in family size research.

159

is currently appearing which evidently has two major aims, namely to review the evidence on the effects of family size from social science research and to persuade the reader that small families will not only solve serious problems associated with population but that they will also provide significant advantages for individual family members. Such writing needs to be analyzed on at least two levels: (1) how valid is the original research upon which the review article is based and (2) has the reviewer faithfully presented not only the information from the original source but also the point of view of the original writer. On both of these counts, the "Case for the Small Family" does not fare well.

The following quote from Lieberman (1970) is illustrative of problems associated with both levels of analysis.

> Other studies have found (1) in discordant marriages, the chance for successful outcome decreases as the number of children increases (Mowrer, 1928; Terman, 1938:173); (2) happiness was associated with the desire for children, whether couples had any or not at the time, and poorest adjustment was found among those with unwanted children (Burgess and Cottrell, 1939:260); (3) an inverse relationship existed between marital adjustment and family size, i.e., more children, less adjustment; also, there was a correlation between marital adjustment and success in controlling fertility according to the desires of the couple (Reed, 1947:383-425); (4) having more than one child early in marriage correlated with poorer marital adjustment (Hurley and Palonen, 1967:483-484).

The second research finding cited by Lieberman in the above quote comes from the Burgess and Cottrell research. Lieberman's restatement of Burgess and Cottrell's findings is not really an accurate representation of the information contained in the original research nor does it portray the "meaning" that the original researchers *saw* in their data.

It is accurate to state that Burgess and Cottrell (1939) found the poorest adjustment in the group of parents who had "one or more children not desired." However, they also go to great lengths to *graphically* illustrate that those married couples who do not have children and desire to have none are the next most maladjusted group. Lieberman does not mention this. One could perhaps excuse Lieberman for not noticing the information in a graph showing that those who do not have children and do not desire any are poorly adjusted, but a more telling criticism is his failure

160

to indicate what "meaning" the original researchers saw in their data. The following quote coming from the beginning and ending of the section cited by Lieberman identifies the relationship the original researchers saw between children in a marriage and marital adjustment.

> The presence or absence of children, or their number, may not be so significant as the attitude of the married couples toward having children. If there are no children, are children desired? If there are children, were they wanted or not wanted? . . .
>
> These findings regarding attitudes toward having children showed a more marked relationship to marital adjustment than any other item included in our study. It is evident that the child is a potent and vital factor in family life. If companionate marriage be defined as a marital union where children are neither present nor desired, it is one which on the average grades very low in marital happiness. Only those unfortunate marriages that produce unwanted children reach a lower level of marital maladjustment.
>
> The question remains open whether the desire to have or not to have children is a cause or an effect of marital unhappiness. In many marriages it is entirely probable that dissatisfaction with the marriage makes for an aversion to having children. At the same time many marriages are entered upon with a determination on the part of one or both of the couple not to have children. In these cases the disposition against having children may be definitely related to marital maladjustment. The desire not to have children may, for example, be an index of a personality type unwilling to assume responsibility (Burgess and Cottrell, 1939:260-261).

The general tone and intent of Burgess and Cottrell do not fit with the general tone and intent of Lieberman's review. One wonders why Lieberman did not mention the idea proposed by the original authors that a person desiring not to have children could well be a problem personality type with a general tendency to avoid responsibility. Clearly, this type of analysis which might have been the order of the day in 1939 would not be popular in a day when a need is perceived to persuade people that the "good" life consists of having few or no children.

Lieberman's statement (1970) that "having more than one child early in marriage correlated with poorer marital adjustment" is based upon research reported by Hurley and Palonen (1967). Lieberman accurately reports a negative correlation ($r = -.39$) between child density (number of children born divided by number of years married) and marital satisfaction. He does not, however, let the reader know that the original researchers had serious misgivings about applying their results to populations other than the 40 student couples they studied at Michigan State University. The tone of Lieberman's review is to generalize wildly even in the face of the original authors' reservation. They say: "A fuller interpretation of this phenomenon requires both confirmation of the present finding and more sophisticated further research." They then go on to urge for an investigation into the "possibility that a religious affiliation encouraging high child density may support a more positive view of such marriages and influence marital satisfaction quite differently than would beliefs which negatively value high child density (Hurley and Palonen, 1967:484)."

Perhaps the most flagrant example of Lieberman's misreporting original research findings is seen in the following quote (1970:88): "Other studies show that (1) successive children do not receive the parental warmth granted their predecessors." Compare the above quote with the following statement from Lasko (1954:133), the original researcher:

> To summarize the major findings:
> 1. Parent behavior toward first children as contrasted to second is on the average less warm emotionally and more restrictive and coercive. These differences are more apparent in the pre-school years than later. A similar differential exists between second and third children, though on a less distinct level.

Lieberman completely reverses the relationship between parental warmth expressed to 1st, 2nd, and 3rd children in a family. It is inconceivable how Lieberman could make the type of statement he does, given the findings of the Lasko research, especially since one of the hypotheses Lasko sets out to test, and one of those the data support, is exactly opposite of Lieberman's statement. Lasko's supported hypothesis is "that parent behavior toward the second child, representing later born children is warmer than toward the first (1954:106-107). One is forced to conclude that Lieberman must never have seen the original research article that he cites.

An unfortunate consequence of rather superficial and sometimes erroneous analysis such as Lieberman's is to create the illusion that social science research has identified what the important variables are and furthermore that the problem of causation

162

has been adequately handled. In reality, the situation is quite different. One writer, after reviewing the research, concludes, "In view of the number of studies which found no relationship and the contradictory results of those with positive findings, it should be concluded that *there is no reliable relationship between the presence or number of children and marital adjustment* (Udry, 1971:428). When Lieberman's article (Rosenfeld, 1971:99) is cited in *Life* magazine, as "The most comprehensive recent compilation of data on the effects of family size on children," there is cause for concern. The possibility of the ramifications of the influence of unfounded conclusions from faulty analysis is sobering. The public deserves more and better information than is currently available on the effects of family size if defensible statements are to be made by the social scientist.

Academic Performance: The Data

If much about the causes and consequences of variation in family size is currently not understood, there does seem to be considerable agreement from research about the relationship between family size and academic achievement. There is research evidence accumulating which shows that as family size increases academic achievement decreases.

Research on selective service rejects indicates:

> ... that about 70 percent of Selective Service mental rejects come from families of four children or more, though only 33 percent of the nation's children come from such families. A further breakdown showed that 47 percent of the rejects came from the 11 percent of the children who were members of families with six or more offspring! Interpretation of these results is difficult because large family size and poverty were associated and could not be separated for analysis (Lieberman, 1970:88).

Lieberman citing this research points out the inadequacy of the data because control of socioeconomic status was not possible. Other research, however, does control for socioeconomic status and still shows an inverse relationship between family size and various dimensions of intellectual achievement.

Wray (1971) presents various findings relative to the size of family and intelligence. Contrary to one of his conclusions, the

163

effects of family size on intelligence are ameliorated by social class in that variation in family size in the lower socioeconomic levels seems to have a more negative effect on intelligence.* What is clear from the bulk of this research (Adams and Meidam, 1968:230-239; Waller, 1971:122-136) is that both family size and socioeconomic level are important variables in the study of academic achievement.

The position is sometimes advanced that children in small families do better because of the intensity of their interaction with their parents. With an increase in size of family comes a diminution of this adult-child relationship, hence poorer academic achievement from the children of the larger families. This theorizing may or may not be accurate, but what is clearly needed is further research to investigate the relationship between family size and intellectual achievement. If family size is negatively related to college attendance as some research has shown (Adams and Meidam, 1968:230-239), would children from larger families receive poorer high school and college grades? Would the inverse relationship between family size and academic achievement hold for a subcultural group such as the Mormons (The Church of Jesus Christ of Latter-day Saints) who place a positive value both on large families and academic achievement? That which follows is designed to explore these and other questions.

The general focus is on the relationship of grades to family size. The assumption guiding this research is that when achievement (grades) is examined, most of the variance can be explained in terms of social class. That is, larger families are generally from the lower classes and their class position would negatively affect the grades they receive. It is assumed that this occurs because the schools tend to be middle class oriented, thus producing social organizational factors which work against the lower class students' getting good grades.

At the family level of analysis, it may be argued that parents who have few children would not only be able to provide more resources such as financial help for each child which could lead to achievement, but they would also be in a position to offer more "adult to child contact." The assumption is made that it is such conduct with adults which should promote better grades. On the

* See the article by Darwin L. Thomas in this book for a discussion of the problems of identifying causal relations in family size research.

other hand, one may argue that a child who has more sibs will have more interaction with them, including perhaps some assistance with school problems which could yield higher grades. A student today with a math problem, for example, may be hard pressed to obtain any help from a parent who has had no training in the "new math" while an older sib may be an important source of information.

Study One

Methodology

Responses from 2,926 male adolescents and 3,127 female adolescents (N = 6,053) from twenty-seven different high schools are reported (Peterson, information unpublished to date). The sample approximates a cluster sample, but strictly speaking, is an accidental sample. An attempt was made to have participating high schools in all major regions of the United States; however, the sample is slightly biased in favor of the Intermountain West. The Northeastern part of the country is underrepresented. Because of the interest of high school administrators in this research, the refusal rate was lower than originally anticipated. Only seven school districts declined the invitation to participate in the research. Three of those districts were in the Northeast.

In some cases all of the students who were invited to participate went into the school auditorium or gymnasium. In other cases the questionnaires were administered in the classrooms. All students were instructed how to complete the questionnaire. Within each of the individual high schools the sample consisted of either the total population in school that day or a cluster sample selected from required classes such as English, mathematics, and health.

Findings and Discussion

Table 1 represents the number of sibs the respondents had, along with their self-reported grades. Examination of the table indicates that for the respondents who reported having no sibs 73.8 percent of the respondents in the "upper class" reported grades of B or better; 47.3 percent of the respondents in the "middle class" and 47.4 percent of the respondents designated as "lower class" reported "hi" grades. Socioeconomic status was obtained using the McGuire Index (1949), which utilizes income, occupation, education and religion to assign social class position. Examination of the other columns, with one to three sibs, four or five sibs, and six or more sibs indicates a similar class difference.

Table 1. Relation of reported high school grades to sibship size by socio-economic status for high school samples.

	Number of sibs											
	0 Grades[a]			1-3 Grades[a]			4-5 Grades[a]			6 or more Grades[a]		
	Hi	Lo	N	Hi	Lo	N	Hi	Lo	N	Hi	Lo	N
Upper[b]	73.8%	26.2%	42	74.2%	25.8%	822	72.5%	27.5%	331	69.6%	30.4%	135
Middle[c]	47.3	52.7	167	58.0	42.0	1969	55.2	44.8	801	52.0	48.0	556
Lower[d]	47.4	52.6	19	39.0	60.9	169	42.6	57.4	122	43.9	56.1	253

[a] Hi grades equal B- or more
Lo grades equal C+ or less
[b] Gamma equals 0.05
[c] Gamma equals 0.04
[d] Gamma equals 0.05

The very interesting point to be made from this table is that there is no significant difference moving across the rows, from "no sibs" to "six or more" sibs, while controlling for social class. Thus, the upper class indicates 73.8 percent of only-child respondents with hi grades; 74.2 percent with one to three sibs, 72.5 percent with four or five sibs, and 69.6 percent with six or more sibs all reported "hi" grades. Gamma as a measure of association is very low—less than .05 for each of the three groups.

These data do not support the position which states that larger numbers of children in a family tend to lower intelligence because of lack of contact with parents. However, neither do they support the position that sibs cooperate and increase performance as far as high school grades are concerned. Understandably, grades and intelligence are not the same, but one would expect a fairly high correlation between them.

Study Two

Inasmuch as we are interested in whether these findings would be mitigated in a subculture which is supportive of large families,

166

an additional study was made using a sample from such a subculture. The Mormon Church is very much in favor of its members having several children and in general not restricting birth, except in a very few situations where health of the mother is involved.

> We seriously regret that there should exist a sentiment or feeling among any members of the Church to curtail the birth of their children. We have been commanded to multiply and replenish the earth that we may have joy and rejoicing in our posterity.
>
> Where husband and wife enjoy health and vigor and are free from impurities that would be entailed upon their posterity, it is contrary to the teachings of the Church artificially to curtail or prevent the birth of children. We believe that those who practice birth control will reap disappointment by and by.
>
> However, we feel that men must be considerate of their wives who bear the greater responsibility not only of bearing children, but of caring for them through childhood. To this end the mother's health and strength should be conserved and the husband's consideration for his wife is his first duty, and self-control a dominant factor in all their relationships.
>
> It is our further feeling that married couples should seek inspiration and wisdom from the Lord that they may exercise discretion in solving their marital problems, and that they may be permitted to rear their children in accordance with the teachings of the Gospel (First Presidency, 1969).

Methodology

A six percent sample of the Brigham Young University student body was randomly drawn by using a computer program. General information contained on the computer file for each of those students was printed. This included some data on the parents such as education and residence as well as information about the students such as grades, high school and university, major for each semester by department and college, and marital status. American College Test scores (ACT) and high school grade-point averages were available for many of these students. University grades were available for almost all of them.

The variable of interest in the present research—family size—however, was not available. As a consequence the researcher and assistants utilized several methods to obtain the number of sibs as well as some additional data to be reported elsewhere. We telephoned the students for whom telephones were available and then mailed a questionnaire to those who had no telephones or who

167

could not otherwise be reached by telephone in order to supplement the file information. In fifty cases both the phone call and questionnaire were used for the same respondent. Comparison of the data from both sources indicates that the data are reliable.

This sample included 661 male and 565 female respondents (N=1,226), all of whom were currently attending the university, or who had attended the previous semester and who were still on file and available to obtain the additional information. The additional information was coded and transferred along with the data from the computer's file to data cards via scanning sheets. Pearson Correlations were then computed for family size by the various measures of grade achievements. In some cases the N varies because of the unavailability of ACT scores which were missing for older students who did not take those examinations. They were not offered when some of them entered the University.

The achieved grade measures studied in this paper included the English-ACT, Math-ACT, Social Science-ACT, Natural Science-ACT and Composite-ACT scores. In addition, there were high school grade-point averages, high school core grade-point averages, and accumulated university grade-point averages. All of the above are familiar to most people except for the high school core grade-point average. The core excludes all classes such as physical education and chorus, and generally includes only academic classes.

Findings

Table 2 presents the various measures, Pearson correlation coefficients, and the number of respondents for each measure. This presentation indicates no significant relationships between family size and grades for university students.

Closer examination of the relationship between the number of sibs and the university grade-point average is shown in Table 3. The only indicator of socioeconomic status was father's education. Using this as a control, we are able to examine the association of family size with grade-point average. Father's education appears to make some difference in terms of the percentage receiving "low" and "hi" grades. While the N for respondents is understandably lower, note the tendency for larger families to have more of the "hi" grades. For the left and right parts of the table, there is no statistically significant difference, however.

168

Table 2. Pearson correlation coefficients for grade measures by sibship size for Brigham Young University sample.

Grade Measure	Pearson r	Number
English-ACT	-0.02	808
Math-ACT	-0.01	808
Social science-ACT	-0.03	808
Natural science-ACT	-0.02	806
Composite-ACT	-0.01	823
High school GPA	0.06	652
High school core GPA	0.06	712
University cumulative GPA	0.02	1227

Table 3. Relation of university cumulative grade-point average to sibship size by father's education for Brigham Young University sample.

Number of sibs	Father's education									
	High school or less					1 year college or more				
	Low[a]			High		Low			High	
	1	2	3	4	N[b]	1	2	3	4	N[c]
0	36.4%	36.4%	18.2%	9.1%	11	25.0%	50.0%	25.0%	0.0%	4
1	30.3	48.5	12.1	9.1	33	34.2	26.3	28.9	10.5	38
2	29.2	35.4	22.9	12.5	48	22.0	40.7	27.1	10.2	59
3	32.7	36.7	22.4	8.1	49	14.5	39.8	32.5	13.3	83
4	37.5	33.3	16.7	12.5	48	20.9	34.9	22.1	22.1	86
5	26.1	37.0	34.8	2.2	46	15.6	44.2	20.8	19.5	77
6	13.3	46.7	26.7	13.3	30	41.2	26.5	26.5	5.9	34
7	0.0	55.6	33.3	11.1	9	23.1	34.6	26.9	15.4	26
8	57.1	0.0	28.6	14.3	7	25.0	37.5	0.0	37.5	8
9	20.0	60.0	20.0	0.0	5	40.0	20.0	0.0	40.0	5
10	40.0	20.0	40.0	0.0	5	12.5	25.0	50.0	12.5	8

[a] 1 equals 0.01 to 2.50 on a 4.00/A scale
 2 equals 2.51 to 3.00
 3 equals 3.01 to 4.00
[b] Gamma equals 0.07
[c] Gamma equals 0.08

Partial correlations of first, second and third order, for number of children, father's education and sex of the respondent also indicate no statistically significant differences. Difference of means tests (using the T-test) for the mean cumulative grade-point average for small, medium and large families while controlling father's education and respondent's sex were also not statistically significant. In short, the data do not support the idea that there are grade-point differences associated with family size.

The argument may be made that students at Brigham Young University do represent a narrow spectrum of Mormon society and therefore cannot be used to indicate the effects of the Mormon culture which has positive rewards for the large family. A closer examination of the data from the high schools, in the first study reported above, will provide data to examine this question.

Data from study one permit us to examine Mormon high school students and to compare them with other religions. Table 4 presents the respondents who either indicated "no" religious affili-ation, or were Catholic, Protestant, or Mormon. Other groups were

Table 4. Relation of reported high school grades to sibship size by religion for high school sample.

	Number of sibs											
	0 Grades[a]			1-3 Grades[a]			4-5 Grades[a]			6 or more Grades[a]		
	Hi	Lo	N	Hi	Lo	N	Hi	Lo	N	Hi	Lo	N
No Religion[b]	38.1%	61.9%	21	59.2%	40.8%	233	52.9%	47.1%	68	44.4%	55.6%	36
Catholic[c]	51.9	48.1	52	55.3	44.7	597	51.0	49.0	310	43.4	56.6	244
Mormon[d]	45.2	54.8	31	66.1	33.9	493	69.3	30.7	358	59.9	40.1	282
Protestant[e]	67.2	32.8	201	60.9	39.1	1799	55.1	44.9	537	54.0	46.0	428

[a]Hi grades equal B- or more
  Lo Grades equal C+ or less
[b]Gamma equals 0.08
[c]Gamma equals 0.13
[d]Gamma equals 0.03
[e]Gamma equals 0.12

not examined here because of their small number. Note the rather curvilinear relationship within each row except for the Protestant. In general, however, there is a very weak relationship between grades and number of sibs. The data in the university sample above

170

showed no curvilinear relationship. Further study of this should be made, but we should point out that the contingency coefficients computed for the data represented in the reported curvilinear relationships were not significant.

A rather interesting point may be observed as one examines the Mormon respondents reporting high grades. When there are "no sibs" only 45.2 percent report "hi" grades, less than the Catholics or the Protestants. In all other categories in the table, however, the Mormons are somewhat higher, which may reflect Mormon emphasis on educational values. This rather intriguing finding may be a reflection of the lack of support for the person who is the *only* child in a Mormon family. The differences between Mormons and the other categories are interesting in any event, with their 66.1, 69.3, and 59.9 percents which are associated with "hi" grades.

Summary

This paper suggests that literature dealing with the consequences of variations in family size needs to be more carefully examined. While the data in this paper examine family size only as it relates to the achievement of grades and American College Test scores, the finding of no relationship between these and family size is important. Further study of the relationship of family size to I.Q. needs to be made inasmuch as this finding is different from what is reported in much of the literature. Also, further research examining the effect of other variables is needed to test the accuracy of statements made by some of the proponents of the superior position of the small family.

References

Adams, Bert N., and Miles T. Meidam
    1968   "Economics, family structure, and college attendance." The American Journal of Sociology 74 (November, 1968):230-239.

Burgess, Earnest W., and Leonard S. Cottrell
    1939   Predicting Success or Failure in Marriage. New York: Prentice-Hall.

171

First Presidency of The Church of Jesus Christ of Latter-day Saints
 1969   Statement of First Presidency of The Church of Jesus Christ of Latter-day Saints (April 14).

Hurley, J.R., and D. Palonen
 1967   "Marital satisfaction and child density among university student parents." Journal of Marriage and the Family 29(August):483-484.

Lasko, J.K.
 1954   "Parent behavior toward first and second children." Genetic Psychological Monograph 49 (February):106-107, 133.

Lieberman, James E.
 1970   "Reserving the womb: case for the small family." American Journal of Public Health 60 (January):87-92.

Mowrer, E.R., et al.
 1928   Domestic Discord. Chicago: Chicago University Press.

McGuire, Carson
 1949   "Index of value attitudes." Unpublished research memorandum.

Peterson, Evan Tye
      "A study of the physician-patient relationship." Conditionally accepted for publication by the Journal of Health and Human Behavior.

 1968   "The adolescent male and parental relationships." Paper given at the annual meetings of the National Council on Family Relations, New Orleans (October).

 1971   "Growing up: Some relationships between adolsecent health and family processes." Paper given at the annual meetings of the Southern Sociological Society, Miami Beach (May).

Unpublished to date
"The impact of adolescent illness on parental relationships." Journal of Health and Social Behavior.

Reed, R.B.
1947   "Social and psychological factors affecting fertility: the interrelationship of marital adjustment, fertility control, and size of family." Milbank Memorial Fund Quarterly 25:383-425.

Rosenfeld, Albert
1971   "What is the right number of children?" Life (December 17):99.

Terman, Lewis, et al.
1938   Psychological Factors in Marital Happiness. New York: McGraw.

Udry, J. Richard
1971   The Social Context of Marriage. New York: J.P. Lippincott, Co.

Waller, Jerome H.
1971   "Differential reproduction: its relations to I.Q. test score, education, and occupation." Social Biology 18 (No. 2):122-136.

Wray, Joe D.
1971   "Population pressure on families: family size and child spacing," in Rapid Population Growth: Consequences and Policy Implications, chapter 11. Prepared by a study committee of the office of the Foreign Secretary, National Academy of Sciences, Baltimore: Johns Hopkins Press.

In Defense of Density:
Its Relationship to Health
and Social Disorganization

Bruce A. Chadwick

Introduction

Given that man is a physical creature, it is obvious that most of his activities are related to the experience of space. Differing cultures have developed distinctive values as to the ideal proximity to others and how to handle the situation of "overcrowding" or "aloneness." For example, during the days of the western frontier the often stated rule of thumb was that when you could see the smoke from a neighbor's chimney it was time to pack up and move further west.

During the past few decades the population of the United States has increased rapidly while the amount of land surface has remained relatively constant, with the exception of adding Hawaii and Alaska. One response to this rising population has been the growing fear, by many, that we are running out of space. This anxiety has resulted in numerous articles and editorials "predicting" that if present trends continue we will eventually arrive at "standing room only." In addition, writers in a variety of scientific disciplines have reiterated the same theme cloaked in the language of science. It is widely accepted in scientific circles that increased population density (more people in a limited space) is related to a host of physical, environmental, and social problems:

There is a clearer evidence that inadequate space standards can disorganize family life (Madge and Maisel, 1968:517).

Crowding generally increases aggressive behavior in man (Russell and Russell, 1968) and in other mammals (Bliss, 1962; Christian, Lloyd and Davis, 1965). (Alexander and Roth, 1971:73.)

Excessive densities unquestionably are a causative factor in some criminal behavior (Schmitt, 1957:276).

The view that crowding and increased population density are deleterious to health is so widespread and generally accepted as to have become almost a medical axiom (Cassel, 1971:426).

As the above examples illustrate it is assumed that population density is directly related to increased morbidity rates of various diseases and maladies and a high death rate. Also it is purported to be a contributing factor in the etiology of mental illness. Among scholars who study the urban scene there is considerable support for the proposition that density leads to "social disorganization" as manifest by increased crime, juvenile delinquency, drug abuse, alcoholism, poverty, illegitimacy, marital conflict, divorce, and suicide.

The purpose of this paper is to examine the empirical evidence about the effects of population density on health, deviant behavior, and the quality of life. Careful assessment of all the evidence is imperative if policy makers and an informed public are to make intelligent decisions about programs affecting population density. The first section of this paper will deal with the problems of defining density and will be followed by sections linking it to health (physical and mental) and social disorganization.

Density

The most frequent definition of population density is the number of individuals per unit of space. The usual practice is to determine the number of people per acre, although occasionally square miles is used. It is obvious that this is a rather crude indicator of density, allowing for considerable variation within the same level of density. This definition does not take into account the number of dwelling units and thus it is possible that an area with many people crowded into a relatively small number of houses will have

176

the same density as an area of high rise apartments with single occupants. In attempting to assess the impact of density on life styles, several researchers have sharpened the focus of the concept. Jane Jacobs (1961) in her work concerning American cities, carefully distinguishes between high density and *overcrowding*, usually expressed as the number of persons per room. She argues quite convincingly that crowding, not density per se, is associated with high disease, death and social disorganization rates.

This distinction between density and crowding is elaborated by Hall (1966) in his excellent book, *The Hidden Dimension*. Hall maintains that "screening" or the number of barriers behind which one can seek refuge is an important intervening variable in the relationship between density and health or social behavior. According to both Jacobs and Hall it is possible to have low death, disease and social disorganization under conditions of high population density *if* crowding is reduced by screening.

A third definition of density to emerge in recent work is that of "social density," which refers to the number of social or cultural roles a person is required to act simultaneously in a given physical space. Students of social density observe the number of social roles such as husband, father, son, lover, provider, etc., that one is forced to play or occupy in a specified limited physical arena. While reviewing previous research in this paper an attempt will be made to specify which type of density is being examined, as it may be that the therapy(s) recommended to alleviate the consequences of each type of density are very different.

Density and Illness

It is a commonly accepted belief that as population density increases so does the opportunity to spread infectious disease organisms which results in higher morbidity rates. An example of this notion that population density is related to the spread of infectious illness is presented by Hall (1966:174):

> ... One of the chief differences between man and animals is that man has domesticated himself by developing his extensions and then proceeded to screen his senses so that he could get more people into a small space. Screening helps, but the ultimate buildup can still be lethal. The last instance of severe urban overcrowding over a significant period of time was in the Middle Ages, which were punctuated by disastrous plagues.

177

Harvard historian William Langer, in his article, "The Black Death," states that from 1348 to 1350, after a period of rather rapid growth, the population of Europe was reduced one quarter by the plague. . . . There is little agreement as to why the plague ended and, while the relationship of man to disease is certainly complex, there is something suggestive about the fact that the end of the plague coincided with social and architectural changes that must have considerably reduced the stress of urban living. . . .

As indicated by the above quote the current hypothesis relating density to the spread of infectious diseases has been expanded to also include noninfectious diseases such as high blood pressure and heart and circulatory diseases. The latter are suspected to occur as a consequence of "stress" generated by living under conditions of high density. Cassel (NAS, 1971) reports that the indictment of density as a causative agent in illness is derived largely from data collected from four sources: animal studies, comparison of urban and rural areas, examination of morbidity rates following industrialization and urbanization, and finally, studies of crowded institutional settings such as military training camps, college dormitories, prisons, nurseries, etc.

Animal Studies

The typical study involves placing a small number of animals in a confined space with adequate food and water (Bliss, 1962). The animals are permitted to reproduce freely until the density increases to the point that a variety of deleterious health effects appear, despite the fact that diet, temperature and sanitation are held constant. The observed effects of density on the health of several species ranging from mice, rats, woodchucks, deer, birds to monkeys include increased incidence of infectious diseases; decreased resistance to drugs, microorganisms and x-rays; increased incidence of noninfectious diseases (heart ailments, abnormal blood pressure, and circulatory diseases); increased mortality rates, especially maternal and infant; and reduced reproduction. Many authors conclude that these phenomena are "nature's way" of reducing overpopulation, and that if man's density ever reaches some unknown threshold, a similar chain of events will bring the human population back into balance with the environment. The interested reader is referred to Christian (1961), who has devel-

178

oped a very complex model linking population change to reproduction and mortality.

At first sight the results of the many animal studies seem extremely convincing. Yet careful examination reveals several important inconsistencies which suggest caution in accepting the link between density and illness reported by ethnologists and particularly in applying the results to humans. First, not all species manifest the same set of symptoms or behaviors. For example, Alexander (Alexander and Roth, 1971) experimented with the density of a monkey troop, and found that "there was no failure of female fertility or maternal protection as is the case with rodents." This interspecies variability makes it an extremely tenuous procedure to generalize the results from one or several species to another, especially when the leap is from animals to man.

Second, most studies of animal populations have been of fairly short duration, and consequently tend to focus on population *change* rather than on stable levels of density. Cassel (1971:467) reports that Kessler at the Rockefeller Institute discovered that "mice under extreme conditions of crowding exhibited no increase in pathology once the population had achieved its maximum density and no further population growth was occurring." Kessler's results are substantiated by Alexander (Alexander and Roth, 1971) who found that for monkeys, population change in either direction (increases or decreases in density) resulted in increased aggression. These findings strongly suggest that rapid change in population density, not level of density, may be partly responsible for the health and antisocial behavior problems reported in animal experiments.

Finally, comment must be made about the dangers of attempting to generalize from animal to human behavior. The behavior of man is extremely complex, especially when compared to that of rodents, birds or even primates. There is simply no justification to make the logical leap that human reaction to density can be predicted from animal responses. In addition, man is extremely adaptable as compared to animals as indicated by his ability to survive in such a wide range of habitats. Thus it may be that he has the capability to adjust to and survive under conditions of rather high density. Indeed, man apparently has the ability to redefine the meaning of density and as Jacobs (1961) maintains this new

179

definition (life in the city) may include important "advantages" for man.

In summary, the inconsistencies in different species' reactions to high density, the failure to look at the effect of stable high density conditions, coupled with the problem of generalization to man's behavior from animal behavior indicate a need to reassess the supposed relationship between population density and health and social behavior.

Urban-Rural Comparison

Historically in the United States the death rate from all causes and morbidity rates for various diseases have been higher for urban (high density) than rural (low density) areas. This trend has been used as evidence that high density is associated with high occurrence of disease and death. But surprisingly, in 1960, the death rate and several disease rate ratios reversed, and rural areas manifested the higher death and disease rates. Furthermore, Cassel (1971) reports data for 1966 which show that the gap between rural and urban disease and death rates is increasing. He reviews explanations usually offered to explain the trend: improved medical care and sanitation in the cities, and the out-migration of the young (and healthy) from rural to the metropolitan areas. Proponents of these explanations state that improvements in the quality of city life have obscured the impact of overcrowding, and thus artificially created the reduced death rates. Cassel (1971) acknowledges that improved medical care and migration contribute to the trend to the favorable urban disease and death rates but he points out that evidence concerning diseases like scarlet fever, for which there is at present no means of prevention, indicate that improved preventative medicine cannot be employed to account for the high incidence of scarlet fever in rural areas as compared to urban areas. Nor can migration account for the reduced urban death rate because the same pattern appears for children as for the total population: rural children have the higher mortality rates. Finally, Cassel (1971:464) reports that this reversal in American mortality rates is consistent with much of the data from other countries.

Data from other parts of the world tend to confirm this seeming paradox. Dubos, for example, reports that despite the fact that Hong

180

Kong and Holland are among the most crowded areas in the world, they enjoy one of the highest levels of physical and mental health in the world. . . .

The reversal in the disease and death rate ratios between urban and rural areas disarms the old argument that density as indicated by urbanization is directly related to high disease and death rates.

An interesting point is that if it is true that improved health conditions were responsible for the reversal in the disease and death rate ratios, then this finding suggests that the effects of increased density can be alleviated without recourse to such drastic measures as compulsory population control. An implication is that sanitation, preventive medicine, and health care are much more important than density in accounting for disease and death rates. An even more important implication is that at present it is easier to provide these things in urban (high density) areas than in rural (low density) areas.

An important and often ignored factor that must be taken into account when making rural-urban or intra-urban comparisons is social class. Banfield's recent and controversial book, *The Unheavenly City* (1968), dramatically illustrates the importance of social class in explaining differing life styles, including illness and reaction to it. Even more convincing is Schmitt's (1966) analysis of census tracts in Honolulu that revealed that when education and income were controlled, crowding had no relationship to death and morbidity rates, although net population density did retain a weak but significant relationship to the dependent variables. If the effects of density on health are to be identified then care must be exercised to separate its effects from those of poverty (diet, sanitation, medical care, etc).

The above-mentioned study conducted by Schmitt (1966) in Honolulu deserves additional attention as he attempted to differentiate the effects of population density from those of crowding. Using 1950 census data for Honolulu he discovered that population density (number of people per acre) was much more strongly related to death from all causes, infant death, TB, and VD rates than was crowding (number of persons per room). As mentioned earlier, after the introduction of controls for education and income the relationship between density and health was reduced but did retain a weak but significant correlation. Freedman (1971) contends that even this weak relationship is questionable as

181

Schmitt's measure of education (percentage of people over twenty-five years of age with twelve or more years of schooling) and income (percentage of families earning over $3,000 per year) are too crude to be adequate controls for the important variable, social class. Nevertheless this finding that density is more salient than crowding is contrary to those anticipated by Hall, Cassel, and other researchers and indicates the need for additional research.

In summary, it is apparent that urban-rural comparisons pertaining to disease and death do not support the contention that density is related to these phenomena. The evidence strongly indicates that other factors are much more relevant in predicting and hopefully controlling disease and death.

Disease and Death Following Urbanization

Cassel (1971) reports that tuberculosis, which has been used as the prime example of the increase in disease following a period of urbanization, reached a peak about 75 to 100 years following industrialization and then spontaneously started to fall. This decrease in TB occurred despite continuing urbanization and also in the initial stages without the benefit of antituberculosis programs. It should be pointed out that urbanization is not synonymous with increasing density. An examination of census and other demographic data reveal that urban densities were *decreasing* precisely during the period of major urban growth. For example, the density of New York City in 1860 was 65,000 individuals per square mile while in 1900 it had fallen to under 40,000. This downward density trend has continued despite the growth of New York City and presently the density is less than 20,000 people per square mile. It is therefore logically inconsistent to point at high disease and death rates associated with urbanization and conclude that population density was the factor responsible.

In addition, Cassel (1971) reports studies conducted in both the United States (Holmes, 1956) and Britain (Brett and Benjamin, 1957) that demonstrate that incidence of TB is not necessarily related to crowding. In fact, in both studies it was discovered that TB occurred more frequently in social isolates (people living alone) than in those living under crowded conditions.

Crowded Institutions and Disease

It is acknowledged that outbreaks of infectious diseases frequently occur under crowded conditions such as military training camps. Cassel (1971), in reviewing studies of such camps, found results that suggest the necessity to revise the accepted link between crowding and disease. First, it was observed that immunization often did not work to prevent outbreaks of upper respiratory infections. Second, in different camps and with different groups of trainees very different patterns were observed concerning the period of training during which the outbreaks occurred. He therefore concludes that some aspect(s) of the training camp experience appears to be connected with the spread of infectious disease. But he does refute the orthodox model which maintains that increased contact led to increased infection and instead suggests that the appearance of a given disease is not necessarily the result of exposure to the microorganism. He maintains that the evidence suggests outbreaks of disease during training camps may be produced "through a disturbance of the balance between the ubiquitous organisms and the host that is harboring them." Crowding may be the factor upsetting this balance but, then again, the blame may rest on the rigors of military training or the intense stress associated with "boot camp" training. The point to be made is that the old model of density increasing contact in turn increasing occurrence of infectious disease is being questioned by medical researchers. Cassel argues that there is strong need for more longitudinal studies which attempt to isolate the factors in the crowded environment that are related to the occurrence of disease.

The above noted emphasis on longitudinal studies emerges from Cassel's feeling that whatever in the environment produces the increase in disease, that after the initial exposure, man is capable of an adaptation which will reduce the morbidity and mortality rates. He reviews three studies that support his adaptation model. Christenson and Hinkle (1961) compared the disease rate for managers of a particular company. They divided the managers into those who had and had not graduated from college. They found that the college graduates almost always had fathers who were in similar occupations, were more prepared for the position and thus did not experience as much stress as nongraduates. The results were in the anticipated direction with the nongraduates evidencing significantly greater incidence of disease. Cassel and Tyroler (1961) studied rural mountaineer factory employees. They secured two matched samples which were from the same mountain coves, did the same work for the same pay, and who were the same age but who differed on familial experience in factory work (fathers had factory experience). "First generation" workers had higher rates of medical symptoms as measured by the Cornell Medical Index and higher rates of absenteeism.

Finally, Haenszel et al. (1962) found that after they controlled for cigarette smoking, farm-born migrants to the city had a higher rate of death from lung cancer than city born individuals. They found this difference despite the city dwellers' lifetime exposure to air pollution.

A careful examination of the evidence provided by animal studies, urban-rural comparisons, urbanization, and crowded institutional settings raises serious questions about the validity of the supposed causal link between density and disease and death. It appears that density, itself, has little impact on morbidity and mortality when compared to other factors. There is even some evidence that is suggestive of *positive* effects of high density living, in that it is easier to control sanitation and provide preventive and corrective medical care. The question of population density's relationship to disease and death is essentially an unanswered one at present and indicates the need for continued research.

Density and Mental Illness

The data concerning mental illness are quite limited in comparison to those for physical illness and death. Mitchell (1971) in an elaborate study of population density in Hong Kong reported conditional support for the relationship between density and superficial levels of strain. Strain was inferred from answers to the questions: "How happy are you?" and "How much do you worry?" When social class (income and education) is statistically controlled the relationship holds for only the lower class, indicating an interaction effect between economic deprivation and density. Also it was a measure of crowding, not density per se, that was related to feelings of unhappiness and worry. More importantly, he obtained data concerning more serious levels of

184

emotional strain and found that these were not related to population density as crowding. On the other hand, Gruenberg (1954) examined the admission rate of elderly patients to state mental hospitals and found that a disproportionate number of first admissions for psychoses were from center-city, high density areas. He did not attempt to control for social class which severely limits the validity of his findings. Mitchell (1971) quotes the conclusion reached in a review of the relevant literature concerning population density and mental illness conducted by Wilner and Baer (1970).

> There is no body of convincing evidence that crowding in a dwelling unit contributes materially to mental disorder or to emotional instability. Nor is there evidence as yet that crowding (or other housing deficits) interferes with a promotive style of life; that because of crowding, family roles and ritual cannot satisfactorily be carried out; or that the development of infants and children is severely impaired (Mitchell, 1971:20).

As is evident from the preceding quotation, this systematic review failed to find any evidence supporting the hypothesis that density contributes to mental illness.

In summary this review of the limited number of studies linking population density to mental health reveals that there is very little support for the hypothesis. As is the case with physical illness and death, when other factors, social class, stress, level of screening, etc., are taken into account the influence on mental illness is negligible.

Density and "Social Disorganization"

Basically, the social disorganization theory states that an increase in population density produces a greater propensity for aggressive behavior, which in turn is manifest in increased crime, delinquency, divorce, suicide, and similar antisocial behavior. An example of the use of density as an explanation of social disorganization is provided by the United States Riot Commission which indicted "crowded ghetto living conditions, worsened by summer heat," as one of the five basic factors involved in civil disorder (1968:325). The data supporting this theory come from three major sources: animal experiments, surveys, and census reports.

Animal Experiments

In the typical animal experiment described in the section on illness, the investigator often performs an autopsy on the animals involved. Significant increases in the various endocrine glands, particularly the adrenal gland, have been reported as a function of increased density (Christian, 1963). Accepting these changes in adrenocortial activity as indicators of increased aggressive tendencies, the evidence is quite convincing for a number of species. On the other hand, Thiessen (1961) in an experiment with mice found that fighting was *not* a function of density. Instead he concludes that close proximity heightened the visibility of "normal" fighting and resultant wounds and "hence neural activation, and that this heightened neural activity stimulated greater behavioral activity and differential physiological responses" (p. 324).

Several researchers have focused on observable aggressive behavior or wounds rather than internal physiological changes. Calhoun (Bliss, 1962) observed more scars on tails and necks of rats after density was increased. Alexander (Alexander and Roth, 1971) witnessed a similar effect with a troop of monkeys as the number of attacks and fights increased significantly in a confined cage.

The abundance of studies and the number of species tested indicate that changing population density is associated with certain physiological changes in animals. But at this time it is not possible to place the responsibility for such changes on density as several other confounding variables have not been controlled. There is the possibility that population *change*, not density, is the causative agent, and longitudinal studies are required to test for the independent effects of change and density. Also Cassel (Bliss, 1971) suggested we need to examine animal populations beyond the first generation to look for a possible adaptation effect. Although the animal research is provocative, there is no evidence that similar physiological changes occur in man. As discussed earlier, extreme caution is required to make the inference from animal to human behavior. Therefore, despite the results of animal experiments there is no basis to conclude that increased population density will produce a similar effect in man. Studies of humans are required to answer the question of the impact of density on human behavior.

186

In a pioneer study, Loring (1956) compared two different groups of families. The first group (experimental) was composed of families who had turned to community agencies or courts for help with one or more of the following problems: parent-child problems; marital difficulties; sibling difficulties; nonsupport by family heads; parental neglect of children; alcoholism; personality problems; adult sex maladjustment; juvenile delinquency; adult offender; and divorce. The second group was composed of "normal" families who had not turned to these agencies. He found that crowding (number of persons per room) and several other measures of "bad" housing related to density were significantly greater for the experimental group than for the control group. He attempted to control for social class by matching the two groups on occupation, but given the occupational categories used, this provided very crude control. Also, almost in refutation of his own data, Loring rejects the importance of density *per se*, and suggests that future research should focus on social density.

In another early study Schmitt (1957) examined the relationship between density and both juvenile delinquency and adult crime in 29 Honolulu census tracts. He found a few inconsistencies in the correlations for juvenile delinquency, adult crime, and density, but basically there was a relatively strong relationship between the five measures of population density and delinquency and crime. He concluded:

> Excessive densities unquestionably are a causative factor in some criminal behavior. While it is true that a high degree of correlation does not in itself constitute proof of causation, and many other factors (such as differential association, parent-child relationships, or economic status) are undeniably operative, it is nevertheless likely, from other evidence, that high densities predispose a resident population, either juvenile or adult to illegal acts. Such densities reduce the availability of land for recreation, curtail privacy, and, by virtue of shared facilities, jammed quarters, and general overoccupancy of housing, tend to promote friction within families with its attendant loss in primary social controls (Schmitt, 1957:276).

In a later study, Schmitt (1966) examined all 42 census tracts making up the Honolulu Standard Metropolitan Statistical Area for 1950. He found significant correlations between several measures of density—including crowding—and suicide, illegitimate births, juvenile delinquency, and incarceration. As will be recalled Schmitt did attempt to control for education and income but his technique leaves much to be desired. Nevertheless, all the relationships persisted after such control, with the exception of suicide. It was also observed that when density was controlled by partial correlation, the correlations between the measure of *crowding* and the dependent variables approached zero, indicating that density is much more important than crowding in explaining social disorganization.

All three of the above-discussed studies were negligent in controlling for confounding variables, particularly socioeconomic class. Since then several additional studies have been conducted in which more adequate control was exercised. Freedman (1971) reports a study by Pressman and Carol, who discovered a positive relationship between density and crime against persons and property in the largest metropolitan areas in the United States. But, when the effect of income was controlled the relationship between density and crime disappeared!

In the fascinating study conducted by Mitchell (1971) in Hong Kong, discussed earlier, it was discovered that population density produced mixed results with social disorganization. He concluded that density had no effect upon husband-wife interaction patterns (conflict and divorce) but that it did influence parent-child relationships. He suggests that in order to alleviate the "uncomfortable" consequences of high density, children are given greater freedom to leave the home. This tends to reduce parental surveillance which in turn may facilitate the youth's participation in various types of deviant behavior.

The National Commission on the Causes and Prevention of Violence reported that crime is primarily a phenomenon of large cities. The rates of crime, particularly crimes of violence, are relatively high for the highly populated centers of the United States. Many generalize from these statistics that density is the causative agent producing the high crime rate. Ehrlich and Freedman (1971:11) contend that "it would, however, be a mistake to interpret these statistics as indicating that higher population density causes higher crime." They point out inconsistencies in this hypothesis by comparing crime rates for the three largest U.S. cities, New York, Chicago, and Los Angeles. New York with the highest density had the lowest crime rate for crime against persons. Also, Los Angeles with the lowest density had the highest crime rate for crimes against property. Finally, comparative data from other countries do not support the density-crime relationship:

> The ever-increasing rates of violent crime are attributed to population growth and density. If crowded conditions cause crime, the most crowded areas of the world might legitimately be expected to have the highest crime rates.
>
> Holland, for example, where people are crowded together at a density of almost 1,000 per square mile (compared with 57 per square mile in the United States), should be a very dangerous place indeed. The Dutch, however, who have one of the lower crime rates in the Western world, seem to be unaware of their predicament. Perhaps they have not yet read such books as Paul Ehrlich's *Population Bomb*.
>
> To take another example, Great Britain has 50,000,000 people crowded into an area smaller than California. On the basis of the explosionists' rhetoric it is hard to understand why there are fewer murders in the entire British Isles every year than there are in Chicago or Cleveland, or greater Kansas City. These examples suggest that population density, *in itself*, does not produce crime (Jermann: 1970).

The studies reviewed, which have attempted to assess the relationship between density and social disorganization, have provided mixed results. Two major points need to be reiterated in attempting to interpret these findings. The first is that much of the research, particularly census analysis, ignored the most fundamental confounding variables. As has been repeatedly stressed, factors such as social class, national origin, etc., have to be controlled. Where this has been done, the results indicate that there is no relationship between density and social disorganization.

Second, even in those few cases where significant relationships have been found it is essential to remember that correlation does not mean causation. The association evidenced in the correlation may be the product of some unknown third factor(s). Also, it may be that the causal chain is in the opposite direction of that hypothesized. In other words, maybe the experience of illness, delinquency, crime, drug use, divorce, etc., prevents the individual from obtaining adequate housing and hence the person is forced into crowded, low-cost living quarters.

In summary, the studies reviewed here do not provide much support for the popular notion that high population density is responsible for various forms of social disorganization. This does not mean that density is *not* related to such phenomena, but simply that at present there is not convincing evidence for arriving at the conclusion that density is causally related to social disorganization.

Summary

The purpose of this paper has been to review the evidence concerning the fairly common acceptance of the deleterious influence of increased population density on health and social organization. Animal studies, comparisons of urban and rural areas, comparisons of morbidity and death rates before and after urbanization, and studies of illness patterns in crowded institutional settings were reviewed to ascertain the amount of support for the hypothesis that density produces illness and death. Inconsistencies in results, recent changes in trends, recognition of intervening variables, as well as methodological inadequacies prevent the conclusion that high density is associated with increased rates of illness and death. It seems that intervening factors such as social class, diet, sanitation, availability of health care, stress, etc., are much more relevant to illness and death rates than is high population density.

The review of the literature concerning high density's relationship to mental illness arrived at the same conclusion; that there is not much support for the idea that high density is causally related to high rates of mental illness. This conclusion is similar to that of other reviews by other scientists.

Social disorganization, as indicated by crime, delinquency, divorce, suicide, drug abuse, alcoholism, etc., was found to be associated with high density relatively infrequently. Animal studies, analysis of census data and surveys produced rather limited and inconsistent support for such a widely accepted relationship. The supposed relationship between density and social disorganization tended to disappear when the effects of social class (income, occupation, education) were controlled for. Surprisingly, some fragmentary evidence emerged suggesting that high density is related to improved health, and reduced death and social disorganization. Considerable research remains to be conducted before a definitive answer can be given to the question of the impact of high density on health, death and social disorganization. At present the jury is out.

References

Alexander, B.K., and E.M. Roth
1971   "The effects of acute crowding on aggressive be-
        havior of Japanese monkeys." Behavior
        49 (Parts 2-4):73-90.

Banfield, Edward C.
1968   The Unheavenly City. Boston: Little, Brown
        and Co.

Brett, G.Z., and B. Benjamin
1957   "Housing and tuberculosis in a mass radiography
        survey." British Journal of Preventative Med-
        icine 11 (January):7.

Bliss, E.L.
1962   "A behavioral sink" by John B. Calhoun in
        Roots of Behavior. New York: Harper and
        Brothers.

Cassel, John, and H.A. Tyroler
1971   "Epidemiological studies of culture change: I.
        Health status and recency of industrialization."
        Archives of Environmental Health 3 (July-
        December):25.

Christenson, William N., and Lawrence R. Hinkle, Jr.
1961   "Differences in illness and prognostic signs in
        two groups of young men." Journal of the
        American Medical Association 177 (July
        29):247-253.

Christian, John J.
1961   "Phenomena associated with population den-
        sity." Proceeding of the National Academy of
        Science 47(April 15):428.

1963   "The pathology of overpopulation." Military
        Medicine 128 (July):571-603.

191

Ehrlich, Paul, and Jonathon Freedman
1971   "Population, crowding and human behavior."
               New Scientist and Science Journal 1
               (April):10-14.

Freedman, Jonathon L.
1971   "A positive view of population density."
               Psychology Today 5 (September):58-61.

Gruenberg, E.M.
1954   "Community conditions and psychosis of the
               elderly." American Journal of Psychiatry 110
               (June):888-903.

Haenszel, William, Donald B. Loveland, and Monroe G. Sirken
1962   "Lung cancer mortality as related to residence
               and smoking histories." Journal of National Can-
               cer Institute 28 (April):947-1001.

Hall, Edward Twitchell
1966   The Hidden Dimension. Garden City, New York:
               Doubleday Publishers

Holmes, Thomas H.
1956   "Multidiscipline studies of tuberculosis," in
               Phineas J. Sparer, (ed.), Personality Stress and
               Tuberculosis. New York: International Uni-
               versity Press.

Jacobs, Jane
1961   The Death and Life of Great American Cities.
               New York: Random House.

Jermann, Thomas C.
1970   "It's time to defuse population 'explosionists'."
               The National Observer (July 27).

Loring, William C.
1956   "Housing characteristics and social disorga-
               nization." Journal of Social Problems 3 (Janu-
               ary):160-168.

192

Madge, John, and Sherman J. Maisel
1968   "Housing and social aspects," in International
                Encyclopedia of Social Science. MacMillan and
                Free Press 6:516-521.

Mitchell, Robert Edward
1971   "Some social implications of high density
                housing." American Sociological Review 36
                (February):18-29.

NAS (National Academy of Sciences, a study committee of the foreign Secretary)
1971   "Health consequences of population density and
                crowding," by John Cassel in Rapid Population
                Growth: Consequences and Policy Implications.
                Baltimore: Johns Hopkins Press.

Schmitt, Robert C.
1957   "Density, delinquency, and crime in Honolulu."
                Sociology and Social Research 41 (March-
                April):274-276.

1966   "Density, health, and social disorganization."
                Journal of American Institute of Planners 32
                (January):38-39.

Thiessen, D.D.
1966   "Role of physical injury in the physiological
                effects of population density in mice." Journal
                of Comparative and Physiological Psychology
                62 (October):322-324.

U.S. Riot Commission Report
1968   Report of the National Advisory Commission on
                Civil Disorders. New York: Bantam Books, Inc.

Wilner, D.M., and W.G. Baer
1970   "Sociocultural factors in residential space."
                Mimeo., prepared for Environmental Control
                Administration of the Department of Health,
                Education and Welfare and the American Public
                Health Association.

V.
MAN THE DESTROYER?
NOT NECESSARILY

Introduction

Pollution has become a very salient word in the vocabulary of most Americans. The rapid insertion of this word into our consciousness has been the consequence of many events, including exposure to numerous books, TV specials, news broadcasts, and speeches, as well as personal experiences of viewing amber horizons or debris-cluttered landscapes. The importance of pollution is presently attested to by its inclusion in school curricula from first grade to graduation. We applaud this concern with preserving and improving a quality environment, but as has been continually stressed throughout this book, caution must be exercised in labelling factors as being responsible for pollution. Pollution is a very complex phenomenon, and simplistic solutions are destined to failure. We reject the popular contention that population size is responsible for environmental problems, and that zero population growth will eliminate pollution from the United States or the world as a whole. It is acknowledged that the number of people living within a given geographical area is one important factor in the creation of waste. We submit that several other factors need to be included in the equation if a viable anti-pollution program is to be developed.

The purpose of the two articles in this chapter is to illustrate the position that variables other than population size are impor-

197

tant in understanding pollution. It is not claimed that all possible factors associated with pollution have been discussed; the intent is to demonstrate that there are other influences involved, and that greater public concern and resources need to be committed to their identification and the design of antipollution programs.

In "Coping with Environmental Damage" Gardner discusses popular notions about environmental pollution: considerable attention has been focused on the relationship between our capitalistic economic system, population size, and environmental damage. Gardner argues that change to a socialistic economic system or stabilizing or reducing population are not the only solutions to the problem. In the case of public ownership of property, he points out that at present greater pollution is occurring in public property than in privately owned property. He therefore suggests that one feasible way to reduce pollution is to decrease publicly owned property rather than to increase it. The possibility of distributing pollution quotas for water, air or land is raised, and if an individual wishes to engage in polluting activities, he can do so until his quota is filled. Then he must purchase someone else's quota, or stop polluting. On the other hand, if someone wishes to reduce pollution below the officially set level, he may purchase quotas and then not utilize them. Other techniques for reducing pollution of the environment such as zoning and taxation are discussed. The point is made that environmental damage is not a necessary consequence of a free enterprise system or of the size of the population. There are additional factors in the pollution equation, and the temptation to oversimplify must not prevent us from looking at all sides of the problem.

The importance of examining any problem and its causes in terms of the total system in which it is situated is discussed by Holt in "Selected Ecological Considerations for an Increasing Population." He demonstrates the danger associated with acting on simple limited-vision solutions to a given problem. Few individuals stopped to consider the ecological ramifications of the eradication of coyotes from the grassland, other than that livestock losses would be reduced. The consequence has been an invasion of sage brush that in turn has taken over former grazing land and thus reduced the number of cattle a given piece of land can support. Holt next considers the implications of the green revolution and makes the point that in order to realize the full

198

potential from new high yield strains of grain, changes must be made in other areas of the society. The necessary fertilizers, pesticides, water, transportation and distribution systems must be provided.

Holt also discusses possible new ways of obtaining the water necessary to support an increasing population, and summarizes proposals for reducing per capita consumption of water and decreasing water pollution. He concludes by discussing pesticides and their impact on the environment. Again creative solutions are presented using a total ecosystem approach.

The necessary technology is available to implement all of the proposals for providing resources for a growing population while at the same time reducing environmental damage. We are confident that if resources of the scientific community are directed at the problem of pollution, additional solutions and technology will be forthcoming. The evidence suggests that despite continued population growth at the current rates, man can develop the means to maintain, protect and even improve his physical environment.

Coping
with
Environmental Damage

B. Delworth Gardner

The so-called environmental crisis has engendered a spate of palliatives and demands for reform of our basic values and the social institutions that perpetuate them. It is almost "conventional wisdom" now to blame the allegedly exploitive free enterprise system, the profit-hungry captains of industry, and the greedy, materialistic consumers for the despoilation and depletion of scarce environmental resources such as potable water, clean air, and unmarred landscapes (Helfrich, 1970). A related argument is that there are simply too many people consuming resources and if the environment is to be protected, population growth must be curtailed (Helfrich, 1970:47-64).

Since entrepreneurs and consumers are the culprits, remedies are strongly promoted that would prevent people from acting in ways that cause environmental damage. Some argue the solution is to manipulate human values so that people will desire goods and services which require smaller amounts of scarce physical and environmental resources (Skinner, 1971). Consumers would thus be enticed to lower rates of consumption of resources and consequently reduce the production of waste. Unfortunately, such manipulation may not be possible in free society and to permit such practices would have serious consequences for personal freedom. It is also suggested that since free enterprise is fundamentally an exploitive economic system, it should be replaced by some form of socialism, which presumably would assure that collective decisions would protect public interest. Some "environmentalists" hesitate to advocate socialism, but do support policies that would strictly regulate private businesses in the hope that more socially optimal decisions would be made. Finally, many have advocated forced population control by limiting family size to two children.

The notion that consumer values and business ethics affect the natural and physical environment cannot be completely discounted. There also is truth in the assertion that five billion profligate human beings will create more waste than three billion. But to put major emphasis on these factors as the primary causes of the environmental crisis is to err grievously by neglecting other important factors which may offer valuable insight into the problems of environmental damage. Imperfections in the legal and political institutions within which resource-use decisions are made are important dimensions of the problems that frequently are neglected. This short essay examines the environmental problem in terms of these institutions and attempts (1) to determine the relationship between these institutions and environmental damage and (2) to suggest possible remedies for these causes of damage. The principle method used in ferreting out the serious causes of environmental damage is to observe where such damage primarily occurs.

Most environmental damage involves resources held as the common property of the community at large, such as air, water, and public land used as roads, streets, and parks (Hardin, 1968). These common-property resources are owned and generally managed by the community, represented by some unit of government. Individual users of these resources have no management responsibilities, they do not bear the costs of maintenance as individuals. The result is that each individual regards these resources as a free good and tends, quite rationally, to utilize the resources intensively, since he knows that if he doesn't get his share or more, other users will. For example, it is precisely the phenomenon of common property control that induced otherwise conservative ranchers to completely denude the range forage on common grazing allotments on public land (Gardner, 1963:109-120), ocean fishermen to reduce some fish populations

202

to near zero levels (Gordon, 1954:124-142), and oil companies to rapidly deplete reserves from a common petroleum pool (McKie and McDonald, 1962:98-121). Examples could be extended almost indefinitely, but these are sufficient to illustrate the importance of this source of damage.

Given the rather frequent incidence of environmental damage whenever property is held in common by the community, it is ironic that "socialism" or greater public "ownership" is so frequently suggested as a solution to environmental damage. Where (1) property rights are well defined and (2) property owners have firm control of the use of environmental resources, and (3) where property owners must fully bear the consequences of their decisions, the damage resulting from production or consumption is generally negligible. As a rule, a property owner will not permit his renewable resources to be irreparably damaged since they are of value to him only if he can maintain their productivity base. Thus, if he can control access to and use of his resources, he will find it in his own best interests to prevent resource damage. Of course, at times there may be sharp differences of opinion between the private owner of resources and the public at large in viewing what uses should be made of the resources. But on the whole, privately-owned and controlled resources are well maintained and relatively free of pollution damage. One possible way to manage public resources in such a way as to minimize environmental damage is to utilize economic incentives to motivate this type of behavior.

By imaginative planning and management, previously squandered public environmental resources could be protected by simulating a private market. Consider the case of an urban airshed. The public authority could create pollution quotas, which would permit the owners of the quotas to put that amount of pollution into the air which the community is prepared to accept. These quotas could then be sold to the highest bidders. Those who wish a lower level of air pollution could also enter the market, buy up the pollution rights, and not use them. This technique of creating private property out of previously public property could permit level of pollution to be controlled at any given level and the community could use the revenues created by the sale of quotas to mitigate any undesirable effects of pollution. It appears that much water and air pollution could be satisfactorily handled in this way (Kneese, 1964; Kneese and Blair, 1968).

The use of property rights as a mechanism for extending personal freedom and for fixing responsibility for protection of resources may generate anxiety over the possibility of some individuals misusing the rights to the serious detriment of society. It must be realized that property rights are granted by society and as a consequence they are almost always conditional; that is, the property owner is never completely free to use his property according to his every whim. The public maintains broad police and regulatory powers that it may invoke to limit personal liberties and property rights in the interest of public health, safety, morals, and general welfare. These powers consist of protection of persons and property; establishment and enforcement of fire, health, and traffic regulations; control of air and water pollution; prohibition of billboards at particular locations; elimination and prevention of public nuisances; enforcement of quarantines; and elimination of diseased animals, etc. It is thus apparent that the blatant private excesses which militate against the public interest, including environmental damage, can be controlled by the police and regulatory power of society.

Additional methods of environmental control in the public interest can be suggested. But they are probably less efficient in producing results than the creation of property rights and generally involve some degree of compulsion—they force people to do things they would prefer not to do. The market, on the other hand, permits largely voluntary exchange, allows for a wide diversity of action, and thus conduces to human freedom (Friedman, 1962).

Zoning is a popular regulating tool and is utilized at nearly every level of government to achieve public purposes. It is a public decision about land use that attempts to prevent undesirable private actions. Thus, exclusive residential areas are zoned against social nuisances such as factory smoke and college students living in multiple-family housing units. Zoning has been used with considerable success in numerous communities.

But while zoning may be effective in eliminating some negative social effects, the cost may be relatively high. By government edict, part of the total demand for a given land parcel is simply ruled out of existence. The land market is, therefore, effectively eliminated as an efficient allocating device. This is at once the advantage and the disadvantage of zoning, since free market allocations may bring with them the undesirable private activity. But on the other hand, it is easy to underestimate the real costs of zoning. The prohibited, undesirable private activity may be quite visible and politically sensitive, whereas the economic products (which may be substantial) the community foregoes by zoning out part of the land demand are usually fairly invisible and easily overlooked.

Zoning suffers from other defects as well, most important being its political limitations. If zoning is to mean anything, it must prevent someone from doing something he would otherwise do. Where local government is weak, zoning simply cannot stand up against the kind of political pressures that inevitably arise. Almost every city council, county commission or any governmental unit involved in zoning is subject to pressure by private interests to change zoning regulations, primarily because of the wealth gains that can be secured. Since those who bring pressure are often developers and large landholders who are already relatively wealthy and because wealth and political influence seem to go hand in hand, there is always some danger that the rich will profit from zoning changes at the expense of the society as a whole.

In addition to zoning, almost every level of government has the power of eminent domain. Privately owned land can be condemned for public purposes such as roads, public buildings, parks, water supply, etc. Condemnation proceedings are brought through the courts and a negotiated compensation is paid to private owners of condemned land. Normally, eminent domain proceedings are used only as a last resort. More usual is the practice of government purchase of land in the market. In some cases, the government may not purchase the land itself, but only buy easements to use the land for public purposes. This is a common practice in making private land accessible to recreation uses. A government easement may permit fishermen to obtain access to fishing waters that would be impossible otherwise. Because compensation is paid, eminent domain may be a more expensive means of social control than zoning. But by the same token, it may also be more equitable. In addition, eminent domain results in removal of private property from the tax rolls whereas zoning does not. Where there are sharp conflicts between private owners of resources and the community at large in terms of what uses are to be made of resources, eminent domain might well be justified as a tool to prevent private resource damage.

Another technique which may be utilized to control misuse of the environment is economic sanctions, such as taxation. Economic sanctions tend to be more flexible than prohibitions such as zoning in giving resource land owners more options (Solow, 1971). Taxes and subsidies may distort market prices, but at least the market still functions to allocate resources. Let us see how a private entrepreneur might react to a taxation program designed to mitigate environmental damage. Suppose we take the situation of a factory on a river where factory wastes impose downstream costs on recreationists. One way to rid the community of these external costs is to zone the river banks to prohibit industrial development. But since these may be the very land sites that yield high location rents, zoning is like throwing out the baby with the bath water, especially if control of the social costs can be accomplished in another more efficient way. A pollution tax could be levied on the factory owner (Kneese, 1964). For every unit of pollutant released into the river, the factory owner must pay a tax. The greater the pollution, the greater the tax. Several options are available to the factory owner to mitigate the effects of the tax on his rents and profits. Since his production costs would rise and rent would decline one option could be to pass on the entire burden of the tax to consumers in the form of higher output prices. This alternative is highly unlikely because he would be competing with other producers of the same product who may not be subject to the tax, and their competition limits the extent to which he could charge higher prices. Even if all producers in the industry were taxed, they could not pass on all of the costs of the tax so long as any products from other industries were competitive.

A second option open is that the producers may find it more profitable to give up production on the river by moving to another site or by ceasing production altogether. In either case, the community controls the external costs imposed on downstream users; but, of course, it gives up whatever rent is earned at the river site. In most cases where the land generates a large rent because of its inherent productivity for the purposes to which it is put, the option preferred by the factory owner will be to pay the tax or escape from paying it by installing pollution control devices. Even if the former option is chosen, the community has the tax revenues available that may be used to mitigate the effects of the external costs on downstream users. If the latter option is taken, the externalities are eliminated, which was precisely the purpose of the tax.

Some have charged that a tax such as the one in our example is ineffective because the land owner will pay it and go right on polluting; that such a tax becomes a license to pollute. The answer to this charge is that if polluters are likely to respond in this way, the tax should be raised. At some level of taxation, the polluter either will reduce the pollution or the community will be luxuriating in revenues with which it can take measures of its own to reduce the impact of the pollution on the community.

The reverse of the tax is a subsidy. If some resource uses bring positive benefits to the community, the community may wish to subsidize these uses in the form of tax rebates. Subsidies may profitably be used to encourage individuals and industries to utilize nonscarce resources in place of those whose production creates environmental damage.

In conclusion, the American people should not regard environmental damage as unavoidable. There are many ways, few of which are presently being utilized, that could be invoked to solve environmental problems. Only a few ideas have been presented in this short essay, but the point has been made that private ownership and population growth are not the only critical factors in protecting the environment. Our planet will be plundered and polluted so long as our system of incentives and institutional arrangements allow and encourage this waste, even if the population were stabilized. The basic problem is not human selfishness. It is not our exploitative enterprise economic system. It is our collective failure to be innovative in designing market and control institutions that could more effectively cope with environmental damage.

References

Friedman, Milton M.
  1962   Capitalism and Freedom. Chicago: University of Chicago Press.

Gardner, B. Delworth
  1963   "A proposal to mitigate misallocation of live-

stock grazing permits." Journal of Farm Economics 45 (February):109-120.

Gordon, H. Scott
1954   "The economic theory of a common property resource." Journal of Political Economy 62 (April):124-142.

Hardin, Garrett
1968   "The tragedy of the commons." Science 162:1243-1248.

Helfrich, Harold W.
1970   The Environmental Crisis. New Haven, Connecticut: Yale University Press.

Helfrich, Harold W.
1970   "Famine 1975: fact or fallacy?" by Paul R. Ehrlich in The Environmental Crisis. New Haven, Connecticut: Yale University Press.

Kneese, Allan V.
1964   The Economics of Regional Water Quality Management. Baltimore: Johns Hopkins Press.

Kneese, Allan V., and Bower T. Blair
1968   Managing Water Quality: Economics, Technology, Institutions. Baltimore: Johns Hopkins Press.

McKie, James W., and Stephen L. McDonald
1962   "Petroleum conservation in theory and practice." Quarterly Journal of Economics 76 (February):98-121.

Skinner, B. F.
1971   Beyond Freedom and Dignity. New York: Knopf.

Solow, Robert M.
1971   "The economist's approach to pollution and its control." Science 173 (August 6):498-503.

Selected Ecological Considerations for an Increased Population

Elvis J. Holt

This article considers three subtopics which have been integrated in an effort to illustrate the relationships existing between the human population and the environment. The first section is an endeavor to establish the necessity for perceiving our earth as a functional, dynamic system rather than "dissecting" it and then attempting to draw conclusions. It is another way to express the fact that the whole is more than a sum of its parts. The subsequent discussions of water quality and use of pesticides illustrate contemporary ecological conditions and perspectives related to an increasing human population.

An Ecosystem Approach to Stewardship

Human society is presently facing an ecological crisis largely because in the past goals and outcomes have been inadequately considered and seldom specified. In retrospect, a portion of our predicament can be justified on the basis of lack of knowledge. But surely today we can refrain from practices which have been demonstrated to be ecologically damaging. A political scientist points to the need for a governmental policy of planning and action based upon ecological criteria:

The crisis of the environment is more a crisis of will and rationality

209

than it is of knowledge or of technical or engineering capabilities. Informed men know what must be done if the world is to survive man's demands upon it. They also know how to accomplish substantial parts of the task of environmental renewal. What remains to be discovered is how to bring human will and effort to bear upon the task in sufficient strength and in sufficient time to safeguard the continuing existence of the living world (Murdoch, 1971:413).

Without looking for ecological ramifications, who would think that the eradication of coyotes from the grasslands could result in the invasion of sagebrush, or that stopping the occasional natural fires from burning off the spruce and fir in some areas of Alaska or Isle Royale in Lake Superior could cause the elimination of moose from these areas? Plainly, people must be educated and oriented toward thinking and acting ecologically. Before acting we must learn to formulate plans which specify expected effects on all facets of the ecosystem and which evaluate alternative actions and their consequences.

From the ecologist's viewpoint we drastically need a resounding public education program on the subject of the environment. One might ask, "What would you include in such a program? How would you know if it were effective?" Murdoch (1971:416-434) has suggested that one criterion for achievement would be the layman's response to proposed projects. A public education program might be considered successful if in answer to a question about possible construction of a large dam on an African river, a layman would answer, "Before making a judgment I would need to know the dam's potential effect on the spread of schistoso-miases, on the local climate, on downstream agriculture and on health, the number of people to be moved, where they would go, the possibilities of flooding and silting in of the empoundment and the specific benefits from constructing the dam."

The functioning of the earth ecosystem must be viewed and planned for in the same way as for ecosystems of smaller scale. When one factor in the system is altered, compensation must be forthcoming in that factor or other factors, or wider system changes may be anticipated. For example, in considering the possibility for increasing food production each resource cannot be considered independent of other resources. The appearance of some new genetic varieties of wheat, rice, and corn have added tremendously to our capabilities for food production. However,

210

the extent to which the potential production actually occurs will be determined largely by factors in the system other than the new variety of grain. To list a few:

1. Advanced technology is required to produce machinery, fertilizers and pesticides.
2. Fertilizers have to be mined or manufactured and distributed, and that presupposes a high level of industrial development.
3. A given amount of water is required to produce a given amount of dry matter. As the new varieties of wheat and fertilizers make possible an increased production of dry matter there must be additional water supplied. (In the example cited, water is not as critical a factor as it might be since the new short stem varieties of wheat and rice have a higher ratio of usable food to total plant biomass than do the other varieties.)
4. When a nation becomes a transporter rather than an importer of cereal grains its economic system must undergo adjustments, and these have an impact on the ecosystem. New distribution systems must be developed because the crops are not grown where the people are concentrated. The people are likely to be concentrated near the old locations of import where goods were more readily accessible.
5. Accompanying the technological and industrial changes will be changes in the educational system so that the needs for trained people to fill the new positions of operation and system management may be met.

Using the Green Revolution as an example is not an endeavor to minimize its significance but to illustrate that the creation of new varieties of grain is only one of many adjustments that must occur in the ecosystem if mankind is to reap the potential benefits.

The importance of basing conclusions on the entire ecosystem rather than some isolated portion merits an additional illustration. The temperature of the earth is determined by three factors: a) intensity of solar radiation, b) amount of energy (heat) reflected by the earth, and c) effective emissivity or the amount of energy which leaves the earth's atmosphere and goes off into space. When any one of these factors is altered the earth's temperature will change unless the other factors change to maintain an equilibrium.

About 42 percent of the high intensity, short wave radiation from the sun is reflected back into space by clouds and dust; an additional 10 percent is absorbed by ozone, oxygen and water vapor in the earth's atmosphere. This leaves about 48 percent which actually reaches the earth's surface. The earth reflects some of this energy, the remainder warms the earth, and is then radiated as longer wave-length energy (infrared), into the atmosphere. Carbon dioxide, moisture, dust and ozone in the atmosphere absorb some of this energy and reflect some of it back to the earth. Were the concentration of CO_2 to increase in the atmosphere, the effective emmissivity of the atmosphere would decrease, and more heat would be maintained within the earth's atmosphere. Unless some opposing factor resulted in less energy reaching the earth, an increase in CO_2 would result in an increase in the earth's temperature. This is one of the factors contributing to the "greenhouse effect".

Since about 1880 atmospheric CO_2 has increased about 11.3 percent. The major portion of this increase has resulted from more and more people desiring more and more goods and services which require fossil fuels. CO_2 is a product of burning these fuels. The CO_2 increase has paralleled population increase. Some "preachers" of eco-catastrophe have used this CO_2 increase as evidence for the need to reduce the size of the earth's population. Moreover, their views become somewhat persuasive and alarming when we are confronted by *their* possible alternatives: If the population continues to grow, more CO_2 will accumulate, and the temperature will increase. This will cause the glaciers and ice fields to melt and the level of the oceans will increase by 200-400 feet. When considered in the abstract and not in terms of all factors affecting the earth's heat balance such views are tenable.

However, several alternative futures are equally tenable when considered in the abstract:
1. If the earth were to increase in temperature, evaporation would increase, and this in turn would increase the cloud density. This could result in an eventual cooling trend because less energy would reach the earth.
2. If the earth's temperature increased and the ice caps began to melt they would break up and spread out. This could result in a cooling trend because less energy would be absorbed (or more would be reflected) by the earth.
3. If the amount of CO_2 increased and the temperature increased there would be an increase in the rate of plant growth and photosynthesis since plants function better in a higher CO_2 environment.

212

The increased rate of plant growth would require more CO_2, and more O_2 would be released than at present. As the O_2 built up in the atmosphere the amount of O_3 (ozone) would also increase as a result of normally occurring chemical reactions. As a consequence, more short wave-length radiation would be absorbed in the outer reaches of the atmosphere, and a cooling trend could be initiated.

What is actually happening? Is there a warming trend associated with the increasing CO_2? According to Mitchell (1961:248) the mean temperature of the earth has been *decreasing* since 1940. Sunspots (which may indicate an increase in solar output) have increased. Mitchell notes that volcanic activity has also increased noticeably since 1940. The observed cooling trend is correlated with increased atmospheric turbidity (dust and suspended particles) from industrialization, mechanization and renewed volcanic activity. Increased turbidity would primarily result in a decrease in the amount of solar energy reaching the earth.

In considering the total heat balance it is most likely that man's activities have altered all three factors which determine the earth's temperature and that presently the effects of the increased turbidity of the atmosphere are more influential than those which might occur from CO_2 increase. The net result is that the earth is in a cooling trend rather than a warming trend.

The rationale for discussing these examples is to illustrate the grand homeostatic mechanisms (counter balances) inherent in the earth's ecosystem and more importantly, to emphasize that we must weigh critically statements about the consequences of particular changes for the ecosystem as a whole. For a more detailed examination of the complex interrelationships involved in climatic change, see the work of Bryson (1968:56-61).

Ecologists, working as a community of scholars, are now able to execute comprehensive studies on a scale which was never possible in the past, when each ecologist was capable of coping only with his own limited specialty. In collaboration with computer specialists and systems analysts, ecologists are creating ecosystem models that make it possible to describe the normal and altered conditions of an ecosystem and to project the influence of a variety of changes on the system. This type of integrated analysis and problem solving must become more common if we are to prepare ourselves to cope with present and anticipated alterations of our earth ecosystem.

If our efforts at establishing appropriate control and utilization

213

of public resources, e.g., air, water, and land, are to succeed, it would appear that more political decisions will have to be based on ecological criteria. For example, decisions could be based on the ultimate good a particular factor could contribute to the ecosystem. Top quality cropland would be preserved and not used, except as a last resort, for freeways or city expansion. Marginal land subject to erosion would be removed from cultivation and used for pasture, housing, or other needs not requiring the best agriculture land.

Thus, we need to consider the total environment in our decision making. The problem is appropriately summarized in the following statement:

> The effective management of environmental quality is dependent upon the development of a broader sense of economic and social responsibility. There is a need to develop an increased awareness of short-run and long-run effects of pollutants. Alternative means of alleviating pollution problems must be evaluated to determine if they are in harmony with our physical, biological, social and economic objectives. There is a need to develop an awareness of the short-run and long-run effects of technological developments. Engineers and researchers usually are engaged in activities directed at the solution of specific problems. They need to develop a keen awareness of the unplanned, or external implications of their research findings, and these implications should be reflected in the decision making process. There is a need to integrate learning from all branches of science into a comprehensive system of knowledge, ideas, and values relevant to environmental quality (Cornell University Conference, 1969:367).

Water Supply, Pollution, and Population Increase

It has been estimated that almost three-fourths of the annual precipitation in the United States is lost to evapotranspiration. Three-fourths of the remainder is presently lost to runoff, and one-fourth (350 times 10^9 gallons per day) is used. The projected 1980 requirement for use is twice that figure, and will represent half of the water available from precipitation after losses to evapotranspiration are deducted (Ehrlich and Ehrlich, 1970:65; Bradley, 1962:489-491).

How Much Water Do We Need?

We are all aware of the two quarts or so of water a man requires

214

daily for drinking. We are undoubtedly less aware of the much larger volumes of equally essential water required to sustain a man's food chain from the soil to his stomach. This includes the water to raise the wheat for bread and for vegetables to fill the salad bowl. There is even a larger volume required to raise the alfalfa necessary to feed a steer to provide us with a daily slice of meat. All this water represents a rather rigid requirement for human life.

An adult human has a daily requirement of about two and one-half pounds of food (dry weight). Let's illustrate the water required to produce a strictly vegetarian diet. It takes about 500 pounds of water circulating through the wheat plant from the soil to the air to produce one pound (dry weight) of wheat plant. The grain to be milled represents only half the weight of the plant so we can say that it takes 1000 pounds of water to make a pound of bread. Therefore, it takes 2500 pounds of water (about 300 gallons) to supply a theoretical, daily, per capita minimum requirement to sustain life (Bradley, 1962:489-491).

What happens to the water requirement when we consider a simplified American diet of one pound of animal fat and protein and two pounds of vegetable foods (bread) per day? It takes about two years to raise a steer that will yield 700 pounds of meat. The animal gains about one pound of meat per day. To provide one pound of beef per day in the diet would require a situation of having about one steer per person being continually produced. A mature steer on a diet of alfalfa consumes 25 to 35 pounds of alfalfa per day (Woll, 1921:274). Assume an average consumption of 25 pounds of alfalfa per day to produce one pound of edible meat. It requires about 20,000 pounds of water to bring 25 pounds of alfalfa to maturity. (This estimate is based upon experiments which show that it takes about 800 grams of water to produce one gram of dry matter [Maximov, 1929:299 and 303].) In other words about 2500 gallons of water per day per capita would be required to introduce one pound of beef protein and fat into a person's diet. This does not include drinking water for the animal or water to process the meat so it is ready for the table. Add to this the 200 gallons necessary to round out the diet with two pounds of vegetable matter and we have a total water requirement of perhaps 2700 gallons per day per person for a substantial American diet.

215

The above figures represent only the food requirement. When we consider the total water "used," we need to add that required to process our food and furnish us fiber, lumber, and newsprint, to operate factories, washing machines, flush toilets, and to sweep our sewage out to sea. The list could go on and on, but it's not difficult to determine that the American standard of living requires a tremendous water supply. Fortunately, pound for pound water is the cheapest item brought into the home. Perhaps in our society an effective way to bring about water conservation would be to increase the price. Then we would tend to value the resource more highly, plan for its use and use it with better discretion than we presently do.

Prospects for Improving the Availability and Quality of Water

Water is a necessary resource for life as we know it. Consequently we would expect man to respond more rapidly and actively to an environmental circumstance which affects the quality or availability of water than he would to some lower priority resource. The declining quality of water in our rivers, lakes and streams is a present reality, and action must not be delayed.

Let us begin with three generalizations relevant to a discussion of future prospects in water resources: (a) There is considerably more water available than we are currently using (However, the solution to pollution is no longer dilution!); (b) Water pollution is not a nationwide problem but instead is related directly to the concentration of humans and/or their livestock; (c) Like most pollution problems water pollution is not so much a matter of technology as of a current lack of human support which is inhibiting progress toward solving water pollution problems.

The most direct effect of man on the quality of his water resources results from domestic sewage. To illustrate that point, take the case of Chicago's sewage treatment.

Around the turn of the century Chicago had a population of about 300,000. The city was rightly proud of its sewage treatment plants which were among the most efficient for large cities anywhere. The plants were achieving about 90 percent removal of organic materials which require oxygen to degrade them. (In other words, the bacteria in the stream which received the effluent from

216

the sewage treatment plants required only 10 percent of the amount of oxygen to break down the organic matter in the sewage that would have been required had the sewage been "dumped" into the stream untreated.) This efficiency resulted in the Chicago River receiving a biological oxygen demand (BOD) load equivalent to the raw sewage from 30,000 people.

Today Chicago has sewage treatment facilities which are still as good or better than most big cities (90 percent efficient in removing BOD). The city has the same river to dump the effluents into and also a population of 3,000,000 plus. Therefore, the river receives a BOD load equivalent to the raw sewage from 300,000 people. This relationship between population and water pollution from domestic sewage is one of the factors which must be taken into account in dealing with increasing population size and concentration.

Gaining taxpayer support for sewage treatment plants is often a difficult task. Many people view sewage treatment as an unnecessary financial liability because they think that once the water and sewage have left the house they are of no value. In fact, the argument goes, the reason we get rid of them is that they are no longer wanted. Since these resources are no longer of value why do we have to pay for them?

Nevertheless, as the population increases, the extent of reuse (recycling) of water will have to increase. Otherwise the supply cannot meet the demand. In fact, without reuse in some geographic areas, the present water supply could not meet the demand. According to some estimates, water in some of our major rivers is presently being used ten or more times before it reaches the ocean.

Table 1 gives us some idea of the potential for water reuse based on the amounts of water used and that actually consumed, that is, passed from the liquid state to the vapor state of the hydrologic cycle.

Except for irrigation, only 10 percent of the water supplied for various functions is actually consumed. (About 80 percent of that used in irrigation is consumed.) Of the total intake about 38 percent is actually consumed. If the water used but remaining were recycled the annual increase in demand for new water would be rather small. Accordingly, Wagner states that "in a very real sense there is no shortage of water in the U.S. nor is there likely to be in

217

Table 1. United States intake and net consumption of water (10^9gal/day 1965)[a]

	Intake	Net Consumption
Irrigation	142	116
Steam generated power	111	1
Industry	74	12
Public water	23	1
Rural domestic	6	4

Source: Dykes, D. R., T. S. Bry, and C. H. Kline, "Water management: a fashionable topic," *Environmental Science and Technology* 1 (October, 1967) p. 783. © The American Chemical Society. Reprinted by permission.

the future, no matter how many people live in the country and make demands on its water supply (Wagner, 1971:98).

Since we need to think more positively about consuming recycled water, let's summarize what takes place in a sewage treatment plant. A good overview of present and prospective sewage treatment processes is presented in a simplified manner in the USDI and FWPCA publication, *A Primer on Waste Water Treatment.* The very thought of using recycled water is not very palatable to most of us. It may be reassuring to learn that sewage which leaves our homes and enters the sewage treatment plant is over 99 percent water. Thus, the quantity of impurity that must be removed to return the water to a "pure" state is relatively small.

Where it exists at all, sewage treatment consists of one or two stages. Primary treatment is a physical process where sewage is held in large settling tanks. Suspended materials, under gravitational forces, settle to the bottom or float to the surface. They are periodically removed from the tank and further treated or disposed. The somewhat murky liquid remaining in the tank is either chlorinated and run into the river or pumped to secondary treatment facilities. Secondary treatment utilizes bacteria to break down the dissolved solids remaining in the sewage water. The various processes available can remove 90-95 percent of the original content of suspended solids which require oxygen to degrade them. An efficiently operating sewage treatment plant can produce water which is visually acceptable. However, the water still contains phosphates, nitrates and other nutrients known to

218

promote plant and animal growth in streams. Some kind of tertiary treatment to remove nutrients must be included if artificial enrichment of surface water is to be controlled. The artificial enrichments are among the components that have potential to cause water pollution.

There are several possibilities for tertiary treatment using existing technology. The effluent can be held in shallow tanks or pools for a time to allow algal growth to remove the nutrients. Algae can then be filtered out, leaving the water relatively free of nutrients. The algae could be processed and sold as a protein feed for livestock or even humans. A more promising solution and one involving less space uses lime or alum to settle out phosphorus. Filtration through a bed of activated carbon will remove additional organic substances which would otherwise affect the odor of water. Unfortunately, nitrates, unlike phosphates, are soluble in water and are more difficult to remove. However, methods using electrodialysis have been effective in removing nitrates in small scale operations and offer good prospects for the future.

Before long the water leaving some sewage treatment plants will be returned to the city and people probably won't notice the difference over untreated water. In fact, recycled water may be an improvement over what we have become accustomed to. The major limiting factor in recycling water for sewage treatment plants is cost. Conservative estimates reveal that primary treatment costs about 4¢/1000 gallons, secondary treatment about 10¢, tertiary treatment to remove nutrients about 20¢. Thus, drinkable water can be produced from sewage for about 40¢ per 1000 gallons. It should be noted that drinking water from tertiary treatment is presently less expensive than desalinated water (Odum, 1971:437).

There are several other possibilities for reducing pollution from sewage treatment plants. One receiving considerable attention at present is the use of the effluent to irrigate land. Nutrients which may be damaging to aquatic systems are filtered out by the soil-vegetation layer of the land. Growth of crops, pasture and young forest plantations are enhanced by this spray irrigation of waste nutrients (Sopper, 1968:471-480; Bouwer, 1968:164-168).

A rather novel idea currently in the experimental stage which enables a better utilization of water is a recycling system for the home. Wagner (1971:99) suggests a model which works something like this. Presently, water piped into our homes is grade A drinking

219

quality no matter what use we plan to make of it. It makes little sense to throw away 3 gallons of grade A water just to dispose of a small volume of waste in a toilet or 30 gallons to get rid of a little detergent with its dirt and lint from clothes. Why not establish a priority system for water, reserving grade A for drinking, cooking, washing and bathing. Grade B, reprocessed from grade A uses would be adequate for outdoor uses such as car washing, or lawn watering. Perhaps a grade C could be used for flushing toilets. Grade A water would be supplied as is presently done. After grade A uses the water would be filtered and stored in a basement tank for grade B and C uses. Experimental setups of a simple recycling device as described above reduced domestic water consumption by almost 50 percent. The capital cost could be offset by reduced water and sewer bills over the years.

The above examples provide some ideas of how technology can be used to reduce pollution and at the same time provide additional water through recycling. Now let's consider a means for reducing the amount of water required by the adjustment of personal habits rather than via technology.

We have already noted that it takes about 25 times more water to put a pound of meat on the table than a pound of vegetables. This is because the further up the food chain we select our diet, the more water it takes to produce it. The same fact applies not only to vegetables and beef but also to differentials in the water cost of wool as compared to cotton, or of butter as compared to margarine. It can be seen that a tremendous water savings would occur were we to adopt a more herbivorous diet. Moreover, from a pollution viewpoint the processing of our meat-centered diets is a tremendous contributor of BOD to our lakes and streams.

Reducing water consumption is only one benefit that would be realized from a general shift toward a more herbivorous diet. In general, plants transform about one percent of the available solar energy into chemical (food) energy through photosynthesis. For every step in the food chain thereafter the available energy is reduced by a factor of 10. For example, consider a linear food chain of pasture—->beef—->man. Assume the forage crop produced 15 kilocalories per square meter per day (this is the amount of energy or heat that is stored in the crop). After utilization by the cow there would be only about 1.5 Kcal/m^2/day available to man. If man were to derive his energy directly from the forage crop rather than the beef, there would be 10 times more energy available to him.

In our present diets we need some meat to provide proper proportions of some amino acids, but with the advent of protein supplements which can curb these deficiencies, *meat becomes a costly luxury* not only as food but also in respect to water supply and pollution.

If and when the need arises there are even additional sources of water that can be tapped. Approximately two-thirds of all the fresh-water (nonsaline) in the world is locked up in ice. A novel proposal has been made to tow icebergs from Greenland or Antarctica to thirsty cities. Consider the potential of supplying some of the arid Australian cities with fresh water from Antarctic ice. Small icebergs may be two miles on a side and be 800 feet thick. It has been calculated that a good sized tug making one knot could tow an iceberg the necessary distance in six or seven months for about 1½ million dollars. Assuming that about half the ice melted during the trip there would still be one billion m^3 of fresh water or enough for four million people for a year at an average cost per family of about a dollar and a half (Murdoch, 1971:135-155).

Such operations are novel but natural. Icebergs float around anyway while they're melting. Why not have them melt where we want them to melt? Neither climate nor ecology would be noticeably affected.

"Importing" water is another means of getting water where it's wanted. But attempts to transfer water from one basin to another may be costly and if operated on an extremely large scale could affect climate. The main problem is cooperation between authorities or owners within the losing basin.

From the snowy mountains south of Canberra, Australia, a river runs south directly into the ocean. A system of gigantic tunnels diverts this water to the north side of the mountains to help irrigate fertile valleys. On its way the water drives underground turbines to provide electricity. In California a similar project operates where waters from the north are diverted to the fertile valleys and dense population of the south. Other similar plans in the offing are proposals to divert water from the Columbia river to the south and to divert huge amounts of water from northern Canada and Alaska to the U.S. and Mexico. Russia has suggested the

221

possibility of diverting two northern rivers which run into the Arctic into the Volga which runs south into the Caspian Sea. All these proposals would provide water for food production and for use by municipalities.

Some of these prospects are close to fantasy. However, let's not predict the future from just what we have today but on the basis of what we have today compared to thirty, twenty, or even ten years ago. Trends are usually more striking than predictions from a specific point in time.

In summary, this statement by van Hylckama (Murdoch, 1971:154) is appropriate:

> We might conclude that there are water problems, but they are not those of quantity and not even necessarily of quality. It is the attitude of people and their concern for each other which becomes the problem. Man will have to learn to live with man, not on a competitive but on a cooperative basis, and this is probably the biggest problem for man and his environment.

Pesticides: Their Relation to Man and His Environment

A large part of human activity, particularly in relation to the environment, is in response to conditions or events. The evolution of technology—invention of clothing, housing, agriculture, energy and medicine, for example—illustrates man's response to circumstances in his environment.

Man is faced with direct competition from his arthropod enemies for food. This is not the result of *new* species of insects coming into existence. These species have probably existed for hundreds or thousands of years. Many of them have not always been regarded as pests, however, because in their natural environments population interactions were such to keep a species under control. The fact that many arthropods are now classified as pests is in part due to man's activities.

In order to meet the needs of his expanding population and advancing civilization man has changed or manipulated the environment and in doing so he has created conditions that permit certain species to increase their population densities. A few examples will illustrate this principle. When the potato was brought under wide cultivation in the United States, a change favorable to the Colorado potato beetle occurred in the environment. Population density of the beetle rapidly increased to pest status in response to the more adequate food supply.

A second way man has assisted arthropods to become pests has been the result of transporting them across geographical or ecological barriers and leaving their specific predators, parasites, and diseases behind. This is illustrated by the cottony cushion scale, introduced into California from Australia in 1868. The scale insect found a new home, a plentiful food supply in the citrus trees, and no predators. In two decades it increased in abundance to the point of threatening the entire citrus industry in California. This pest was completely suppressed by introducing into California two of its natural enemies, one a ladybird beetle and the other a fly (Doutt, 1958:119-123).

A third factor for increasing the number of arthropod pests has been the establishment of progressively lower (more stringent) economic thresholds. For example, not many years ago, lygus bugs were considered only a minor pest because of the occasional blotches they caused on one of their main food sources, the lima bean. With the frozen food industry came an increased emphasis on product appearance and a demand for a near perfect lima bean. That meant that the presence of occasional blotches on lima beans was a condition which exceeded the established economic-injury threshold and made the beans unacceptable for market. Consequently lygus bugs are now considered a serious pest, not because their damage is any more prevalent, but because of a change in the definition of what is an "acceptable" bean.

Faced with an increasing number of pests, man has responded and has made remarkable advances in their control. A major contributor to this feat has been the new developments in pesticide chemistry and application.

The insecticidal properties of DDT were discovered in 1939. It, along with the herbicide, 2,4-D, was made available to the public about 1945. The success of DDT in halting a typhus epidemic in Italy in 1943-44 was an unprecedented achievement which heralded in a new era in the use of pesticides. From that start a host of new materials has been produced, a new industry has come into being, and agricultural and public health practices have been changed drastically.

Pesticides contribute significantly to increasing production of food, feed, and fiber and to their protection and also to the prevention and spread of disease. Additional positive factors, present but immeasurable, derive from the personal satisfaction one receives from having or viewing a beautiful field, yard, or lawn.

Benefits derived from the use of pesticides are too numerous to attempt extensive classification here. But a few examples may be offered. The United States Department of Agriculture has estimated that a complete stop in the use of pesticides could result in a 25-30 percent drop in crop and livestock production in the U.S. (Bloom and Degler, 1969). In natural grass areas of Argentina one hectare will support a cow. It has been estimated that 8 grasshoppers/square meter will consume as much grass as one animal/HA (U.S. Department of Health, Education and Welfare, 1969). More than sixty countries in Asia and Africa are liable to invasion by locust swarms. Medium sized swarms may have three billion locusts which consume 3,000 tons of food/day. In the four years prior to 1944 over 15 percent of American apple crops were lost each year to the ravages of the codling moth. In the four subsequent years use of DDT reduced the loss to only 4 percent (Murdoch, 1971:302-325). It is suggested that one-fifth of the world's malaria has been eliminated by the use of pesticides. Moreover, these drastic reductions have occurred at the same time that the population has been expanding; India had 100 million malaria cases in 1933-35 and only 150,000 in 1966 (U.S. Department of Health, Education and Welfare, 1969).

In spite of the incalculable benefits to mankind attributed to the use of pesticides the consensus is that education and research on the impact of pesticides on the total ecosystem have not kept pace with their expanded production and utilization. As a result there has developed a genuine public concern, even fear on the part of some, over the usage of these new chemicals. Through their widespread and sometimes indiscriminate use, the components and intricate relations of crop environments have been altered, and a number of serious environmental problems have resulted. Three general problem areas are discussed below: the non-selectivity of most pesticides, the development of resistance to pesticides, and the "human element" in pesticide use and control.

Nonselectivity of Most Pesticides

The cause of many pest control failures and also environmental damage is that most pesticides affect nontarget organisms. Pesticides are dispersed by air, water, and the movements of organisms. Even though the most significant concentrations are found in the areas of use, trace amounts have been found even in the polar regions. A study of the amount of DDT reaching a cornfield after aerial application showed that a maximum of 38 percent actually ended up on the corn plants or in the soil.

To place the problem in perspective let us refer back to the case of the scale insect on the citrus trees in California. The natural predators succeeded in keeping the insect under control until the mid 1940's, when the newly discovered DDT was applied to the citrus groves. The nontarget ladybird beetle proved to be highly susceptible and died off. As the number of ladybird beetles decreased, the scale insect increased in number and again became a major pest. Cessation of DDT use and time (three years) restored a satisfactory balance to the predator-prey populations.

Once applied, pesticides may become concentrated and remain in the bodies of organisms. The concentrating effect is often enhanced as one species feeds upon another and passes the pesticide from one link in the food chain to another. This effect is also enhanced by the fact that many pesticides (especially the organochlorines) are relatively long-lived. Examples of nontarget species which have been affected include:

1. Phytoplankton: Laboratory experiments show a reduction in photosynthesis at concentrations greatly exceeding those presently measured in the oceans (however, local conditions of high pollution exist in some bays and estuaries).

2. Lake trout and salmon: inhibited reproduction as the young fry are killed at the time of final absorption of the yolk sac.

3. Birds: reproduction of some raptorial hawks and eagles is inhibited because of a decrease in egg shell thickness traced to pesticides; robin populations were drastically reduced in areas applying pesticides to control the Dutch Elm disease. Their death was due to convulsions, either by receiving the DDT directly or indirectly through eating worms and insects which had concentrated it from the soil and plants.

4. Mammals: a few wild mammals have been sampled and the data are scarce but it appears that damage has not been as frequent or serious as in birds and fish.

5. Humans:

225

On the basis of present knowledge the only unequivocal consequences of long term exposure to persistent pesticides [DDT and related compounds] at the levels encountered by the general public is the acquisition of residues in tissues and body fluids. . . . There is not evidence to indicate that pesticides presently in use actually cause carcinogenic or teratogenic [cancer or malformation-causing] effects in man. Nevertheless, the fact that some pesticides cause these effects in experimental mammals indicates cause for concern and careful evaluation (U.S. Department of Health, Education and Welfare, 1969:35-36).

A reduction in nontarget species tends to decrease the diversity of an ecosystem and decreased diversity reduces the stability of the system. Documented examples where decreased diversity has taken place show a greater probability of insect population outbreaks and an increase in the number of small organisms which feed directly on plants (Pimental, 1961:78-86).

Resistance to Pesticides

Resistance is a character developed by selection within a population of a species normally susceptible to a particular pesticide. It is an inheritable characteristic developing only in populations that already have the factors for resistance in their genetic makeup. Resistance is *not* induced by exposure to the pesticide. A population becomes resistant because a few individuals possess a genetic structure which allows them to survive a pesticide exposure, while those which are susceptible die. Since the survivors are mostly the resistant type, the next generation will be mostly resistant. The rate of this selection process depends upon the generation time, the type of pest, and how often the pesticide is applied. Resistance in some cases has been attributed to a mechanism in the individual which detoxifies the pesticide.

At least 224 species of insects and acarides (spiders) throughout the world have developed resistance to one or more groups of pesticides. Of these 127 are agricultural pests and 97 are pests of medical and veterinary importance (U.S. Department of Health, Education and Welfare, 1969).

The most widespread resistance has been shown by pests which breed rapidly and have been subjected to the most intense pesticide pressure, e.g., houseflies, cockroaches, bedbugs, flies of cattle, and twenty-one species of the mosquito genus *Anopheles*!

The list also includes cotton pests and the brown rat (Murdoch, 1971:302-325).

An additional aspect of this problem is that cross-resistance to pesticides is common. For example, if an organism is resistant to DDT it may also have resistance to related organochlorine pesticides. In view of our dependence upon the effectiveness of pesticides these factors of nonspecificity, persistence, food chain magnification, and resistance add up to many serious problems.

The Human Element in Pesticide Use

There are examples in the recent past where whole regions of our country were sprayed unnecessarily and indiscriminately. The extermination projects on the fire ant in the southeastern U.S. and the Japanese beetle in the northeastern U.S. are good examples. Although the fire ant does not destroy livestock, wildlife, or crops to any important extent, the pesticides which were sprayed at a rate of 2 pounds/acre, over 2.5 million acres, did affect the ecosystem. After a $15 million outlay the South still had the fire ants and an abundance of residual pesticides. A new chemical applied in bait near ant hills now yields the type of control that should have been used from the beginning.

It is easy to look across the state or nation and condemn the actions of our fellow human beings and turn right around at a later time and support in our own "backyard" what we had previously condemned. Such has been the case with pesticide application. For example, in the late 1950's when the Northeast was having its bout with the gypsy moth the city people were all up in arms about the use of pesticides in the woods for control. Now many of these same people take vacations or live in the rural areas affected and are appalled by the denuded hills and the droppings of insects on the picnic tables. They often fail to realize that it was their action which prevented the control of the moth.

It is difficult to be informed sufficiently on all topics and to be able to discriminate between fact and fantasy. When people get caught up in a cause there arises a need for "facts" to bolster whatever aspect of the cause is espoused. In issues such as the effects of pesticides on the environment, there is considerable emotion and competition involved and various factions are anxious to "beat each other to the punch" with their supporting

227

data. Under such circumstances of expediency we should be on the lookout for inaccurate reporting, claims, and suppositions.

Consider the horror story circulating about DDT polluting the oceans and thereby destroying the oxygen supply. This inaccurate account is usually based on extrapolations made from legitimate research data which show that concentrations of 10 ppm of DDT seriously hindered photosynthesis in four species of phytoplankton. Since phytoplankton produce considerable amounts of oxygen someone (not the original researcher) extrapolated from these results and concluded that DDT was destroying the phytoplankton and that our oxygen supply was in jeopardy. On the surface this sounds reasonable, and many people boarded the bandwagon to ban DDT for no other reason.

As it turns out, every plant consumes as much oxygen during its decay or during its being metabolized by an animal as it produces during its growth. Our oxygen supply has been built up over geologic time by plants that have died and were buried before they were oxidized. Moreover, most of this buried carbon is not in fossil fuel deposits but is found in shale and other rocks which have little chance of ever being burned. Our oxygen supply is in a rather stable and abundant supply irrespective of DDT. A final erroneous conclusion to the argument was that the DDT content in the oceans was reaching a critically high level. It is reported however to be closer to 1 pptrillion than 1 ppmillion. In the research referred to, concentrations of 1ppm had no measurable effect on photosynthesis. An alarm was sounded on both inaccurate ecosystem dynamics and inaccurate suppositions (Strobble, 1971).

Pests, Pesticides, and the Future

The production and use of pesticides continues to grow throughout the world. There are now in the U.S. some 900 active pesticidal chemicals formulated into over 60,000 preparations, including insecticides, fungicides, herbicides, and plant growth regulators. The World Health Organization indicates that control of many of the most important vectors of human disease is still entirely dependent on insecticides and that most food production programs are similarly dependent.

Among the current endeavors which foreshadow future changes

228

are the development of new and better pesticides, improvements in the methods of application, and the substitution of biological control for chemical control. We will consider each of these briefly.

Development of New Pesticides

To meet the residual problems of organochlorides a wide range of organophosphates and carbamate insecticides have been developed. Malathion and carbaryl are presently more useful where it is essential that crops or livestock not be treated with persistent materials. New soil insecticides have replaced alrin and dieldrin. It is reported by well-informed scientists that there are no insect vectors of disease, normally susceptible to DDT, that cannot be controlled with a substitute (U.S. Department of Health, Education and Welfare, 1969).

New "short lived" pesticides, however, are not without their problems. Parathion is an extremely poisonous chemical that can be absorbed through the skin. Most organophosphate pesticides break down quite rapidly but they affect various enzyme systems (cholinesterase inhibitors) in man and domestic animals in very low concentrations. The persistent properties of DDT are essential to malaria eradication. It is impractical and extremely expensive to maintain an insecticidal residue in the large, often inaccessible areas concerned. With DDT, one or two treatments per year is sufficient.

Improvement in Methods of Application

Direct incorporation of pesticides into soil has resulted in a reduction of such hazards as spray drift and residue on standing foliage. By direct furrow application, a smaller amount of pesticide can be used and still provide effective control. A greater understanding of the relation of pests to their environment enables improved forecasting of outbreaks of infestations and has resulted in a reduction of pesticide applications necessary for adequate control.

Biological Control

This category encompasses both the manipulation of the pest

229

and its environment. A pest in a cultivated field was probably not of pest status in its natural environment. By restoring diversity to our monoculture methods by crop rotation, establishment of hedgerows, etc., we can approach a natural ecosystem where more natural population controls exist. Another cultural practice that has been effective is the development of insect and/or disease-resistant plant varieties. Perhaps the most successful cases of biological control to date have involved the use of parasitic or predaceous insects. There are at least 18 successful examples in the United States where noxious insects have been controlled by other insects. The control of the scale insect in California citrus groves is an excellent example.

Other methods of biological control which have proven successful and hold promise for the future are the sterile mating technique, genetic control, and the use of substances produced by the pest species.

The screw worm fly, a serious pest of cattle in the southeastern U.S., was brought under control in about one year by the sterile mating technique. Large numbers of male flies were reared in the laboratory, sterilized by irradiation and released in the field. Each ensuing generation was smaller because many matings produced no offspring (Baumhover, et al., 1955:462-466). Genetic control involves the introduction of lethal genes into pest species. By introducing sufficient numbers of individuals with these mutants into natural populations, it is theoretically possible to bring about eradication.

As for substances produced as part of the chemistry of pests themselves, pheromones, or sex lures, have the potential to attract great numbers of insects to a small area where they can be destroyed. Hormones which control the molting of insects can be used to prevent or induce major changes in the life cycle which prove fatal. Early results have been promising but many questions have to be answered before hormones and pheromones can assume a major role in pest control.

Prospectus for the Future

The above discussion clearly indicates that we are very dependent on chemicals for the eradication and control of pests. They are not only effective in pest control but also in the creation of new pest and environmental problems. It should be obvious that

230

since pests are only one factor of many in any ecosystem, their control is not a chemical problem but a biological problem. It should follow that an integrated approach to pest control will be more beneficial than most current practices.

Our major efforts should be oriented toward solving two major problems of current pesticides, nonselectivity and noncontrollability. Integrated control involves not just alternatives to chemicals but moderate use of all controls. A rational, balanced approach which considers ecological factors includes the following elements: (1) Before control is attempted it must be determined that the supposed pest is actually causing the damage attributed to it. (2) A survey should then be made of the natural control agents which work to limit the pest population. (3) If the pest has been introduced and has no "enemies" in the new locale locate such from its place of origin and screen them carefully to avoid adding two or more pests instead of one. (4) Every effort must be made to preserve and increase the number of natural control organisms. We must not panic at the first appearance of a pest, but rather give natural controls some time to work. (5) If chemicals prove necessary, we should use the smallest amounts that will bring effective control rather than seeking eradication, and we should apply them only when necessary with the most specific and least resistant chemical available (Wagner, 1971:244-245).

The following quotations from reputable sources provide, in my opinion, an optimistically oriented summary of the current status and projected outlook for our environmental "crisis." Most of these statements are related to pesticides, but each conveys an attitude applicable to a wide range of problems.

Pollution of the environment from agricultural sources is of serious current concern in the highly developed countries. Particular attention is focused on insecticides and other toxicants as well as on animal wastes. Closer controls are needed. To accomplish these controls is a test of a society's capacity to avoid despoiling the environment. More attention must be given to methods of biological control of pests, and to the problems of making pesticides biodegradable, more pest-specific, and less toxic to man. Pesticides are one of the most effective innovations of our time. Without pesticides, the future of food production in the tropics would be most unpromising. To use them correctly in controlling a pest without undue contamination of the environment is not an insuperable problem but demands constant vigilance (NAS and NRC, 1969:80-81).

231

Included in our view of health is the feeling of well-being and capacity for happiness that derives from a suitable environment: suitable in the sense that it makes possible the enjoyment of nature and her bountiful provision of flora and fauna. From this standpoint therefore any factor or activity that detracts from the variety of the environment, that reduces its capacity to contribute to health, is fundamentally undesirable. This broad generalization must, however, be tempered by the practical realities and priorities of human existence on the earth.

The need to provide food and other crops and to prevent or eradicate insect-borne disease constitute problems which many countries must necessarily regard as outweighing in importance the potential or even actual hazards to health involved in the use of pesticides. Hence we must recognize that protection of human health involves a system of priorities, which are necessarily different from place to place (U.S. Department of Health, Education and Welfare, 1969:243-244).

I do not agree with the defeatist attitude that to protect our agricultural crops we must inevitably sacrifice wildlife values. If we take a positive rather than a negative approach and develop procedures and techniques through appropriate research, I believe we can have both good crops, clean water, and wildlife. Surely we can find selective and specific pesticides which we can use to control pests without significant detrimental effects to other public values or to other members of the biota which are of high economic, social, or recreational importance. It has been done before. The possibilities are there and the promised rewards are worthy of our best efforts (Maxwell, 1970:280).

The dizzying changes induced into the earth's ecosystem in the last two or three decades constitute an experiment out of hand, whose consequences now seem ecologically catastrophic. Restoring control requires perspective and judgment. Sufficient facts are available. The scientist must not only seek facts; he must judge facts in entire systems, including those within the human community. Ecologists are obligated to serve this human expectation. Through them the primary goal—the reestablishment of a WORKING CONTROL SYSTEM—can be achieved (Murdoch, 1971:300).

We are becoming more conscious of the fact that proper management of the earth involves paying attention to more than present convenience and the maximizing of returns. Rational ecologists and conservationists are endeavoring to establish in our value system that in the ecosystem of which man is a part *he* is the best able to adapt and perhaps less sensitive to the environment than other physical and biological components of the system. By disrupting the very system which sustains him, he endangers his own vitality as well as that of the entire ecosystem. The underlying basis of environmental problems is not pollution, technology, or population, but the value systems of men. The question is not one of capability but rather whether men will use their abilities to achieve success.

References

Baumhover, A. H., B. A. Bitter, D. E. Hopkins, W. D. New, F. H. Dudley, R. C. Bushland
    1955   "Screw worm control through release of sterilized flies." Journal of Economic Entomology 48 (August):462-466.

Bloom, Sandra C., and Stanley E. Degler
    1969   Pesticides and Pollution. Washington, D.C.: U.S. Government Printing Office.

Bouwer, Herman
    1968   "Returning wastes to the land, a new role for agriculture." Soil and Water Conservation 23 (September-October):164-168.

Bradley, Charles C.
    1962   "Human water needs and water use in America." Science 138 (October 26):489-491.

Bryson, Reid A.
    1968   "A reconciliation of several theories of climate change." Weatherwise 21 (April):56-61.

Cornell University Conference
    1969   "Livestock production vs. environmental quality—an impasse?" by Joseph P. Binick in Animal Waste Management: Cornell University Conference on Agricultural Waste Management (January 13-15):367.

Doutt, Richard L.
    1958   "Vice, virtue and the vedalia." Entomological So-

ciety of America Bulletin 4 (December):119-123.

Ehrlich, Paul R., and Anne H. Ehrlich
1970 Population, Resources, Environment: Issues in Human Ecology. San Francisco: W. H. Freeman and Co.

Maximov, N. A.
1929 The Plant in Relation to Water. New York: The Macmillan Co.

Maxwell, Kenneth E. (ed.)
1970 "A conservationist's views on the new pesticides." by Clarence Cottam in Chemicals and Life. Belmont, California: Dickenson Publishing Co., Inc.

Mitchell, J. Murray
1961 "Recent secular changes in global temperature." Annals of the New York Academy of Science 95 (October 5):248.

Murdoch, William W. (ed.)
1971 "Better methods of pest control," by Gordon R. Conway in Environment. Stamford, Connecticut: Sinauer Association, Inc.

1971 "Environment and administration," by Lynton K. Caldwell in Environment. Stamford, Connecticut: Sinauer Association, Inc.

1971 Environment and the equilibrium population, in Environment. Stamford, Connecticut: Sinauer Association, Inc.

1971 "Pesticides," by Robert L. Rudd in Environment. Stamford, Connecticut: Sinauer Association, Inc.

234

1971   "Water resources," by Tinco E. A. van Hylckama in Equilibrium. Stamford, Connecticut: Sinauer Association, Inc.

NAS and NRC (National Academy of Sciences and National Research Council)
   1969   Resources and Man. San Francisco: W. H. Freeman and Co.

Odum, Eugene P.
   1971   Fundamentals of Ecology. Philadelphia: W. B. Saunders Co.

Pimental, David
   1961   "Species diversity and insect population outbreaks." Annals of the Entomological Society of America 54 (January):78-86.

Strobbe, Maurice A. (ed.)
   1971   "An ecologist views the environment," by D. R. Spencer in Understanding Environmental Pollution. St. Louis: C. V. Mosby.

U.S. Department of Health, Education, and Welfare
   1969   Report of the Secretary's Commission on Pesticides and their Relationship to Environmental Health. Washington, D.C.: U.S. Government Printing Office (December).

USDI and FWPCA (U.S. Department of Interior and Federal Water Pollution Control Administration)
   1969   A Primer on Waste Water Treatment. Washington, D.C.: U.S. Government Printing Office (October).

Wagner, Richard H.
   1971   Environment and Man. New York: W. W. Norton and Co.

Water Research
   1968   "Waste water renovation for reuse," by William E. Sopper in Water Research, vol. 2. New York: Pergamon Press.

Woll, F. W.
   1921   Productive Feeding of Farm Animals. New York: Lippincott.

VI.
THE "CRISIS"
IN
FUTURE PERSPECTIVE

Introduction

Few times in this world's history has man been more preoc-
cupied about future states than he is now. In a variety of disciplines, national and international organizations have arisen
whose primary purpose is to understand and outline the probable
conditions projected to exist. In contemporary discourse about
population and resources no theme is more ubiquitous than the
shape of the future. Indeed, only when the future dimension is
included may population size and resource depletion be considered worldwide problems. Not surprisingly, the probabilities
usually are quite low that estimates about the state of the future
will be correct. To make predictions about the future one must
not only possess the relevant information about present social
conditions, and current rates of change, but he must also make
assumptions about potential quantities of resources and about the
basic nature of man. Anyone willing to enter such an arena should
be simultaneously congratulated for his courage and warned about
his ignorance. To amass knowledge about man and his social and
physical world sufficient to be able to forecast the future is post-
industrial man's premier challenge, for it is only the post-industrial
man who has come to realize that he is the great determiner of his
own future. In an existential sense man is not only destined to be
free but is also destined to determine, either through action or
inaction, the nature of tomorrow.

239

Edwards' intriguing article on "Population Goals and Controls"
demonstrates the critical nature of the limiting assumptions which
of necessity must be built into any model predicting future states.
He correctly notes that population control proposals have notori-
ously avoided the question of what goals *man should have. He*
presents a modest population control goal, "to bring to earth,
under conditions allowing a happy and satisfying life, the greatest
possible total number of people," and then constructs mathe-
matical models designed to maximize that goal. In Edwards'
model, the most important variable in the realization of that goal
is not rate of population growth but rather rate of increase in per
capita energy consumption.

Edwards does not play mathematical games with no attempt to
touch base with reality. He questions whether any proposed
solution to the "population problem" will be successful. He then
accepts his own challenge and attempts to look realistically at
contemporary world conditions, adjusting his model to take into
account differences between rich countries and poor countries. His
prognosis for success is indeed dismal; he concludes that it seems a
questionable objective for "rich nations to seek to govern popula-
tion size in order that they might continue their over-consuming
ways." Certainly rich nations cannot expect poor nations to
reduce their efforts to catch up in the resource consumption race.
He asks, "Are the rich nations sufficiently enlightened to let them
catch up, or even to help them to do so?"

One of the assumptions built into Edwards' model is that there
is a fixed quantity of resources available to man. He takes an
estimate of available resources from reliable sources and then cau-
tions that because experience has shown that resource estimates
are revised upward "almost exponentially," his working estimate
should be considered as a lower limit. What would mathematical
models designed to predict the future look like and what predic-
tions might derive from them if energy sources were seen as
approaching infinity rather than as a finite quantity? Or if one
assumes, in keeping with our contemporary Einsteinian world
view, that energy is never lost but merely changed, and that man
as part of geosocial reality is an infinite source of ideas for orga-
nizing energy transfers, then what kind of prediction about future
states might the models produce?

In his "Report on the 'Geosocial Revolution' " Buckminster

240

Fuller does not present models but does make the case for an optimistic view of the future, based on some assumptions he makes about the nature of man as well as the nature of his physical world. An example of how Fuller's perspectives on the future may affect the extent of resource utilization and the very nature of what may be considered a resource is his idea for turning the seas into habitable space. The proposal demonstrates the dynamic quality of resource assessment, or even the literal creation of resources via the interaction of human intellect and physical environment. Let us quote him at some length:

We have learned that the most stable structure is the tetrahedron. Following this design-science clue, we find that a tetrahedronal city, to house a million people, is both economically and technologically feasible. Such a vertical tetrahedronal city can be constructed so that all of its 300,000 families have balconied "outside" apartments. All of the organic operative machinery can be housed within the tetrahedron.

Programed for 1,000,000 occupants, a tetrahedronal floating city would measure two miles long for each of its base edges. Such a city is so structurally efficient and therefore so relatively light that, together with its hollow box-sectioned reinforced concrete foundations, it can float. The city could be anchored in triangularly patterned canals or floated out into the ocean at any point and anchored. It would be earthquake-proof and, because the depth of the tetrahedron's foundation would be below the turbulence level of the seas, it would be a floating triangular atoll with a harbor that is always calm and protected. The cities will generate their own energy requirements using atomic reactors. The by-product of heat from these reactors will be used to desalinate water supplies.

Tetrahedrons are unique geometrically, he explains, in that they may be added to on every one of their four equilateral triangle faces and increased symmetrically in size by additions to any one of the faces. Thus the cities can begin with a program for a thousand occupants and grow to hold millions without changing their shape.

Salvage of materials from obsolete buildings on the land can produce enough of these floating cities to have relays of them in various sizes around the oceans of the earth, at distances negotiable by relatively small boats such as those that operate between the Florida coast and the Bahamas. This will allow new habitation possibilities on that three-fourths of the earth's surface that is covered by water. It also will permit mid-ocean cargo transfer within the cities' calm harbors, extraordinarily increasing the efficiency of distribution of the world's raw and finished materials as well as aiding passenger traffic (Fuller, 1967:14-18).

Elsewhere Fuller has observed that "You and I are essential

functions of Universe. We are exquisite anti-entropy" (Fuller, 1966:70). If the wealth of World Man is, as Fuller maintains, man's "organized intellectual ability to protect and satisfy his forward regenerative needs," then any predictions about the future which do not take these "resources" into account will undeniably sell man far short of the future he has the potential to create. Does the optimistic view of the future through the "design and invention revolution" espoused by Fuller contain a more noble view of man than the dismal projections of many neo-Malthusians?

References

Fuller, Buckminster R.
    1967   "Man with a chronofile." Saturday Review (April 1):14-18.

Fuller, Buckminster R.
    1966   "How little I know." Saturday Review (November 12):70.

Report
on the
Geosocial Revolution*

R. Buckminster Fuller

A half-century of subconsciously developing world revolution is now crossing the threshold into human consciousness and ultimate popular support. Though dwarfing all history's revolutions in relative magnitude of its transformation, this twentieth-century revolution has been unapprehended for fifty years. So vast and historically unfamiliar are its ramifications that the narrow foci of contemporary specializations have failed to perceive and integrate its components. It is the one revolution which is politically welcome the world around. It is the Geosocial Revolution.

Human myths and self-deceptive rationalizations have, historically, prevented the social scientist from seeing the larger patterns of human behavior which were not consciously premeditated by man. While recognizing the individual's subconsciously controlled behavior, they do not extend this to subconscious coordination of man's ecological behavior. Yet these human-ecology-transforming forces are as real, as important to life, as are the Van Allen radiation-inhibiting belts surrounding earth. Both have been unknown to man in all but the last decades of human history.

This is a tentative inventory of those hitherto invisible techno-

---

economic world-social-force fields now looming into view. These invisible evolutionary systems, once discovered and studied, apparently disclose nature's scheme, not only for successfully sustaining human life but also for permitting man henceforth to participate consciously in his prosperous continuance on earth.

First, it should be stated that this greatest single revolution in human affairs has been the sum of a series of human inadvertencies. The inadvertent actions were executed separately and unbeknown to one another by approximately 100,000 of the world's industrial complexes—both private corporations and state undertakings. These, during the past fifty years, have been largely contracted to supply the world's powerful nations with the multitrillion-dollar flow of technological goods which constitutes the swiftly evolving weaponry systems of those nations. Priority of access to man's highest capability has thus far always gone to weaponry; the home front has always been the anti-priority area. From man's personal home and family life the reserves of effort and capability to meet crisis have always been commandeered to meet the commonly seeming enemy. The inadvertencies occurred as various separate contracts were terminated by the world nations' defense departments as a consequence of progressive obsoleting of weaponry components. These obsoleted weaponry systems' tool capabilities were then second-handed onto the "home front" by the contractors.

A typical focus of such "secondhand" manufacture for the home market has been the building industry. Because all that the ex-weaponry contractors ever attempted to produce were those domestic items most easily suited to profitable processing with their unique tools, it was in such areas that they were usually successful. Giant electric generators, steam boilers, electric lights, radios, oil burners, refrigerators, and air conditioners were originally developed and used only as battleship equipment. Such items were easily converted to domestic use—as were marginal products such as improved wall panels, partitions, stoves, window hardware, and aluminum shingles. But many of the potentially useful domestic capabilities were originally not so obvious.

The ex-weaponry prime contractors, as the cast-off "kept mistresses" of the sovereign nations, had never had to risk their own judgment on the selection of weaponry to be produced. That was the often "top-secret" prerogative of national defense authorities. The contractors, therefore, naïvely assumed that their new masters, e.g., the U.S. building industry, like the "defense" master, must have a grand, logically coordinate strategy. They didn't know that the building industry was so inefficient and uncoordinated that it went bankrupt in 1929; and that anarchic plunging in real estate since then has been subsidized by the several hundred billion dollars of U.S. Government mortgage-guarantee underwriting. The prime contractors also accepted the so-called building industries' product categories as having been scientifically conceived. But no Ph.D. scientist has been retained to consider a general-systems theory governing establishment of the potentially successful life of all men on earth—let alone look at a toilet. No architect or builder knows what buildings weigh; they have never heard of performance per pound.

Unlike the homebuilding industry, both the communications and the transportation industries have benefited by the general systems controls adapted to weaponry systems—simply because mails, telephones, telegraphs, wireless, railroads, ships, autos, and trucks were and are themselves vital parts of the operational weapons-delivery and support systems.

In further contrast to the ex-weaponry contractors' piecemeal ventures in home building is the most forward development in man's ecological capability—again, as yet little recognized for its "geosocial revolutionary" nature. This is the rocket capsule that will keep man living successfully in space for protracted periods, entirely remote from sewer and other service mains—the first "scientific dwelling" in history. The prototype of a little 300-pound black box which will reduce the metabolic regenerative system, as now operative on earth, from an ecologically accomplished chemical-energy exchange complex one mile in diameter to a four-foot-diameter rocket-capsule, energy-regenerating accessory, will cost about $7 billion. Once produced and successfully "operative," it may be mass-reproduced for $2 per pound—$600. With such an integrated chemical-energy regenerator taking care of all sanitary and energy-generating requirements of family living, men may deploy almost invisibly to remote beauty spots about the earth in air-delivered, geodesically enclosed dwelling machines, and survive with only helicopter and TV communication at luxuriously simplified high standards of living—operative at negligible land-anchorage cost similar to telephone-service charges.

Because of the dawning awareness which accompanies such an advance—that the weaponry phase and its quarter-century lag can now be eliminated—this second half of the tool-invention revolution may be described as the consciously undertaken continuance of the accelerated doing-more-with-less by world society. We now can see that man's comprehensive physical success can be accomplished only through design-science competence. We can also see that design science now emergent in university research activities and encouraged by the International Cooperation Year (1965) will first develop the comprehensive, computerized programing of these general living systems. World coordination of such developments will progressively displace the sovereign nation's political authorities who, until recently, have administered the regeneratively self-improving *more-with-less* system exclusively on behalf of their respective separate national defenses, on the assumption that there were not enough world resources to take care of even half of humanity, and, therefore, that war for survival was and would forever be a necessary characteristic of mankind.

This, the ultimate revolution—now to be resolved only by scientific inventing and engineering competence instead of by now outmoded political initiatives—will swiftly bring about a high standard of survival for all, and thereby eliminate the former political recourse only to weaponry, and to the now-untenable assumption that survival can be justified by elimination—on the battlefield, or in the slums' lower-velocity rot-rate—of the "unsupportable excess" of human population.

Responsibility for development of scientific-invention competence has been spontaneously assumed, in ever-increasing degree since 1961, by students in the professions—at first in architecture, engineering, and science, and now by university students of all kinds. The students see that the world's *prime, vital* problem bears repeating a million times. It is: how to triple—swiftly, safely, and satisfyingly—the overall performance realizations, per pound, kilowatt, and man-hour, of the world's comprehensive resources. To do so will render those resources—which at the present design level can support only 44 per cent of humanity—capable of supporting 100 per cent of humanity's increasing population at higher standards of living than any human minority or individual has ever known or dreamed of.

To thus concentrate on the mastery of the physical service of man will also have its inadvertent profit increment, for to master the physical—intellectually—will bring into human intercourse a level of integrity of exploration of the metaphysical capabilities of man and the metaphysical ramifications of universe also heretofore undreamed of by man. Science and engineering say this is eminently feasible.

The students comprehend, first, that any invention can be realized; second, that the majority of the world's people are faced with starvation, ignorance, and suffering; and third, that there is an ideological struggle of the world's major political systems which, in idealistically convinced self-righteousness, exploits to the limit men's lethal dilemmas by every manner of subversive and guerrilla warring. Each assumes that the poverty-stricken peoples' problems can be solved only by political organization. Each seeks to prove its respective political system to be superior to the others. Each hopes to gain the largest world support for its equally lopsided and mutually obsolete political biases. Each spends far more to frustrate the other side than it spends in developing any realistic plans to make the world work. Each distributes lethal weapons en masse.

Take the technological tools of industrialization away from the United States, Russia, France, China, England, West Germany, Japan, and Italy, and leave them all their respective ideologies and, within six months, two billion world humans would die of starvation. Contrawise, take away from those eight sovereign states all their political ideologies and political leaders, and leave them their industrial tools and human operators and habitual daily production and distribution systems, and no more will starve than are starving now. New gap-filling pro tem leaders would spring up everywhere, with emergency authority that would make things work as well and probably better.

Only as a consequence of such politically transcendental and industrially informed observation is it now apparent that the only difference between all of the unsuccessful yesterdays and the half-successful today is the presence of a worldwide industrial network and its regeneratively multiplying scientific and technical know-

247

how. Due, however, to the inordinately low level of mechanical efficiency of the world's production and distribution system as now designed and operative, not even half of humanity can now survive for half its potential life span. The problem is primarily one of performance-upgrading by scientific invention; of doing more with less; of extracting progressively higher performance per unit of invested energy.

This progressive "ephemeralization" of the industrial process may be viewed in the return of all the world's metallic scrap into reuse. Up to 1940, recirculation of this scrap, released by progressive obsolescence of earlier inventions, was utterly unrecognized by economists, businessmen, or politicians as constituting a fundamental factor in the doing-more-with-less process. It is virtually unknown even today that the world's total mined metals resources recirculate every twenty-two-and-one-half years. Employing this "recirculation yardstick," we may safely predict that from July 1967 to 1976, the world's recirculating, scrap-derived metals resources, coming uninvited onto the world's metal markets, will be more than doubled again. This massive metals supply will make easy the design-science conversion of the world's resources from the service of only 44 per cent of humanity to service of 100 per cent of the world's population.

We may swiftly review several other major economic world trends which are as surprising as they are vast—and which also are heading full speed to integrate with and compound the "big economic surprise" that overnight will render man on earth a total physical success.

Of top importance among these trends is that of big business's moving operations permanently out of its home country—out of the United States, out of any one sovereign nation. So powerful is this trend that *in 1964, $4 out of every $5 that the 100 largest U.S. corporations put into new capital equipment investments went into their foreign operations.* Quite clearly, as IBM's international operations chairman, Arthur Watson, says, "The trend is already a reality, and big business is no longer 'national' in character but is identifiable only as a 'world' phenomenon."

The effect of this on labor will become more important as there are progressive increases in foreign wage rates and time-payment financing to accelerate world-buying. Organized labor's inadvertent contribution to world industrialization success was that its widely distributed, stepped-up wage rates made possible mass purchasing—which made mass production an economic success. It will now have to consolidate its gains by welcoming automation to further advance the general energy-wealth capability. Organized labor in this country will have to persuade Congress to underwrite 50,000,000 university scholarships, with life benefits of every type, to persuade its rank and file to fully mandate automation. In turn, in order to make universities capable of accommodating such an avalanche, a revolution in use of television in education will have to take place. All this, and more, is possible because the true wealth of World Man is mathematically inventoriable as his physically organized intellectual ability to protect and satisfy his forward regenerative needs.

It is an inherent characteristic of Man's intellect-organized energy-wealth that the larger the numbers served, the more swiftly the apparatus is amortized and becomes replaceable. The larger the energy-wealth system, the more efficiently does it operate. Conversely, as energy systems grow larger they lose energy more slowly. The combined energy and intellect-wealth may be distributed from natural energy sources which are remote from where energy is needed. We know, for example, that electrical energy delivered today by wire (and tomorrow, possibly, by radio or light or laser beams) is by far the most efficient, profuse, and speedy wealth-distributing system. And within such an increase in energy-transmission capacities there is a further large-scale economic-trend "surprise." Costs go down and profits go up rapidly with transmission network integrations.

Technological improvements now permit transmission-voltage step-ups of importantly improved magnitude—to 380,000, to 500,000, and to 1,000,000 volts. This new era of transmission is spoken of in the electrical industry as UHV—ultrahigh voltage. Contracted UHV installations are now underway throughout the United States which, within a decade, will for the first time completely interconnect the nation's electrical generation and transmission systems, bringing such important cost reductions and profit increases that both the public and private ownership sectors will be vastly advantaged.

Such UHV long-distance energy transmissions as from generators in Newfoundland to New York City will mean elimination of smog, not only from New York City but from the majority of all cities. Step-ups to 1,000,000 volts also will make economically feasible the intercontinental linkage not only of Europe, Asia, and Africa, but also of the American continents, and, in the not-too-distant future, of North America with Kamachatka (linked over or under the Bering Straits), and thence with both the Russian and Chinese networks. This will occur in time to greatly accelerate step-ups in the Eastern Siberian and, above all, the swift Oriental energy-intellect-wealth distribution. The energy-intellect-wealth advantage accruing to these last interlinkages will be the optimum because they will link low nighttime loads of one hemisphere with the high daytime loads of the other.

Such energy-wealth advantages will be so vast as to tend swiftly to cancel out ideological differences. "If that's Socialism—I'm a Socialist," and, "If that's Capitalism, it's ideal for the common-wealth augmentation of the masses," will be heard where dogmas to the contrary once prevailed.

Revolution by design and invention is the only revolution tolerable to all men, all societies, and all political systems anywhere. Every nation welcomed and employed the transistor. All will welcome technical-economic desalinization. All the world, properly informed of the significance of the design and invention revolution, will applaud it.

250

Projecting Future Trends

W. Farrell Edwards

In the controversy over population, pollution, and diminishing resources, models are constructed in order to predict the future state of the earth. Assuming that present trends will continue, they predict calamitous conditions within a few decades. Awakened to a sense of urgency, millions of people are asking how controls can be placed so as to change the predictions.

Undeniably, research and technology related to science, engineering, agriculture, and medicine, in their awesome and successful effort to improve the lot of humankind, have brought us to our present dilemma, and few wish to fully return to a preindustrial society with its high mortality rates, debilitating illnesses, and low standards of living. How then, can the predictions be changed? Some of the typical answers will be questioned here.

The debate suffers from a lack of clear population goals without which we are unable to use effectively the models to identify those variables that matter. A goal is suggested: optimize the number of people having inhabited the planet before it becomes unsuitable for life. As we shall see, under no conditions can the habitable period for the earth be extended indefinitely, and time is otherwise a questionable variable to maximize.

Through a very simple mathematical model relating population and energy resources, we will find that the rate of increase of per

251

capita energy consumption is presently a more critical variable than population growth as far as energy resource depletion is concerned. Also, the efficacy of trying to reduce resource depletion time either through population or resource management is questioned. Because of the differences between the rich and the poor nations, we will find that very little global advantage should be expected through such a management effort.

The Ultimate Future of the Earth

Writers in the population controversy seem to assume that the useful lifetime of the earth, the survival time, can be extended indefinitely through wise management of resources and population. The assumption, however, is wrong. Under no circumstances will the earth exist indefinitely as a habitation for man.

Astronomical data indicate that our sun will remain in somewhat the same state for approximately five billion more years, after which its internal heating processes will change, instabilities will arise, and it will expand, becoming a red giant star. During the expansion the surface will cool, but the size will increase. Mercury, Venus, and perhaps even the earth will be engulfed. Even if the sun's surface does not reach the orbit of the earth, it will be so near that the temperature of the earth's surface will increase to several thousand degrees, and life as we know it will cease.

Other uncontrollable calamitous conditions such as a collision with another celestial body, profound surface changes, atmospheric perturbations, or large temperature shifts may arise earlier, but the five billion year figure forms the upper limit.

As children, it was extremely difficult for any of us to become concerned about our own deaths. The issue was academic. Seventy years seemed to spread before us as an unlimited eternity. Five billion years for the earth may appear that way to us right now, so we talk as if there need be no end to the habitable period of the earth. Those developing a population policy should avoid any such implicit assumption of unlimited time, and should carefully question any conclusion based upon such an assumption.

Goals: What Should We Optimize

Related to this is a second implicit assumption that is even more common. It is that the basic population goal is to increase the survival time—the length of time for humankind to live under favorable conditions. The justification apparently is that by extending this time more people are allowed to come to earth under favorable conditions. But this generalization is correct only under special conditions. As will be shown later, lengthening the survival time by reducing the population growth rate may actually result in fewer people having inhabited the planet.

Because of the uncertainty in the mathematical relationship between the two, we should try to optimize directly the conditions for increasing the number of people having inhabited the planet under favorable conditions, subsequently called the *habitation figure. The basic purpose of a population policy should be to bring to earth, under conditions allowing a happy and satisfying life, the greatest possible total number of people.*

We have a serious problem with the definition of "happy and satisfying." One group talks of "our way of life" and demands a quiet walk through the hills. Another speaks of the right to bear children, and a third, the private ownership of property. Maintaining our "way of life" with all of its familiar advantages, at least to Americans, will be impossible for more than another few generations. What will we decide to compromise? How will they be compromised? These difficult questions must be left for other discussions. At present we will only consider the relatively more simple question of maximizing the total number of people.

Calculations of the habitation figure and the survival time require the construction of reliable population models, respectable examples of which now seem to be appearing (Meadows et al., 1972). But to illustrate our points, a very simple model will be assumed. Using the model, values of survival time and habitation figure will be obtained, and the relative importance of different quantities for maximizing these will be discussed.

Illustrative Model

For the example we will consider the earth's fossil and fissionable fuel reserves. How long they will last will depend upon (1) the available reserves, (2) the present consumption rate per person, (3) how the consumption rate is increasing, (4) the total Earth population, and (5) how the population is increasing. Because reliable

253

data were available for the year 1965 as well as for several years before that, the zero of time will be set at 1965.

A recent estimate (Hauser, 1969:132) for the energy reserves of the earth in the form of fossil fuels and fissionable materials is the equivalent of 12,000 billion metric tons of coal. This does not take into account either (1) the energy potentially available from controlled fusion reactions, the feasibility of which awaits demonstration, (2) the technological development of entirely new energy sources, or (3) the fact that conventional fuel reserve estimates are constantly revised upward in an almost exponential manner. Therefore, any calculations of energy depletion times should be thought of as lower limits. In spite of this the points are amply illustrated through the exercise.

For this highly oversimplified model the data justify the assumption that population and energy consumption per person both increase exponentially, that is, they double every fixed number of years. The rate of resource depletion at a given time is proportional to the product of the population and the energy consumption per person at that time. From these basic assumptions we can obtain the expression for resource reserves as a function of time, the energy depletion time, and the habitation figure. The equations are developed in the appendix of this article.

Steady State Earth

Here we will establish some limiting conditions by assuming that both population and energy consumption per person are constant (zero increase).

At the 1965 figure for average per capita energy consumption for the earth,* 1.67 metric tons per person per year, what population could be sustained for five billion years? The answer is 1400 persons. The 1965 earth population of 3.3 billion persons could be sustained at that energy consumption value for 2,100 years.

What of the habitation figure? *With a population level remaining constant through time and with a fixed energy consumption per person, the total number of people who can be sustained on an energy reserve is independent of the population level.* If the average individual lifetime is fifty years, the figure is 140 billion

---

*See the population and energy consumption data table near the end of this article.

people, regardless of population level. If the population is higher, the energy is used up faster; if lower, the reserves will last longer, but the total number of people sustained is the same.

Mathematical Controls: Time Maximized

Data gathered over the past fifty years indicate a doubling of the earth's population approximately every thirty-four years. Per capita energy consumption is doubling every twenty years (Hauser, 1969: Tables 2 and 4). The mathematics of the model show that for calculating depletion time the number representing population increase and that representing energy consumption increase always appear as a sum. Without knowing their numerical values one couldn't say which would have the greatest effect on energy depletion. But from the fact that the doubling time for energy consumption per person is much less than the doubling time for population (twenty years compared with thirty-four years), it is clear that, at the moment, *the most critical quantity is per capita energy consumption increase, not population increase.*

If the estimate of the reserves is accurate and the population and energy consumption both increase according to the trends, the reserves will be used up in approximately 86 years. If zero population growth had been achieved in 1965, the time would be increased to 122 years, a saving of 36 years. If instead, zero per capita energy consumption growth had been achieved, the depletion time would have been increased to 188 years—a total saving of 102 years, which is a factor of three over the saving achieved by going to zero population growth only.

If the reserve estimate is not accurate, and we actually have one thousand times that energy reserve estimate, the number of years for depletion time will change, but the basic pattern remains the same. With the present population and energy consumption increase the depletion time would be 212 years. With zero population growth only, this would increase to 320 years. With zero per capita energy consumption growth the figure would increase to 533 years.

A more thorough study taking into consideration food supply, crowding, pollution, etc., would be required to obtain reliable quantitative data on possible catastrophic situations of which energy depletion is only one. In any event, to maximize time it is

255

not at all clear that population control is presently most critically needed. On the contrary, resource consumption control is probably the most critical need. We hear both mentioned, but quantitative comparisons should be made.

Mathematical Controls: Habitation Maximized

We can accommodate more people on the earth using a high population increase rather than a low one because with increasing per capita energy consumption, the longer we wait the more violence each person does to the planet.

The analogy of the Spaceship Earth is a good one. In a spaceship there is a fixed and well-known quantity of consumables. Knowing that termination of life is without question the final end of the crew, would we agree to a policy allowing fewer people a life on the ship? If it were inevitable that succeeding generations would use a proportionately higher share of the consumables, would we likely encourage as high a population as the spaceship could manage in the earlier generations?

With the present values of our five variables the total number of people who will inhabit the planet between 1965 and the year energy resources are depleted is about five times the present earth population. Maintaining a level population gives us thirty-six more years, but reduces the habitation figure to approximately one half the former value. But maintaining a level per capita energy consumption results not only in 102 extra years but also increases the total habitation figure to approximately 40 times the present population.

For the earth, if we could be sure that the present energy reserve estimates were accurate with no hope for additional resource developments, and if crowding, food or pollution would not become limiting factors, our policy directs our efforts *away* from population limitation and *toward* energy consumption control. Of course, few of us believe those conditions will obtain exactly, but once we have determined a population policy we must seek the best ways to administer it regardless of our prior prejudice.

Real World Controls: The Rich and Poor Nation Dilemma

All this up to now might turn out to be academic. Mathematically, it is simple to change a variable; just substitute the new number in the equation. But can we change them in the real world? Before engaging in a tense and expensive campaign to alter or control population, energy consumption, or any other quantity, we should have at least some understanding of the probability of success. With our present model let us consider just one control problem and its implications.

The prospects for making truly significant changes in the energy depletion time are diminished because of the differences between nations. The "rich" nations of the world all have relatively low birth rates and high per capita energy consumption. The "poor" nations have relatively high birth rates and low per capita energy consumption. The reduction in birth rate as a nation reaches higher average living levels is well established.

But the per capita energy consumption rate is growing faster in the poor nations. Furthermore the possibility of reducing through education or legislation the rate of population increase in the poor nations is low. It seems that the rich nations and the poor nations alike have participated in the demographic transition whereby mortality is reduced through improved sanitation, personal hygiene and more advanced medical and public health programs. The fertility rate of the rich nations has correspondingly reduced, but that of the poor nations has not. Even an intensive birth control program in India over the last two decades has produced little overall reduction in fertility. Philip M. Hauser (1969:22) says that "at least two human generations will be necessary to achieve appreciable progress in the reduction of the birth rate among the mass peasant populations of Asia, Latin America and Africa."

Table 1 shows a division of the world into four rich and four poor areas. As can be seen from the table the population doubling time for the poor nations is almost one-half that of the rich nations. The actual energy consumption levels of the poor nations are much lower than those of the rich nations, but their per capita energy consumption doubling times are again almost one-half that of the rich nations.

The model was adjusted to take the rich-poor variations into account. Assuming the accuracy of the present energy reserve estimates and the present values of the population and energy consumption figures, the depletion time is approximately eighty-

257

Table 1. Population and energy consumption data for the earth, by areas.

	Population		Per capita Energy consumption	
	1965 Value (millions)	Doubling time (years)	1965 Value (metric tons of coal per person per year)	Doubling time (years)
North America	214	43	9.53	41
Western Europe	324	133	3.36	23
Eastern Europe and USSR	352	50	3.50	14
Oceania	17.5	35	3.50	24
Rich nation composite	907	58	4.87	21
Latin America	246	24	0.81	19
China and Communist Asia	730	37	0.44	10
Non-Communist Asia	1100	27	0.35	10
Africa	311	24	0.30	32
Poor nation composite	2387	28	0.42	12
World composite	3294	33	1.67	20

six years. If the rich nations successfully achieved zero population growth in 1965 and the populations of the poor nations continued to grow as at present, the energy depletion time would be increased by *one year. Even if both the population and the energy consumption per person remain level in the rich nations, without corresponding changes in the poor nations, only three years would be added to the energy depletion time.*

The problems concern the whole Earth. Any nation that seeks unilateral solutions needs clear evidence from the models that thereby something can be accomplished. It seems particularly questionable for rich nations to seek to govern population size in order that they might continue their over-consuming ways. Poor nations likely won't reduce their efforts to catch up in the resource consumption race. Are the rich nations sufficiently enlightened to let them catch up, or even to help them do so?

It is depressing to consider the absolutely profound political, economic, and social issues that would need to be faced if policy makers really pursued courses of action for the good of the whole earth, and not simply for what they thought was the good of their

258

separate nations. We probably can't expect such action, but the alternative is even more gloomy.

In any event those constructing population models and those formulating policy must consider the real problems and not simply encourage those who, without support of statistics, rush around trying to convince us that if we "stop at two" or legalize abortion the problems will go away. The dilemma has been anticipated because of modeling and statistics. We must try to find realistic solutions using those same statistical techniques, adding to them wise consideration of the problem of controls.

Appendix

The Mathematical Model

The equations expressing the exponential behavior of population and per capita energy consumption are

$$P = P_o \, e^{pt} \qquad (1)$$

$$C = C_o \, e^{rt} \qquad (2)$$

where P is the earth's population, p is the index related to the doubling time, C is the energy consumed per person per year, r is the corresponding doubling time index and the subscript zero indicates the value of a variable at time zero.

The equation for the earth's energy resources, R, is obtained by equating the rate of decrease of R to the per capita energy consumption times the population.

$$\frac{dR}{dt} = - CP \qquad (3)$$

From the above three equations R may be found,

$$R = R_o + \frac{C_o \, P_o}{r + p} \, [1 - e^{(r+p)t}]. \qquad (4)$$

The depletion time t_d can be found by setting $R = 0$ in Equation 4 and solving for t.

The habitation figure N, for any survival time t_s can be found approximately from

259

$$N = \frac{1}{T} \int_{o}^{t_s} P \, dt \qquad (5)$$

where T is the life expectancy, assumed constant.

Substituting from Equation 1 we obtain

$$N = \frac{P_o}{pT} (e^{pt_s} - 1) \qquad (6)$$

References

Hauser, Philip M. (ed.)
1969   "Natural resource adequacy for the United States and the world," by Joseph L. Fisher and Neal Potter in the Population Dilemma. Englewood Cliffs, New Jersey: Prentice Hall, Inc.

"World population growth," in The Population Dilemma. Englewood Cliffs, New Jersey: Prentice Hall, Inc.

Meadows, Donell H., Dennis L. Meadows, Jorgen Randers, and William W. Behrens III
1972   The Limits to Growth, A Potomac Associates Book. New York: Universal Books.

VII.
POPULATION POLICIES:
IMPLICIT VALUES
AND
ETHICAL PROBLEMS

Introduction

Most programs for change include two vital elements: an assessment of what is and a picture of what ought to be. Most of this book has been concerned with the first of these; in this final chapter we shall pay more attention to the second. Determinations of right and wrong, what ought and ought not be, are not based upon scientific observations, but rather upon value systems or, if you like, moral positions. Decisions about the course of actions governments ought to take with respect to population growth and population control derive from a combination of an assessment of the present situation and the value positions of those in power, or of the pressure groups behind those in power. Accordingly, we decided to include in this final chapter an overview of some of the values manifest in the writings of some leading spokesmen for positive population control. Bahr's "Values and Population Policy" is an attempt to meet this objective.

The ethical problems posed by explicit population policy have been addressed by several writers. One of the most noteworthy pieces, Arthur Dyck's "Population Policies and Ethical Acceptability " is reprinted as the final selection in this chapter (see also: Brewster, 1972; Callahan, 1972). Dyck notes that a population policy is based on an assumption about "what is wrong with the world," and that the policy itself contains judgments about what

263

is ethically acceptable. He contends that assessments of given recommendations should include questions about whether a policy ought to be adopted as well as about whether it is likely to be adopted and to be effective.

Criteria for assessing the ethical acceptability of policies include questions of distributive justice, questions of freedom, and questions of benefits and harms. In the matter of distributive justice—the equity of the division of goods and benefits—even some of the proponents of positive and negative incentive programs have admitted that injustices would be perpetrated thereby. The negative incentives would make poor people still poorer; the wealthy would still be able to have as many children as they wished. The children of the poor probably would suffer if negative sanctions were applied. In any population policy special attention must be given to the problem of poverty, not mainly because of the higher birth rates of the poor but instead "because the conditions under which it is just and rational to expect anyone to curtail family size do not occur in dire poverty." Finally, there is no assurance that injustices that might be perpetrated through the use of incentives would be worth the price.

The case against coercive measures is even stronger. Especially troubling is the problem of punishment; how does one sanction offenders without thereby inflicting suffering on innocent children? Compulsion discriminates against the poor just as incentives do. Finally, coercive programs are incompatible with self-direction and personal freedom. Both the relative absence of government interference and compulsion and equality of opportunity are values as strong as survival itself. Sometimes freedom is not incompatible with compulsion, as in the case of compulsory traffic regulation, compulsory education or compulsory vaccination. But Dyck argues that compulsion in limiting the number of one's children is not comparable to any of these examples, because having children is one of the ways people try to satisfy their longings for immortality.

Some have challenged the individual's right to determine for himself how many children he shall have because this right conflicts with that of society to keep the number of children at some specified level. Dyck suggests that just as it is in society's interest to encourage free expression generally, society has the obligation to see that one's right to decide about the number of his children

264

is honored. In circumstances of oppressive growth rates, a government may provide information and materials which will assist individuals to limit their births voluntarily, both for their own and the public good.

Dyck states that some types of compulsory measures might be justified only as a last resort, in the most pressing of circumstances, after everything else has been tried. On the other hand, he affirms that "not every compulsory measure can be justified even as a last resort."

Finally, there is the question of benefits and harms. Population control will not in itself eradicate nutritional deficiencies or ecological imbalances. He concludes that the extension of family planning and the continued overall social and economic development of underdeveloped nations are the most ethically acceptable ways of reducing high birth rates.

Values
and
Population Policy

Howard M. Bahr

This paper is divided into two sections. In the first, we shall identify certain values and assumptions which characterize the policies proposed by some of the leading spokesmen for population control. Then we shall discuss the nature of the suggested programs for national and world population control.

Values and Assumptions

The essence of Malthusian population theory is that population growth tends to outrun the earth's capacity to produce sustenance. In its simplest form, it consists of the notion that population size increases geometrically while food supply increases arithmetically. Population growth in itself is identified as a primary cause of war, famine, and pestilence. Other variables, such as technology, social organization, or cultural values, are seen as relatively unimportant in comparison with the inexorable finalities that man's capacity to reproduce is greater than his capacity to increase the means of subsistence and that the ultimate check to population size lies in food supply.

We will not attempt to assess the original theory or the neo-Malthusian modifications of it here. Extended treatments are readily available (cf. Hutchinson, 1967). Instead, we will focus only upon selected value assumptions or priorities apparent in the proposals for population limitation advanced by some of the modern spokesmen for this point of view. Specifically, we shall consider the presumed precedence of biological factors in social causation, the anticipation and acceptance of violence as a positive population check, the imputation of "guilt" to those who have contributed to the "population problem" by improving death control, the devaluation of human life implicit in the notion that there can be "surplus people," a moral elitism which refuses to acknowledge the legitimacy of other perspectives on the problem, and the transformation of ideological statements into "facts."

We have not attempted to represent the views of all, or even a cross-section of those who speak and write on the need for curtailment of family size in the interest of "zero population growth" or even negative growth. Instead, we have focused on the published statements of some of the more outspoken proponents of population control. While this emphasis may be unfair to many scientists who urge "zero population growth" with more moderation in rhetoric and perspective than those whose statements and assumptions we have assessed, it is the more strident, immoderate spokesmen who receive the greatest attention in the mass media and whose views seem to have the greatest impact on the uninformed. Moreover, the more "radical" statements about the "population explosion" sometimes highlight assumptions present but not made explicit in more moderate recommendations.

The immoderate pronouncements about the "population explosion" filter into the attitudes and, presumably, the family behavior of young people, but the tenuous chain of assumptions and hypotheses upon which the pronouncements are based are lost to view. Too often the reader accepts on faith such statements as "there are too many people," "zero population growth will solve our problems," "humanity is breeding itself into extinction," without assessing the validity of such statements or the assumptions implicit in them. As a consequence, an influential segment of the population now "knows," with moral certainty, that "overpopulation" is one of the greatest social problems of our time, and with energy and dedication they seek to convert others to their "responsible" perspectives. Note, as examples, the following statements by university students:

Each baby born in the U.S. represents an extra burden upon our natural resources. I wouldn't say that my conscience has dulled due to extreme self-indulgence, but rather that it has been whetted, cognizant of the problems of our country and the world due to increasing overpopulation.

As a woman, I am interested in giving my child a full life, not just nine months in the womb, or until old enough to die on a battlefield or feel the full effects of malnutrition. What is the "life" of one fetus compared with that of hundreds of thousands of those in the world already starving and suffering from malnutrition. No woman should be forced to bear a child she does not want and no child should be forced to be brought into a world plagued with overcrowding and not enough resources (Bartel, 1972).

One of the most depressing aspects of the problem is that we cannot escape unscathed. Dr. Paul Ehrlich (1968) and others say that immediate action must be taken simply to minimize the consequences. I AM TERRIBLY SADDENED BY THE FACT THAT THE MOST HUMANE THING FOR ME TO DO IS TO HAVE NO CHILDREN AT ALL.

As an ex-potential parent, I have asked myself what kind of world my children would grow up in. And the answer was, "Not very pretty, not very clean. Sad, in fact." Because, you see, if the population continues to grow, the facilities to accommodate that population must grow, too. Thus we have more highways and fewer trees; more electricity and fewer undammed rivers; more cities and less clean air. Mankind has spread across the face of the earth like a great unthinking, unfeeling cancer (Mills, 1970).

The Presumed Precedence of Biological Factors

The controversy over whether biological or social factors are the primary determinants of human behavior has a long intellectual history. The argument still tends to be drawn along disciplinary lines, with physical and biological scientists opting for greater salience of the "nature" or "hereditary" factors, and social scientists stressing the primary role of "nature" or "environment."

For many the issue has been resolved via the admission that in most situations both kinds of factors are operative. Thus, biological facts are elements in an interactive situation along with social facts; but as a rule they are not the primary determinants of social structure or collective behavior. Climate does not explain personality; the presence of natural resources does not explain industrialization; and population size does not explain either the incidence or the nature of social conflict. Biological or environmental factors set limits; but sometimes even those limits prove temporary and may be extended by those culture complexes we designate as technology.

269

Marx's (Kammeyer, 1969:461) critique of Malthusian thought involved the precedence of social over biological factors. He opposed Malthus

> ... as a peculiarly vicious and obsolete defender of capitalism. "Over-population" was a bourgeois invention, designed to justify the poverty of the working classes. Improved production and distribution, not restriction of births, was the answer. A socialistic economy could thrive under all conditions of population growth, while an economy based on scarcity and high prices required birth control to mitigate its glaring deficiencies.

While it is unlikely that modern observers would go so far as to say that any system could thrive under "all conditions of population growth," the notion that social organization and not sheer number determines the condition of human populations is widely accepted. "Under-," "over-," or "optimum" population all are relative terms in an equation which includes culture and all its components, and we have only hypotheses about which terms of that equation are the best ones to vary to improve the lot of humanity in the long run. The proponents of population control claim to know the answer—population is the key, they say—but that "knowledge" derives from an act of faith, not of empirical fact.

Wertham (1966:102-105) asserts that disaster is assured if men look to biological factors such as fertility to explain social problems:

> ... Mass starvation is not made in bedchambers but in council chambers. Social and economic problems cannot be solved with biology. We are dealing here with a general law of political sociology: every reactionary political tendency of modern times ... contains Malthusian elements.

> ... a surplus population is never absolute. It is always relative to other factors of production, distribution, and social organization. It is relative also in respect to occupation, sex, and age. There may be a surplus population of workers, of unskilled laborers, or women or children, and so on. It is never, however, an absolute overgrowth. *It is not that there are categorically too many people and that this explains economic conditions. The reverse is true. There are definite socioeconomic conditions that explain why at certain times and in certain places there are too many people.*

Questions of population are an international matter. There are no absolutely supernumerary people. There are only relatively surplus and superfluous, having been made so by social, economic, and political conditions. . . . Better planned economy would do away with a lot of the problems of planned parenthood. . . . People are not poor because they are superfluous, they are superfluous because they are poor.

. . . What poor farmers need most are not antifertility measures in their beds but fertilizers for their fields. . . . Taking an international point of view, we can say that it is not that people cannot find the means of subsistence, but rather that the means of subsistence cannot find them. For through social conditions, the means are kept from them. Exclusion from multiplication is a drastic step to make up for exclusion from the market (emphasis added).

To summarize, the assumption in question may be broken into two parts. One is that biological facts such as population size in and of themselves determine social outcomes. The other is that the single factor of population size or rate of growth is the most important one determining whether the future holds contentment or catastrophe for mankind. Both of these are assumptions only; both are highly questionable. Almost all human events are consequences of a complex interaction of many biological and social facts. Moreover, within the combination of variables which determine societal well-being, the priority of population size as a causal factor is an open question. The available evidence suggests that, far from being the most critical factor, population size is a relatively unimportant determinant of variation in the quality and length of human life when compared to the impact of technological development and the nature and efficiency of a society's social organization.

The Inevitability of Violence

The psychiatrist Frederic Wertham has assessed some of the values implicit in the statements of the neo-Malthusians in a chapter, "The Malthus Myth," of his best-selling *A Sign for Cain: An Exploration of Human Violence* (1966). More frightening than the attribution to "overpopulation" of all the inequities and inefficiencies of modern production and distribution systems is the "self-fulfilling prophecy" which the rhetoric of the neo-Malthusians sets into motion. Social scientists have known for a long time that one of the best ways to create a given situation was to predict it and to act as if it were going to occur. Treat a child as

271

if he is inferior, and he will become inferior; treat a nation as an enemy, and it becomes an enemy. Behave as if tomorrow a great disaster shall occur, and the forces which can produce that disaster may be set into motion.

Undergirding the writings of many of those who cry for immediate population control is the suggestion—the expectation— of death and violence. Malthus justified the existence of poverty, famine, and war, arguing that misery was "natural" among human populations. Similarly, the neo-Malthusians justify a miserable future. Their simple message: unless man's "runaway fertility" is brought under control, there is no way famine, war, or international cataclysm can be averted.

One of the most vocal neo-Malthusians expressed his pessimism and his moral certainty about the *true* cause of man's problems in the book *The Population Bomb* (Ehrlich, 1968). Speaking of the chances of "success," by which he means reducing the earth's population to between one and two billion persons, Paul Ehrlich says:

> ... the chances of success are small. ... But partial programs can help. Indeed, even if the worst happens, short of the end of civilization, efforts toward solving the population problem may not be in vain. Suppose we do not prevent massive famines. Suppose there are widespread plagues. Suppose a billion people perish. At least if we have called enough attention to the problem, we may be able to keep the whole mess from recycling. *We must make it impossible for people to blame the calamity on too little food or technological failures or "acts of God." They must at least face the essential cause of the problem— overpopulation* (p. 174, emphasis added).

What are the underlying moral implications of the neo-Malthusian perspectives? Dr. Wertham (1966:107-110; emphasis added) identifies several of them:

> —*However concealed under a cover of moralisms, the whole idea includes a depreciation and devaluation of human life.* ... A high birthrate is an unmitigated evil and the sole cause of further evils. A high death rate is a boon. ... Mass deaths as an asset is a dangerous idea.
>
> —*It is a dehumanization to speak of the procreation of people as barnyard activity or rabbitlike behavior.* The equation is simple: poverty is equal to superfluousness, superfluousness is equal to a crime. The consequence is punishment. You may have the right to

272

exist, but you lose the right to procreate. *If someone in authority tells us that we have no right to procreate, it is only one step further for him to tell us we have no right to live.*

—*Controlling the size of a whole nation, although the avowed motive may be to bring about a better life, comes perilously close to forcible elimination....* It is strange how few people realize the close connections—psychological, social, and political—between the very term "population explosion" and the extermination of populations.

—Historically, Malthusianism has from its very beginning "explained" war and seen beneficial results from it. According to Malthusian reasoning, wars do not come about through political, economic, and social circumstances. Their main cause is overpopulation.... The neo-Malthusians consider *war an inevitable consequence of what they assert are "the controlling laws of nature." They have popularized the idea that sexual improvidence is what propels us into war....* In other words, nobody is responsible for war unless we shift the blame on the shoulders of those who make too many babies and those who fail to provide the parents with enough contraceptives and sterilization operations. If we accept such propaganda, we are already absolving from guilt all those who would unleash the next world war.... *This attitude justifies the existence of war—and if we justify something, we help to bring it about.*

A depreciation of human life, a dehumanization of procreation, an affirmation of a "forced choice" between the prevention of millions of births and the mass deaths, a justification for wide-scale violence and war; these are some of the values implicit in neo-Malthusian thought. Sometimes the specter of mass violence is held up as the negative but inevitable option. Other statements include it as an alternative, along with the option of a "low-quality" life, if population size does not stabilize. In either case, the violence is there, a corollary of the notion that there are too many men, that either births must stop or more men must die.

The Ignorant Doctors

Most people grow up believing that advances in medical science have benefited the world, and that to be a dedicated physician is one of the nobler human callings. To some of the neo-Malthusians, however, the advances in death control fostered by modern medicine are the causes of the "population explosion," and hence are not regarded with total admiration. Thus, for example,

273

Wertham quotes a scientist who wrote: "One of the greatest national assets of Chile, perhaps its greatest asset, is its high death rate" (Wertham, 1966:107-108). Even more revealing of the underlying values of some of the proponents of population control are their statements "forgiving" physicians for their ignorance in creating the population "crisis" and assuring them that their good intentions are applauded regardless of the apparently negative consequences of the activities. Garrett Hardin (1970b:42) writes in the official journal of the California Medical Association:

> Should medical men feel guilty because they help to increase the population of the world, and hence presumably its misery as well? I think not, for several reasons. In the first place, even though intentions *are* the paving blocks of Hell, intentions *do* matter. It does matter that medical researchers and practitioners have intended well. They did not foresee the ultimate consequences of saving lives—but then, who did? The physicians' ignorance was mankind's ignorance. It is not the past, but the future to which we must give our attention.

Another way the ignorant doctors have contributed to the problem is by their almost exclusive focus on death control. Ehrlich criticizes the effective lobby in Washington which has promoted death control, lamenting that this "health syndicate" has not received effective criticism for their preoccupation with lengthening life, especially in promoting the support of massive research on cancer and circulatory diseases. He complains that even biologists are oriented toward the preservation of life rather than its prevention:

> One might think that American scientists, especially biologists, would be using their influence to get the government moving. Unfortunately they are all too often a retrograde influence. The establishment in American biology consists primarily of death-controllers: those interested in intervening in population processes only by lowering death rates. They have neither the background nor inclination to understand the problem (Ehrlich, 1968:92).

The "ignorant physicians" may be a powerful influence in the battle for population control if they assume their medical responsibilities. Hardin, who is willing to overlook their past folly, outlines his program by which enlightened physicians of today may avoid the blunders of the past. His suggestions include the institution of "complete," i.e., perfect, birth control. In other words, the

274

birth of unplanned or unwanted babies is not to be permitted. Abortion must serve as a back-up measure for whatever contraceptive measures are used, and it must be permitted for *all* "failures," not merely for proven contraceptive failure. Another responsibility of the physician is to discourage childbearing among his patients:

> . . . to discourage fertility itself . . . in order to diminish the amount of adult stupidity, which itself is a form of social pollution, and a most dangerous one. It may be difficult for an obstetrician to bring himself to discourage exuberant fertility among his patients, but his civic responsibility is clear (Hardin, 1970b:45-46).

A third "civic responsibility" urged upon physicians is a willingness to sterilize patients who desire sterilization as a method of contraception. Hardin (1970b:46) is highly critical of prevailing attitudes of physicians in this matter:

> Many physicians have a great reluctance to operate on a person who has few or no children. The medical attitude is clearly contrary to public interest in this day of overpopulation. Why do physicians make this difficulty?
>
> The reason many physicians drag their feet in performing sterilizations is not that they are physicians, but that they are partakers of the general culture, for they breathe in the atmosphere of the entire community. . . .
>
> It will not be easy for many physicians to accept the legitimacy of sterilization as an individual decision, especially for a person who has no children; it will not be easy for the medical profession to divest itself of such now maladaptive resistance. Fortunately, the recent emergence of sterilization from a long taboo is helping to create the climate of opinion that is needed for rationality.

The world is already overpopulated, he concludes, and medical doctors must do their part to correct the situation. In the past, they have "played God" by bringing about "death control." Now, they must again "play God" by "fully controlling births," in the name of the good of posterity.

"Surplus Babies"

Let us emphasize again that not all proponents of population control incorporate into their statements the devaluation of life implied in the intemperate language of the more strident spokesmen. Two eminent demographers, Leslie and Charles Westoff (1968:345-351), identify Paul Ehrlich as "the most visible proponent of the view that the world is coming apart at the seams and that U.S. population growth is a leading villain," and partially refute his position, but it is Ehrlich, not the Westoffs, whom the young people read and quote. The moderate voices receive less public attention and ultimately seem to have less impact than the more "radical" positions.

Sometimes the devaluation of human beings is direct and specific, as in Hardin's (1970b:42) statement that "Every babe's birth diminishes me," for example. Devaluation of human life also accompanies references to human populations as if they were lower animals, as in Ehrlich's description of a growth rate which leads to a population's doubling every thirty to forty years as "multiplying like rabbits" (Ehrlich, 1968:84).

Writing to teachers in *The American Biology Teacher,* Howard uses a geological—but no less demeaning—analogy:

> Since *overpopulation is the erosion of civilization,* it behooves all scientists to act now, utilizing all available resources, *to help check this flood of human beings* (Howard, 1971:149; emphasis added).

Later in the same piece he applies the term "surplus" to infants:

> . . . if a surplus baby does not die at birth, it means that another child or person somewhere else is going to be unable to live a full life because of the resources consumed by the surplus baby (p. 151).

The very notion of "surplus babies" implies that they can be discarded, pruned away with no loss to society.

Ehrlich (1968:166-167) takes the notion of excess people even farther; to him, they are not merely redundant humans, but malignantly so; not a neutral excess, but a positive threat to be eradicated, cut away, and destroyed.

> A cancer is an uncontrolled multiplication of cells; the population explosion is an uncontrolled multiplication of people. Treating only the symptoms of cancer may make the victim more comfortable at first. but eventually he dies—often horribly. A similar fate awaits the world with a population explosion if only the symptoms are treated. We must shift our efforts from treatment of the symptoms to the cutting out of the cancer. The operation will demand many apparently brutal and heartless decisions. The pain may be intense. But the disease is so far

advanced that only with radical surgery does the patient have a chance of survival.

The possible consequences of the widespread acceptance of such ideas about human life, especially in cultures already steeped in traditions which support violence, are most unsettling. Convince an entire society that the most critical problem is overpopulation and that many of them are surplus, and the stage is set for population policies reminiscent of those of the Third Reich. If human life is valuable, if the individual human life has meaning, then there are no "surplus babies."

While the logical conclusions of the train of thought beginning with the idea that human beings may be equated with cancer cells may be to raise the possibility of the elimination of populations, the neo-Malthusians are quick to point out that they too reverence human life that has already been born. Their campaigns are largely against the unborn, or, if they have their way, the never-to-be-born. The term "surplus babies" then refers to those who should not be born because the earth is "too crowded" for them. If an entire society can be convinced simultaneously that when any family produces more than two children, the subsequent children are "excess" or "surplus," then the consequences may be drastic for the nonborn but not too severe for the living. What is frightening, however, is the specter of the social controls that will have to be designed to assure that all families in the society conform to the norm. There are almost always lags in socialization; certain groups accept new norms more rapidly than others.

Thus, mass acceptance of the notion of surplusage leads inevitably to public decisions about just who shall be defined as surplus and what shall be done with the surplus. Hardin's (1970a) recommendations for positive population control foreshadow the mechanisms whereby births would be prevented among those whose definition of "surplus babies" differed from that of the enlightened majority:

> Our experience with Prohibition has taught us that positive control is not feasible unless the *vast* majority is convinced of its necessity; when this stage is reached the recalcitrant minority that would have to be sterilized would be small (p. 261-262).

Who shall determine when members of a viable subculture no

277

longer have the right to hold values which deviate from the majority's with respect to ideal family size? In the end, the devaluation of infant humans may become a devaluation of the right of minorities to exist, for to deny distinctive values is to deny the essence of minority status.

The Illegitimacy of Other Points of View: The "Insane" and the "Stupid"

The vast accretion of publications urging population control cannot be summarized without distortion. Some scientists carefully take other points of view into account. But many of the most influential writers, especially when writing for the general public, treat perspectives other than their own and alternatives to their programs with great disdain. Committed to their own ideas about how to save mankind, the "true believers" among the advocates of population control frequently dismiss other points of view or treat them as beneath notice. Hoffer (1951:23,107) noted that "There can be no mass movement without some deliberate misrepresentation of facts," and has pointed to the consequences for self-esteem of having a "burning conviction" that one has a holy duty toward others: "The vanity of the selfless, even those who practice utmost humility, is boundless." Evidence of the vanity of those whose holy duty is to save the world from procreating itself into extinction is apparent in their intellectual ethnocentrism.

Thus, Ehrlich (1968:192) proposes that his proselytes write critical letters to scholars "who are proposing idiotic panaceas to solve the food problem." He classes attempts to improve food production from the oceans among these "idiotic panaceas." Even the suggestion that the sea may be more fruitful than we have supposed are to be avoided. He urges that letters be sent to scientific journals "to ask the editors to stop accenting advertisements that imply that a technology for mining or farming the sea can save humanity."

He characterizes an editorial which cited "hopeful experts" to the effect that much of the earth's surface is uncultivated and that the sea could yield "unmeasurable riches" as "an absurd extreme of technological optimism," representative "of the attitudes of a large number of uninformed Americans, 'experts' and non-experts alike." In fact "the notion that we can extract vastly greater

278

amounts of food from the sea in the near future is quite simply *just another myth promoted by the ignorant or the irresponsible."* Moreover, it is worse than futile to try to bring desert land, the tropics, or other marginal land into production: "The Russians have recently given us a graphic example of the *stupidity* of trying to put marginal land into production." Finally, to want more people is sure evidence of mental incompetence: "no *sane* society wants to promote larger population size today" (Ehrlich, 1968:95-96, 97, 99, and 137; emphasis added).

The moral certainty is so intense that the existence of other reasonable viewpoints cannot be admitted. It is not a matter of parties with different emphases, but of the "innocent" and the "guilty," the good and the bad. The bad are those who "over-breed" and produce "surplus" or "excess" children, or who provide social support for such "irresponsible" behavior. Thus, Ehrlich (1968:182) urges that people, organizations, and companies impeding population control be "blacklisted," that action groups for population control boycott products of "guilty" companies, and work for opponents of "guilty" politicians. Think as we think, is the message, or you are guilty.

Other writers manifest comparable intellectual arrogance. We have already noted Garrett Hardin's patronizing attitude toward the "guilty" physicians who in their ignorance made death control too effective. Harrison Brown (1971:11) divides mankind into two camps, those who care about the environment and believe that the earth's population is perhaps already too large, and "those who don't care how they live or what dangers they create for posterity" who believe that the earth can support many more people. Former Secretary of the Interior, Stewart Udall (1967:11), places in this last category the scientists and engineers who are working to make our technology more efficient. He complains:

> Regrettably, a segment of the scientific community abets the forma-
> tion of a bearable world of teeming billions. Certain brilliant men are so
> engrossed in engineering techniques that they have seemingly lost sight
> of their own species.

How have these traitors to their own kind betrayed us? By devising means that more people can live comfortably on the earth—by abetting the formation of a "bearable world of teeming

279

billions." Apparently they would better serve mankind if they made certain that the future would be unbearable for more than the present population.

Some demographers are even more severe in their indictment of those who do not share their values. Sripati Chandrasekhar (Ismach, 1971), an internationally known proponent of population control and a visiting lecturer at the University of Washington, was quoted as identifying as "the greatest criminals of all time" any church or ideology which opposed population control.

The point of all this is that the public does not get an unbiased, critical examination of the issues and of the evidence which supports certain points of view. No one denies that our cities and many of our other facilities are crowded and inefficient. Few deny that environmental pollution, the growing demand for energy, and the problem of feeding the increasing population of the earth are serious problems. But too many of the proponents of population control have decided that they know the answer to the problems, that the primary variable is population size, and that anyone who does not agree is blind, willfully perverse, or incompetent. At base, the position that increasing population size is the chief culprit, or even an important element in the etiology of our social and environmental problems, is an untested hypothesis. But it is an hypothesis whose time has come, and it has been exalted into an article of faith. The tragedy is that so many accept uncritically affirmations based upon this ideology as scientific fact.

The Transformation of Ideology into "Fact"

We should not be surprised that advocates for population control use familiar propaganda techniques nor distort the facts to fit their objectives. Such ploys are common in most attempts to mold or mollify public opinion, and government leaders, politicians, advertising executives, lawyers, and salesmen are among those who seek to influence our attitudes and behavior by telling us half-truths or outright falsehoods. Optimists presume that, despite the misinformation to which the public is subjected, the critical faculties of the intelligent citizen, combined with his access to information from a variety of sources, will operate in such a manner that in the end "truth will out." In any event, the interests of the public at large are served by the identification of misrep-

280

resentation or error in the statements of those who would persuade us to abandon values held by many people as fundamental rights, such as the individual right of parents to determine the number of their progeny.

A few examples will suffice. The alleged "fact" is listed first, followed by an alternative point of view for which there is at least as much empirical evidence.

Allegation

> ... it is impossible to expand it [agriculture] fast enough, for population grows geometrically, whereas agriculture can only be increased arithmetically (Taylor, 1968:53).

Response

This is the Malthusian hypothesis, unadulterated. Taylor states it as fact; it is hypothetical at best, and there is substantial evidence that Malthus was wrong. In fact, some who urge population control for "quality of life" reasons argue that "there is a strong case to be made for a stringent population policy on exactly the reverse of the basis Malthus expounded" (Mayer, 1969). Moreover, the historical experience of mankind over the past two centuries is in direct refutation of Malthus' hypothesis. The population has increased dramatically, and *at the same time* the average standard of living has improved rather than deteriorated. How many centuries of such evidence is necessary before the inaccuracy of the Malthusian hypothesis is admitted? Here are two expert assessments which contradict the Malthusian position.

> Neither Malthus nor the neo-Malthusians have ever been able to give scientific proof or documentation for what is the cornerstone of their theory, namely, that the population has a permanent inherent tendency to outgrow the available means of subsistence. The accumulated facts and the scientific reasoning based on those facts contradict their theory. It is not accidental that from totally different points of view both Marx and Freud disagreed with him (Wertham, 1969:104).

> I trust that I have demonstrated how dangerous it is to link constantly in the mind of the public the concept of overpopulation with that of undernutrition. I believe that it is dangerous to link it necessarily with poverty. It is absurd on the basis of any criterion of history, economics, or esthetics (Kammeyer 1969:13).

281

Allegation

Taking into account present population densities and the other factors involved in carrying capacity, we arrive at the inescapable conclusion that, in the context of man's present patterns of behavior and level of technology, *the planet Earth, as a whole, is overpopulated* (Ehrlich and Ehrlich, 1970:201).

Response

To the Ehrlichs, this conclusion may be inescapable. But the conclusion is, and should clearly be understood to be, the result of their personal calculus based on their own notions of what an optimum population is. It is vital that it not be accorded the status of scientific fact. Day and Day (1964:35,37), who themselves argue for population control on "quality of life" grounds, make plain the essentially personal nature of such assessments of earth's "overpopulation":

Any claim that a country's population is too large or too small implies some idea of an optimum size, and some standard by which to measure deviation from it. . . . There is no exact formula for determining optimum population. One man's optimum may be another's overpopulation; and not even the demographer has an ultimate way of determining which is right.

Allegation

. . . this earth does not have the resources necessary to provide even the present world population with the degree of affluence now enjoyed by the middle-class American (Howard, 1971:149).

Response

This is a simple value judgment, a matter of faith (or, rather, lack of it). To claim otherwise is to suppose that the writer is familiar with all of the earth's resources, and of the ways they may be used for the benefit of man. Other population experts disagree with the above allegation. For example, Fisher and Potter, (NAS, 1971b:240-241) compared projections of demand for resource commodities with a review of supply possibilities for both developed and underdeveloped countries and concluded that developed countries "should be able to accommodate the maximum popula-

282

tion growth projected for them with due allowance for increasing levels of living, at least as far as *quantities* of resource products are concerned." And for the less developed countries:

> ... the outlook is not as dark as it is frequently painted although the possibility of securing enough food for the underfed 2 billion or more people will remain in doubt for some years to come. ... In energy and metal commodities the outlook is more favorable, based on recent production trends and on the outlook for discoveries and development, although even here there will be difficulty at times with regard to particular items.

We have listed a few sample affirmations and presented alternative perspectives to illustrate the general point that those whose holy cause is population control, like advocates of almost any ideological or political position, frequently exaggerate or misrepresent in their anxiety to gain adherents to their position.

A "Moderate" Approach

We have highlighted some of the values apparent in published statements of certain leading spokesmen for population control. However, the discussion thus far has emphasized proposals or assumptions which are in sharp contrast to many of the traditional attitudes about population size, family responsibility, and human freedom. More moderate approaches to the "population explosion" also deserve attention. Accordingly, we shall briefly discuss some of the arguments and values apparent in Day and Day's (1964) *Too Many Americans*, a work by professional demographers which one authority (Wrong, 1964:64) on "Population Myths" has characterized as "refreshingly free from the strident alarmism that characterizes the writings of so many of the amateurs who have dealt with the subject."

Day and Day (1964:34) affirm that at some point in the future population stability must come, and that if by conscious choice men do not limit their numbers, then they will be limited by the impersonal operation of factors which increase the mortality rate. Since population stability must come, they suggest, why not bring it about at a point which maximizes freedom, dignity, and aesthetic, ethical, political, and material benefits. Besides, they argue, even though the United States is in a position to grow for some time without experiencing many direct negative consequences, our ethical position with reference to less developed countries requires that we set an example: ". . . for a nation with our incomparable wealth and living levels, with our opportunities for leading world opinion . . . to uphold a double standard of population growth is surely insensitive and undiplomatic in the extreme."

Although they cannot demonstrate that the increasing United States population is directly responsible for "checking improvements in the quality of life," Day and Day (1964:45-74) insist that continuing population increases "can hardly escape" having negative consequences. They say that population threatens many aspects of the present American way of life, and hypothesize that the larger the population, the more difficult it will be to maintain that standard of living. Five kinds of losses in quality are discussed: less accessibility of space and recreational facilities, increasing economic costs of resources, greater pollution, declines in the availability and quality of social services, and loss of personal freedom because of a hypothetical direct relationship between population density and social regimentation.

The "quality of life" argument for support of population control is of questionable validity. The idea that population increases "can hardly escape" having negative consequences is an interesting research hypothesis, but it lacks empirical support. Both negative and positive consequences are likely to derive from population changes in either direction, and there are no logical or scientific reasons—only ideological ones—to anticipate that the negative consequences will predominate. In fact, none of the anticipated declines in quality of life necessarily follow from an increase in population size; there are too many intervening variables. Furthermore, even if it were granted that with respect to those indicators the quality of life might decline, there are other measures of "quality" living which might be enhanced by increased population size. Would opportunities for interaction with children increase or decrease? Would respect for life, altruism, and sensitivity to the needs of others be fostered or made less relevant? The answers to these questions depend, in part, on the particular value system of the society experiencing population growth. In human societies, to a great degree, "thinking makes it so." Social values and priorities mediate the cold facts of population size and rate of increase.

Thus, on two counts—an inadequate conceptualization and impoverishment of measurement of life "quality," and an undemonstrated and unknown relationship between the quality of life and population size—we must conclude that *Too Many Americans* presents insightful arguments for a value position, but certainly does not demonstrate that there now are or soon will be too many Americans, nor that population size is an important, let alone dominant, determinant of the social problems which confront modern society.

Current Proposals for Population Control

Within the past decade an increasing number of governments—including at least twenty-three developing nations, the U.S., and Japan—have made official or semi-official statements favoring control of population growth. Moreover, advances in techniques of contraception—particularly the development of the intrauterine contraceptive devices and of oral contraceptives—have provided governments with the means for instituting programs of positive control. Consequently many governments have or are preparing to embark on officially sponsored programs of population control.

There are various answers to the question, "what is an optimum population," but as we have already noted, many of the writers currently publishing on the subject suggest that the United States has already passed its optimum. Often the argument for stringent national policy *now* is couched in language like the following:

> ... unless we wish to live in a completely ordered state of the most restrictive type, we must discuss and plan an optimum population and a national policy designed to achieve it. Our responsibility to ourselves, to future generations, and the total biosphere that is our world requires it (Prindle, 1969:568).

Many of the most vocal spokesmen are biological scientists, and perhaps their professional training has minimized their perceptions of the interaction between social organization and physical environment in man's use of resources. Statements like "Every day, month, and year reduces the potential carrying capacity of this earth by man's overexploitation of the soil and the non-renewable resources" (Howard, 1971:150) reflect a lack of understanding of social and economic perspectives to the problem, and

285

illustrate what Barnett (1971:545) has referred to as "fuzzy thinking and colorful propaganda."

> A great deal is being written today about population growth, its economic and social effects, and the prospects for these. Much of what is written is nonsense. . . . Misplaced alarms divert attention from more urgent social questions. From invalid diagnosis, wrong prescriptions are concocted. . . . The propensity for slogans, lack of objectivity, and absence of scientific analysis is disturbing to social scientists. . . .

Despite the absence of clear sociological and economic thinking in many of the pronouncements about the causes of our current problems and the disaster that waits in the future, pressures for both worldwide and national programs for population control are mounting. Everyone is aware that our society faces serious problems, that our cities are in many respects almost unlivable, and that the unnecessary pollution of the environment needs to be stopped. The cry "the problem is people—too many people" is a seductive one. It is easily understood: one need not admit the complex origins of our troubles; and with the identification of the problem comes a simple remedy—stop having children, and prevent others from having so many children. No matter that the invalid diagnosis may lead to wrong prescriptions. The phrase "population explosion" catches on, and valuable energies are devoted to reducing family size in developed as well as undeveloped countries on the basis of the assumption that it is the biological factor—too many people—that is causing the social problems.

It is ironic that population growth is identified as, next to the threat of thermonuclear war, the most serious problem of our time; this, at a time when the earth is supporting more people at a higher standard of living than ever before in history. Given the importance ascribed to population per se as a cause of the world's evils, it is astonishing that our histories of earlier, uncrowded periods do not reveal more peace and harmony.

The political realities of the situation, however, are that vocal and organized minorities exert influence; that popular opinion may swing behind the oft-voiced urgency to do something about population "before it is too late." The shape of the population policies which have been proposed may give us some idea of the directions legislation may take.

286

Several excellent summaries of the types of population policies which have been proposed are available (National Academy of Sciences, 1971:70-99; Berelson, 1969). One of the simplest is Nash's (1971) four-fold typology with reference to compatibility with the norms of "individualism" or voluntariness.

Nash's first category includes those programs which "simply heighten the possibilities for self-determination by the individual mother or by the married couple." Programs of this kind are non-compulsory and consist largely of information dissemination, although laws which liberalize availability of abortions are included here. The traditional activities of "family planning" programs fall almost entirely under this heading.

The next category includes proposals for including material on population growth and family planning as part of the public school curriculum, thus essentially making exposure to "sex education" compulsory.

Third are the creation of inducements to encourage voluntary restriction of fertility, such as payments for childlessness, child-spacing, or voluntary sterilization. Combined with these is the provision of negative incentives such as modifying the income tax structure to penalize families with many children, or simply the neutralization of the "pronatalist" tax incentives which many nations maintain.

Finally, there are the nonvoluntary controls, such as requiring licenses to have children, temporary or permanent compulsory sterilization at certain stages of the life cycle or after a certain number of births, and the placing of antifertility agents in public food or water supplies.

Categories one and two both involve education. Voluntary controls can work, it is asserted, only if the people learn to want fewer children. Accordingly, relevant to both types of policy are massive educational programs designed to create the necessary antipopulation norms and to establish a climate whereby compulsory sex and population courses will be accepted by parents. The objectives of these educational programs are to change the nature of the family, particularly women's role in the family, and to increase the availability and the ethical acceptability of contraceptives and abortions. By means of appropriate education the range of tolerance in family size is to be reduced, so that a family of three children is considered large.

287

Some of the proposed programs for redefining family roles and responsibilities via appropriate education are outlined below. After treating them, we shall comment on the methods by which advocates of population control hope to neutralize opposition to population control programs. Finally, there is a brief description of some of the more positive modes of population control which have been proposed, including anti-natalist incentive systems and direct control by government.

Redefining Family Roles and Responsibilities

One of the chief aims of those who would stabilize or reduce our population is a redefinition of woman's role, to be accomplished primarily by reeducation:

> Women need to be shown the many values of not becoming pregnant, rather than be instructed throughout their early years that a woman's role is primarily that of wife and mother and that children are life's greatest fulfillment. . . . we especially need to broaden the perspectives of girls—show them the many economic and social advantages today for the one-child or no-child family. . . . We need to extol the virtues of late marriage and the single life, in contrast to the drudgery of early pairing and many children (Howard, 1971:150, 154).

Another goal is to highlight the nonreproductive functions of marriage. One avenue for accomplishing this end is to make divorce easier to obtain. However, the relationship between this proposal and decreased fertility is not obvious, since presumably persons who had dissolved unsatisfactory marriages would form new liaisons with more compatible partners. At any rate, the call is for laws which "permit the easy termination of unsuccessful marriages," and the justification is that "present divorce laws encourage the continuation of unsuccessful marriages and the birth of unwanted children into unhappy families" (Howard, 1971:153).

Compulsory sex education in the schools will offer—in the name of the goodness and wholesomeness of human sexuality as a gift of God's creation, the sanctity of natural environment, and the sacredness of life—the following:

1. A shift in emphasis away from procreation to understanding sexual satisfaction;

2. Emphasis on the individual's right and responsibility to limit his reproduction;

288

3. Dissemination of birth-control information; and

4. Provision by the health professions of "free and easy access to voluntary birth control, including sterilization, abortion, and other services related to sexual expression, as the right of all people, regardless of age, sex, or marital or socioeconomic status" (Howard, 1971: 154).

Supplementing the modifications in attitudes about family responsibilities, procreation, and marriage stemming from sex education of this kind will be a broader range of tolerance for forms of sexual expression now considered deviant. In fact, because these forms of expression do not lead to procreation, some have urged that they be approved and affirmed. "Let's face it, homosexuality is pretty good birth control," one author asserts. Another writer suggests that "the time may yet come when homosexuality is practically compulsory and not merely fashionable." Instead of censuring such activity, it is suggested that society must "stress the immorality of irresponsible human reproduction." (Howard, 1970:154; 1971:109; Clark, 1958:57).

In Paul Ehrlich's (1968:140, 147) blueprint for the future, the sex education required by federal law would include:

1. Instruction in the need to regulate the birth rate;

2. Teaching the techniques of birth control at the earliest age recommended by professionals in the area, certainly before junior high school;

3. Emphasis on sex "as an interpersonal relationship, as an important and extremely pleasurable aspect of being human, as mankind's major and most enduring recreation, as a fountainhead of his humor, as a phenomenon that affects every aspect of his being";

4. Deemphasis of the reproductive role of sex by (a) finding substitutes for the satisfaction women derive from childbearing and men from "excessive fatherhood" and (b) promoting a "rational" atmosphere which will make it easier to deal with venereal disease and illegitimacy;

5. Emphasis by biologists of the "biological absurdity of equating a zygote (the cell created by joining of sperm and egg) or fetus (unborn child) with a human being."

In addition, there would be laws guaranteeing any woman an abortion if a physician agreed, and guaranteeing to both sexes the right to voluntary sterilization. Both the "reform" in abortion and sterilization laws and the legislation necessary to insure compul-

289

sory sex education would be drafted, "sold" to the public, and pushed through congress by a powerful "Department of Population and Environment." This Department would also sponsor research on mass sterilizing agents and be responsible for informing the public about the need for population control. Its mandate would be broad and its powers immense; it would have the power "to take whatever steps are necessary to establish a reasonable population size in the United States and to put an end to the steady deterioration of our environment" (Ehrlich, 1968:138).

Not all the neo-Malthusians are enthusiastic about the consequences of proposed changes in family structure. Bentley Glass (1971:160), a leading geneticist and President of the National Association of Biology Teachers, is deeply concerned about the future of the family:

> ... the conscious control of human population increase by means of effective contraception will inevitably loosen our sexual mores. The sex life, permitted to become promiscuous, will threaten marriage and weaken the stability of the family. I do not see how this can be prevented, but I am fearful of the consequences unless some satisfactory social alternative to the family rearing of children can be devised. ... The family group has been the basis of his finest emotional qualities of love and altruism. The plight of the mother and the child lacking husband and father is exceeded only by the ultimate loneliness of the predatory male and the abandoned child. Man will cease to be the *human* species when this has occurred.

Arthur Dyck, who is Professor of Population Ethics at the Harvard School of Public Health, takes issue with those who have suggested an attack on the institution of parenthood as a mode of population control. Instead, Dyck (NAS, 1971c:634) argues that motherhood and the need for family solidarity should receive *more* emphasis than at present.

> ... we would do well to think of motherhood even more positively and to emphasize the tremendous responsibility entailed by it. If much more than they now do, societies came to measure the quality of parenthood and motherhood by the achievements and the quality of life of children, the constraints on family size would operate even more effectively. ...

It would seem to be a shortsighted policy to attack the institution of motherhood and parenthood generally. *Stressing the quality of mothering and parenthood and, at the same time, providing women with alternative forms of vocation and self-realization would appear to be a morally and demographically superior policy* (emphasis added).

Neutralizing Opposition to Population Control Programs in the United States

The backers of population control legislation recognize that changes in public opinion must precede changes in statute. They affirm that "in time, of course, government controls must come." In the meantime, they seek an indoctrinated populace, so that fertility levels may drop "from free choice of an informed populace." To help that free choice along, and to insure that the "right" choices are made, social pressures are encouraged. The intent is that large families be stigmatized so that "people will be embarrassed to have more than one or two children" (Howard, 1971:154).

Values about parental sacrifice must be changed so that parents of more than two or at the most three children are viewed as irresponsible or selfish:

> Regardless of what individual couples may think they have to offer a child, a large family can no longer in itself be viewed as a social contribution. In fact, children in excess of the number necessary for replacement will increasingly become a liability to our society. If the parents of three children decide to have a fourth, it should be with the full awareness that they are choosing to indulge their personal desires at the expense of the welfare of their society. In short, we must change our ideas about what constitutes social responsibility and what constitutes parental sacrifice. No longer can a parent's contribution be measured in terms of the number of his offspring, however much time, energy, and money he may expend on them. The willingness to keep one's family within an upper limit of three will have to be considered the more socially responsible act; and the couple with but one or two children accorded recognition for the social importance of the sacrifice it makes by not bearing any others (Day and Day, 1964:233).

Other actions aimed at "informing" the populace are recommended by Ehrlich (1968:179-181) in a chapter entitled "What Can You Do?" The reader is asked to:

—"Bombard with mail any elected official who opposed liberalizing abortion laws."

—"Complain bitterly [to magazine or newspaper editors] about

291

any positive treatment of large families. Attack the publicizing of 'mothers of the year' unless they have no more than two children or have adopted the extra ones."
—Assail television or radio programs which feature large families.
—Attack advertising which implies that it is socially acceptable to have more than two children.
—Catholics (or others whose church policies favor large families) are to "let your Church know that you strongly disapprove of its policies on birth control."

Proponents of federal population policy in the United States have identified the American political ideology as the most critical structural barrier preventing a comprehensive policy. The idea of nonvoluntary methods of population control seems "unAmerican." A second barrier is the unfavorable attitude to voluntary birth control held by significant minorities in the population.

After reviewing the various types of proposals, Nash (1971:19-20) concluded that perhaps the most effective route to effective population control, given the American political structure, will be to liberalize abortion laws "so that couples have freedom of choice with respect to carrying pregnancies to term" and at the same time to build courses on population into the public school curricula.

He recognized the problems professionals have encountered in trying to introduce "sex education" in the schools, but feels confident that there is a strong long-term movement toward more permissive abortion laws and toward the incorporation of population courses into school programs. His confidence has several bases. He argues that: (1) resistance to abortion reform is linked to "neofundamentalist" fears of increases in promiscuity following, and such fears will not weather either the altered attitudes toward sex in the "post-Kinsey generation" or the "greater political truth of the relation between poverty, large families and urban unrest"; (2) "neofundamentalist laws against abortion clash with yet another fundamental tenet of American political beliefs—the virtue of individual self-determination"; (3) the opposition to "sex education" may not carry over to courses labeled "population problems." Apparently it will not matter that the content of the course will be much the same; changing the title may suffice to get it past the parents and local school boards; and (4) the college youth of today will set the public opinion of tomorrow, and they are far more liberal than their parents in matters of sexual expression and population control.

Incentives for "Reproductive Responsibility"

Proposed incentive systems for population control may provide positive incentives (rewards for childlessness), negative incentives (punishments for fertility), or a combination of both. Positive incentive programs which have been proposed include payment for sterilization or contraception, payment for periods of nonpregnancy or nonbirth, bonuses for childspacing or nonbirth, "responsibility prizes" for each five years of childless marriage or for voluntary sterilization, public lotteries where only the childless could obtain tickets, and guaranteed pensions for poor parents with few or no children.

The imposition of negative incentives would create antinatalist systems of social services in place of the pronatalist systems which currently prevail. Suggested negative incentives are withdrawal of maternity benefits or child-support allowances after a specified number of births, a tax on births after the "Nth" child, limitation of use of federal social welfare facilities and services to small families, and limiting free public education to a certain number of child-years per family (Berelson, 1969:2).

Ehrlich (1968:137) believes that for the United States, at least, the financial reward and penalty system would be the most workable policy. He recommends that the first and second child would each add $600 to a family's taxable income, and after the second child the "reverse deduction" would double. In addition, he would add luxury taxes to diapers, cribs, layettes, and other baby furnishings—always allowing that the essentials were available to the poor—so that there was enough financial pressure to discourage "reproductive irresponsibility."

> In short, the plush life would be difficult to attain for those with large families—which is as it should be, since they are getting their pleasure from their children, who are being supported in part by more responsible members of society.

Direct Control—"Coercion in a Good Cause"

The direct control by government of the right to bear children is frequently raised as a specter of last resort if people don't

293

conform to the neo-Malthusian's ideas about ideal family size: "People must develop much greater voluntary restraint in reproduction—or conception itself will have to come under government control" (Howard, 1971:153).

Some of the experts go even farther, substituting declarative for conditional statements. Hardin (1970b:44) asserts that "over-population cannot be stopped by individual consciences," and cites Kingsley Davis' (1967) studies of desired family size as evidence that women want more children than nations need to achieve zero population growth. The conclusion is that making every child a wanted child is simply not enough: "If only wanted children are born the population will grow out of control." Accordingly, coercion will be necessary:

> If we try to control population by an appeal to individual consciences, we set up a selective system that favors the conscienceless. That is, those members of society who resist the call to have fewer families will leave more descendants than will those who respond to such a call. Therefore, in the long run, *a purely voluntary system of birth control cannot achieve the goal of national (or international) population control. In the long run, some form of community coercion—gentle or severe, explicit or cryptic—will have to be employed* (Hardin, 1970b:45; emphasis added).

The coercion could be achieved by mass use of a "fertility control agent" designed to lower a society's fertility by a given level, or by the addition of temporary sterilants in water or food supplies. Antidotes to the temporary sterilants might be rationed by the government. Other proposals include the requirement of licenses to have children; temporary sterilization of all girls and of mothers after each delivery, with reversibility allowed only after government approval; compulsory sterilization of men with three or more living children; or compulsory abortions for all illegitimate pregnancies (Berelson, 1969:2; Ehrlich, 1968:135-136).

The technology for introduction of mass sterilizing agents does not yet exist. But we do know how to sterilize, and Ehrlich (1968:165-166) argues that the United States, in the absence of effective international machinery for population control, should take unilateral action when opportunities arise.

> A good example of how we might have acted can be built around the Chandrasekhar incident. . . . When he suggested sterilizing all Indian

males with three or more children, we should have applied pressure on the Indian government to go ahead with the plan. We should have volunteered logistic support in the form of helicopters, vehicles, and surgical instruments. We should have sent doctors to aid in the program by setting up centers for training para-medical personnel to do vasectomies. *Coercion? Perhaps, but coercion in a good cause. . . . We must be relentless in pushing for population control around the world.* (emphasis added).

Another writer who rejects voluntary family planning as a solution to population control is Garrett Hardin, who asserts that "Retaining a measure of freedom of choice is always desirable, other things being equal. *But other things are not equal. . . .*" (Hardin, 1971:567). Family planning, he says, might work in a system where the children's survival depended entirely on the family which produced them. But our present society has introduced a social welfare system with the consequence that:

The family has the children, and the community feeds them. . . . Adopting the philosophy of a welfare society does not merely ensure that children shall not starve; it also makes it certain that family planning cannot achieve population control (1971:570).

Accordingly, there is only one solution: "Only by making parenthood a privilege, to be enjoyed under specified conditions and to a specified extent, can society achieve population control" (1971:570).

Moral problems which Hardin's proposed compulsory system of population control might raise are handily dealt with:

Increasing control of "natural" processes has loaded new responsibilities on mankind in moral matters. *Absolute ethics must be replaced by situation ethics.* . . . The essential doctrine of situation ethics is this: the morality of an act is a function of the state of the system at the time it is performed. (1971:573; emphasis added).

Some of the moral implications of the compulsory population control programs are discussed in the following section of this paper. But let us emphasize now that the writers urging the adoption of such drastic measures are presently in the minority, although many more suggest that some form of coercive control may be necessary if other types of population control are not effective. However, the publicizing of proposals for coercive con-

295

trol may have important latent functions: ". . . the more extreme or controversial proposals tend to legitimate more moderate advances, by shifting the boundaries of discourse" (Berelson, 1969:12).

In summary, there seems to be a "natural" progression in state efforts to achieve population control, with recognition of population growth as a problem followed by research by experts and then establishment of family planning programs. If "success" is not achieved by voluntary programs, the progression then seems to be to move from "soft" programs to the more coercive approaches. Among the proposals Berelson (1969:12) has identified as most likely to be adopted are institutionalization of maternal care, population study in the schools, use of television satellite system for dissemination of population control information, better contraceptive technology, and liberalization of abortion. He argues that testing the effectiveness of such measures will take time, and suggests that adoption of the more coercive approaches be postponed, perhaps forever.

References

Bartel, Sherly
    1972   A letter to the editor. Washington State University Daily Evergreen (February 16):4.

Barnett, Harold J.
    1971   "Population problems—myths and realities." Economic Development and Cultural Change 19 (July):545-559.

Berelson, Bernard
    1969   "Beyond family planning." Studies in Family Planning. The Population Council No. 38 (February):16.

Brown, Harrison
    1971   "After the population explosion." Saturday Review (June 26):11-13,29.

Clark, Arthur C.,
    1958   "Standing Room Only." Harpers (April):57.

Davis, Kingsley
1967   "Population policy: will current programs suc-
               ceed?" Science 158:730.

Day, Lincoln H., and Alice Taylor Day
1964   Too Many Americans. Boston: Houghton
               Mifflin.

Ehrlich, Paul
1968   The Population Bomb. New York: Ballantine
               Books.

Ehrlich, Paul R., and Anne H. Ehrlich
1970   Population, Resources, Environment: Issues in
               Human Ecology. San Francisco: W. H. Freeman.

Glass, Bentley
1971   "The human multitude: forces in the rising
               tide." The American Biology Teacher 33:3
               (March):145-149,160.

Hardin, Garrett
1970a   "Choices of parenthood." Science 170 (October
               16):259-262.

1970b   "Everybody's guilty: the ecological dilemma."
               California Medicine 113 (November):40-47.

1971   "Population, biology, and the law." Journal of
               Urban Law 48 (April):563-578.

Hoffer, Eric
1951   The True Believer. New York: Harper and
               Brothers. Perennial Library edition, 1966.

Howard, Walter E.
1971   "The population crisis." The American Biology
               Teacher 33 (March):149-154.

Hutchinson, E. P.
1967   The Population Debate: The Development of

Conflicting Theories up to 1900. Boston: Houghton Miflin.

Ismach, Judy
1971   "Population curb in sight." Seattle Post Intelligencer (August 5):39.

Kammeyer, Kenneth (ed.)
1969   "Food and population: the wrong problem," by Jean Mayer in Population Studies: Selected Essays and Research, Chicago: Rand McNally.

Mayer, Jean
1969   "Toward a non-Malthusian population policy." Columbia Forum 12 (Summer):5-13.

Mills, Stephanie
1970   "Saving the human race." The Family Planner (January-February):11.

NAS (National Academy of Sciences)
1971a   Rapid Population Growth: Consequences and Policy Implications. Baltimore: Johns Hopkins Press.

1971b   "The effects of population growth on resource adequacy and quality," by Joseph L. Fisher and Neal Potter in Rapid Population Growth: Consequences and Policy Implications. Baltimore: Johns Hopkins Press.

1971c   "Population policies and ethical acceptability," by Arthur J. Dyck in Rapid Population Growth: Consequences and Policy Implications. Baltimore: Johns Hopkins Press.

Nash, A. E. Keir
1971   "Going beyond John Locke? influencing American population growth." Milbank Memorial Fund Quarterly 49 (January):7-13.

Prindle, Richard A.
1969   "The population crisis." Archives of Environ-
              mental Health 19 (October):564-569.

Taylor, Gordon Rattray
1968   The Biological Time Bomb. New York: World
              Publishing Company.

Udall, Stewart L.
1967   "Our perilous population implosion." Saturday
              Review (September 2):10-13.

Wertham, Frederic
1969   A Sign for Cain: an Exploration of Human Vio-
              lence. New York: The Macmillan Company.

Westoff, Leslie Aldridge, and Charles F. Westoff
1968   From Now to Zero. Boston: Little and Brown.

Wrong, Dennis H.
1964   "Population myths." Commentary 38 (Novem-
              ber):61-64.

Population Policies
and
Ethical Acceptability*

Arthur J. Dyck

Population policy proposals advocate ways of coping with problems associated with rapid population growth. Defining the problematic charactë. of rapid population growth is an assessment of what is "wrong with the world," or "what is bad for people." Without defining what is harmful about a given demographic situation and specifying the benefits that would follow from changing it by means of a given policy, a recommendation would lack legitimation. Population policy proposals and population analyses alike make judgments about what is ethically acceptable and unacceptable. In assessing any given population policy recommendation, therefore, it is appropriate to ask not only whether it is likely to work and likely to be adopted, but also whether it is ethically acceptable, that is, whether it is a policy we *ought* to adopt (Berelson, 1969:1-16).**

*Reprinted by permission from *Rapid Population Growth: Consequences and Policy Implications,* published for the National Academy of Sciences by The John Hopkins Press, Baltimore and London, 1971, pages 618-638.

**Berelson delineates ethical acceptability as one of six criteria by means of which he evaluates population policy proposals. Berelson does not restrict ethical acceptability to normative meaning but uses it also in a purely descriptive way by asking whether a given proposal is congruent with the values of those who will be affected, whatever those values may be.

The purpose of this essay is to evaluate the ethical acceptability of population policy proposals and, at the same time, to suggest a framework for making such evaluations.

The Meaning of Ethical Acceptability

In this paper, "ethical acceptability" has two meanings. First, it is used as a normative criterion. One can ask of any given population policy whether it corresponds to what people *ought* to value and whether it resolves conflicts of value in the way that these *ought* to be resolved. These are questions for normative ethics, questions as to what things are right or wrong, good or bad. Among the most universally recognizable normative criteria identified by ethicists are freedom, distributive justice, veracity, and the calculation of benefits and harms, including, at one extreme, harms that threaten survival (Ross, 1930).*

However, normative assessments of the rightness or wrongness of given population policy proposals may differ. Where disagreements exist, it is necessary to specify criteria for adjudicating moral disputes. This brings us to the second meaning of "ethical acceptability." It can refer to what is specified by meta-ethical criteria, i.e., criteria that provide us with reasons, or a set of procedures, for preferring one moral judgment over another.

There is growing agreement among ethicists that the rationality of moral claims is to be judged by the extent to which they satisfy the following criteria: knowledge of facts; vivid imagination of how others are affected by our actions; and impartiality with respect to both our interests and our passions, so that what obtains for one person obtains for another and for ourselves as well. These criteria are derived from an analysis of moral discourse and

---

*See Ross's work for a more complete list, one which is widely used and referred to among professional ethicists. Ross calls these norms "prima facie duties." Prima facie duties specify recognizable right- and wrong-making characteristics of actions. Specific actions or policies will be right or wrong insofar as they exhibit one or the other of these characteristics. For example, the act of telling a lie to save a friend violates the prima facie duty of truth-telling but satisfies the prima facie duty of not harming others. To decide the rightness or wrongness of particular actions or policies will usually involve a process of weighing conflicting moral claims upon us. The normative criteria I have specified are to be understood as prima facie claims.

describe the kinds of considerations that arise in the processes of formulating or reformulating our own moral judgments, and of attempting to resolve disputes (Baier, 1958; Brandt, 1959; Firth, 1952:317-345; Frankena, 1963; Hare, 1963; Mandlebaum, 1955). They are embodied in our social and institutional practices and appear in classical attempts to describe an ideal moral judge (Firth, 1952:317-345).

Using these normative and meta-ethical criteria, this paper will explore the ethical acceptability of some major population policy proposals.

Questions of Distributive Justice

The ethical acceptability of any population policy will certainly hinge on the relation it bears to distributive justice—to the way in which goods and benefits are to be divided. In terms of this paper, achieving a just distribution of goods is governed by two principles: each person participating in a practice or affected by it has an equal right to the most extensive liberty compatible with a like liberty for all; and inequalities are justifiable only where it is reasonable to expect that they will work out for everyone's advantage and provided that the positions and offices to which they attach or from which they may be gained are open to all (Rawls, 1958:164-194).

Distributive justice is a strongly held value. Gross inequalities with respect to one's share in a society's goods or one's opportunity to change a disadvantageous position (as in slavery) can prompt people to risk death. It is in the interest of society as well as individuals to satisfy the principles of distributive justice.

Population policy proposals that advocate the use of positive or negative incentives are very directly involved in questions of distributive justice. "Positive incentives" means the governmental inducements that take the form of direct payments of money, goods, or services to members of the target population in return for the desired practice of limiting births. "Negative incentives" are tax or welfare penalties exacted from couples that exceed a specified number of children.

Ketchel (1968:687-703) has described very well some of the forms of injustice that would be generally perpetrated by population policies resorting to positive and negative incentives:

303

In underdeveloped countries practically no financial inducements to have children now exist to be reversed, and the imposition of further taxes upon the many poor people would depress their living standards even further and probably only succeed in raising the death rates. In developed countries people in higher economic groups could still afford to have as many children as they wished so the economic pinch associated with having children would be felt mainly by middle-class and lower-middle-class people, to whom the cost of having children, though somewhat eased by government economic favors, is still relatively high. In order to be effective, economic pressures would probably seriously affect the welfare of the children who were born in spite of the pressures. It seems to me that the same arguments apply to the use of economic pressures to lower the birth rate as are used to argue against the issue of suppressing illegitimacy by cutting off aid to dependent children. If children become a financial burden, there will be fewer of them, but those that are born will be punished by being deprived of precisely those economic advantages they should have, both for humanitarian reasons and for their growth and development into worthwhile citizens. The same objection applies to the use of financial rewards to induce people not to have children because such programs would make the families with children the poorer families. A further objection to the use of economic pressures or rewards is that, since they would be primarily effective against certain economic groups, such methods are discriminatory.

Among the variety of specific proposals to use positive incentives is one that advocates the provision of pensions for poor parents with fewer than N children as social security for their old age (Ohlin, 1967; Samuel, 1966:12-14; Spengler, 1969:1234-1238). This particular policy recommendation is perhaps the least unjust of all the proposals involving incentives, especially in less developed countries where pensions are largely unavailable at present and parents depend upon their children for social security.

If social security were provided for those parents who had no more than some specified number of children, this provision would not severely, or directly, affect the lives of children in economic conditions where it is not normally possible to save money. Similarly, it would not discriminate much against parents who exceeded the specified number of children for they would, as has been the custom, look to their children for social security.

It is true that the whole society would bear the cost of this pension plan, but such a cost could be seen as enhancing the general welfare of the society, and, therefore, as a mutually advantageous burden to bear, even though it would discriminate some-

304

what against the grown children of large families if they were required to support their parents and contribute to the cost of the pension plan as well.

In any estimate of the benefit/harm ratio that would obtain should some policy of positive or negative incentives be initiated, it is important to consider the way in which these benefits and harms are distributed, and to take care particularly not to discriminate against the poor. Generally, the chances that the children of the poor will get a good education, that they will survive to adulthood, and that they will have a good and productive life and thus realize the hopes for the future that the parents have invested in them are not nearly as good as for the children of people at higher incomes. Having only two or three children may, from the vantage point of the poor, look precarious.

In *Children of Crisis,* Coles (1964) asks whether many of us understand what a new child means to many of our poverty-stricken mothers, to the men in their lives, and to their other children. To further our understanding, he cites the following very dramatic and articulate account by a black mother:

> The worst of it is that they try to get you to plan your kids by the year; except they mean by the ten-year plan, one every ten years. The truth is, they don't want you to have any, if they could help it. To me, having a baby inside me is the only time I'm really alive. I know I can make something, do something, no matter what color my skin is, and what names people call me. When the baby gets born I see him, and he's full of life, or she is; and I think to myself that it doesn't make any difference what happens later, at least now we've got a chance, or the baby does. You can see the little one grow and get larger and start doing things, and you feel there must be some hope, some chance that things will get better; because there it is, right before you, a real, live, growing baby. The children and their father feel it, too, just like I do. They feel the baby is a good sign, or at least he's some sign. If we didn't have that, what would be the difference from death? Even without children my life would still be bad—they're not going to give us what *they* have, the birth control people. They just want us to be a poor version of them only without our children and our faith in God and our tasty fried food, or anything.
>
> They'll tell you we are "neglectful"; we don't take proper care of the children. But that's a lie, because we do, until we can't any longer because the time has come for the street to claim them, to take them away and teach them what a poor nigger's life is like. I don't care what anyone says: I take the best care of my children. I scream the ten commandments at them every day, until one by one they learn them by heart—and believe me they don't forget them. (You can ask my min-

ister if I'm not telling the truth.) It's when they leave for school, and start seeing the streets and everything, that's when there's the change; and by the time they're ten or so, it's all I can do to say anything, because I don't believe my own words, to be honest. I tell them, please to be good; but I know it's no use, not when they can't get a fair break, and there are the sheriffs down South and up here the policemen, ready to kick you for so much as breathing your feelings. So I turn my eyes on the little children, and keep on praying that one of them will grow up at the right second, when the schoolteachers have time to say hello and give him the lessons that he needs, and when they get rid of the building here and let us have a place you can breathe in and not get bitten all the time, and when the men can find work—because *they* can't have children, and so they have to drink or get on drugs to find some happy moments, and some hope about things.

This graphic description of the feelings of one poverty-stricken mother underlines the claims of distributive justice. In any population policy, attention must be given to the problem of poverty—not so much because the poor have relatively high birth rates but rather because the conditions under which it is just and rational to expect anyone to curtail family size do not occur in dire poverty. Infant mortality rates are high enough, educational opportunities scarce enough, job opportunities uncertain enough to undermine the usual rationale for careful family planning. Alleviating conditions of poverty and delivering better health care to the poor must be part of any population policy, if it is to be just and effective.

Clearly, population policies that employ positive and negative incentives will create injustices by discriminating against the poor and by bringing about less advantageous economic conditions, or even poverty where penalties are severe, for the children of parents who are subject to penalties or who fail to gain rewards, unless special adjustments are made for these groups. However, making these adjustments may reduce the effectiveness of incentive programs. In any event, there is no direct evidence that incentives reduce birth rates and, therefore, no assurance that any injustices that might be perpetrated through the use of incentives would be worth the price.

What about the use of compulsion to secure the goals of population policy? Compulsion, on the face of it, is the most predictable and rational way to achieve the exact birth rates considered desirable or necessary for a given nation. Boulding has suggested marketable licenses to have children in whatever number that would ensure a zero growth rate, say 2.2 children per couple: the unit certificate might be the deci-child, and accumulation of ten of these units by purchase, inheritance, or gift, would permit a woman in maturity to have one legal child (Boulding, 1964:135-136). Another proposal by Ketchel advocates mass use by government of a fertility-control agent that would lower fertility in the society by 5 to 75 percent less than the present birth rate, as needed (Ketchel, 1968:687-703). Such a substance is now unknown but would, he believes, be available for field testing after 5 to 15 years of research. It would be put in the water supply in urban areas and introduced by other methods elsewhere. Variants of compulsory sterilization, both temporary and permanent, and compulsory abortions have been proposed as well (Davis, 1969:730-739; Ehrlich and Ehrlich, 1970).

Aside from the obvious technical and administrative difficulties of all of these proposals, especially in less developed countries, the effectiveness of a policy of compulsion is directly dependent upon its ethical acceptability. Any law can be disobeyed, or subverted, and the problem of punishing offending parents is especially acute. Could it be done, for example, without inflicting suffering upon innocent children? Obviously fines and jail sentences would be a hardship for children as well as parents no matter what provision society would make for the children. Compulsory sterilizations and abortions could be used to enforce a specific quota of children per couple, but these methods are ethically unacceptable for reasons that will be discussed later.

Compulsion, like incentives, discriminates against the poor. Restricting the very poor to two or three children would render their lives much less joyous, much less hopeful, and much more precarious. In less developed countries, such restrictions for the poor mean economic losses in the form of reductions both in labor and in security for their old age.

Suppose, however, that the gross poverty in a given population group were virtually eliminated. What other ethical objections to the use of compulsion would remain? The most conspicuous argument against compulsion is that it is incompatible with the freedom to pursue our own happiness and forge our own destiny. How cogent is this argument?

Questions of Freedom

Freedom refers in part to the relative absence of government interference and compulsion concerning those actions that are not harmful to the public interest. It refers also to what we sometimes call equality of opportunity, that is, the opportunity to determine and change one's economic, social, and political status within one's society. Freedom in both the senses I have specified is as strong a value as survival itself. People will risk death to obtain it for themselves and others. They will not trade it off completely for some other actual or potential benefit. Moreover, freedom serves public interests as well as private ones. Some freedom of speech, for example, is an essential component of any society; it is a necessary prerequisite to social intercourse.

However, freedom is not always incompatible with compulsion. One of the ways in which freedom is secured through compulsory regulations is illustrated by the laws governing traffic. Without such laws, it is difficult to imagine how the freedom to drive private automobiles in crowded areas could be maintained. Compulsory education also guarantees and enhances freedom. Compulsion can prevent great harm both to individuals and to society. One example is compulsory vaccination to prevent epidemics, as well as individual suffering. In all of these examples, certain choices are taken away from the individual, and yet his total freedom is increased. Would compulsion in limiting the number of one's children be comparable to any of these examples? To answer this question, one must try to characterize more nearly the kind of decision involved in choosing whether or not to have children and how many to have.

In Plato's *Symposium,* Socrates notes that there are three ways in which people can try to satisfy their deep longing for immortality (Dialogues of Plato, 1937:332-334). One way is to have children. Another is to commit a deed or deeds noble and heroic enough to receive the attention of one's community and become a part of its collective memory. A third way is that of scholarly pursuit and authorship. Each attempt to achieve immortality depends for its success upon the receptivity and support of one's community. Children, therefore, provide a deeply gratifying link to the human community and to the future. Decisions about how we will use our reproductive powers are decisions about our own future and about our own contributions to the future of the human community, about how one's life is to count, and how far its influence is to extend.

308

Sexuality is at once an expression of our individuality, and a gift that each of us receives from others, his parents most immediately, but also from the wider community. Indeed, it is a gift from the human species to the human species. We owe a debt of *gratitude* to these wellsprings of our unique genetic and social individuality for the very possibility of experiencing sexual pleasure, and for the considerable rewards of childbearing and child rearing.

As those who have been chosen to live, we incur an awesome but joyous obligation to see to it that these gifts of life—sexual expression, procreation, and child rearing—have a future. Our obligation to the larger community is particularly vital insofar as each of us has unique genetic endowments and unique talents to offer and to perpetuate. No one else can give to the species what we bring to it. Failure to reproduce is both an individual and a communal act that requires a special justification if it is to be morally responsible. Individual decisions to refrain from having children of one's own are presumably easier to justify in times of rapid population growth.

If these are the values guiding our reproductive decisions, the very dignity and identity of the person as a moral being is at stake in any decision to use compulsion in controlling reproductive behavior. There are those who believe that the dignity and autonomy associated with reproductive decisions is a human right provided for in the United States Constitution. As part of its successful effort to defeat the birth control laws of Connecticut in the Supreme Court, the Planned Parenthood Federation of America argued that these laws, by forcing couples to relinquish either their right to marital sex relations or their right to plan their families, constituted a deprivation of life and liberty without due process of law in violation of the Fourteenth Amendment (Griswold vs. Connecticut, 381 U.S. 479, 1965). Earlier Supreme Court decisions were cited affirming the right "to marry, establish a home and bring up children" as among "those privileges essential to the orderly pursuit of happiness by free men" under the Fourteenth Amendment (Meyer vs. Nebraska, 262 U.S. 390, 399, 1923; Skinner vs. Oklahoma, 316 U.S. 535, 1942; United Nations General Assembly, 1961). In a "Declaration on Population" presented at the United Nations in 1957, thirty nations, including the United States, affirmed their belief "that the opportunity to decide the

309

number and spacing of children is a basic human right" and "that family planning, by assuring greater opportunity to each person, frees man to attain his individual dignity and reach his full potential" (Studies in Family Planning 26, 1968:3).

But it is precisely on this point that the battle has been enjoined. Davis has directly challenged the right of any person to determine for himself how many children he shall have, because, in his view, the assertion of such a right conflicts with society's need to keep the number of children at some specified level (Davis, 1969:730-739). In this instance, Davis, like many others, sees a conflict between individual rights and interests on the one hand, and societal necessities and interests on the other.

But has Davis correctly characterized those interests we call human rights? I am convinced that it is not correct to think of a human right as something that can come into conflict with our public interests. To identify a human value as a right is to claim that something of value is *so* valuable and *so* precious that society has a stake in it—for example, freedom of speech, which is generally considered to be a human right (United Nations General Assembly, 1961:Article 19).

Rights imply duties.* When we say that freedom of speech is a right, we imply that it is our duty, and the duty of others, to see to it that freedom of expression is generally honored and protected. In claiming that freedom of speech is a right that society should protect, we are not claiming that every utterance ought to be sanctioned regardless of its consequences. Clearly, the right to free speech is not abrogated by considering it a crime to cry "fire" falsely in a crowded theatre (Holmes, 1919). The important thing, however, is that the interests in encouraging certain utterances, and in discouraging others, are both public and private. It is of benefit both to individuals and to society to encourage free expression generally, and to discourage certain forms of it under special circumstances.

This is true also of decisions regarding the nature and the number of one's children. In asserting that it is the right of individual couples to make such decisions voluntarily, we are positing

---

*See, for example, books by Carritt and Ewing. I would abstractly define a right much in the way Ewing does, to refer to powers or securities that an individual or group can rightly demand of other individuals or groups that they should not normally interfere with them.

both an obligation and an interest of society to see to it that this right is honored. At the same time, it is in the interest both of individuals and of society to curtail the extensive expression of this choice should the consequences of rapid growth rates become too oppressive or threatening. If, therefore, society is to avoid a conflict between two public interests—the interest in maintaining the quality of life against the interest in maintaining the right to decide voluntarily the number of one's children—every effort must be made to provide the information, materials, and conditions that will assist individuals to limit their births voluntarily for their own welfare and for the common good.

For the sake of argument, let us imagine a hypothetical situation in which a particular government has used every conceivable program to bring down its population growth rates, and these programs have failed. As a result, the nation must attain nothing short of zero growth rates very quickly or face consequences that the government and its people feel they must avoid, even at great cost. Under these circumstances, compulsory measures to curb birth rates might be justified as a last resort.

However, I wish to argue that *not every compulsory measure can be justified even as a last resort.* The continuation of human life depends upon the exercise of our reproductive powers. To maintain a population at a replacement level requires slightly more than two children per couple at the death rates now prevailing in affluent nations. In principle, every couple in this world could be granted the right and privilege to have at least two children of their own.* The threat of overpopulation is not in itself a sufficient argument for singling out any given type of individual for compulsory sterilizations or compulsory abortions. The suggestion by Davis (1969:730-739) that abortions be required in cases in which the child would be illegitimate not only dries up the most

---

*In the United States there are sterilization laws in some states that permit the sterilization of certain classes of people. In North Carolina, for example, the mentally ill, the feebleminded, and epileptics may be sterilized (Woodside, 1950). Presumably these are voluntary sterilizations in the sense that the consent of guardians is required, but the state can appoint such guardians. The constitutionality of this procedure in the case of the feeble-minded was upheld in Buck vs. Bell, 274 U.S. 200 (1927). The North Carolina law and others like it are ethically very questionable. In *Skinner vs. Oklahoma,* 316 U.S. 535, (1942), the Supreme Court did declare a law permitting the sterilization of "habitual criminals" to be unconstitutional.

311

important source of children for sterile couples but also denies the unwed woman any right to a moral decision regarding either the fate of her fetus or the physical risks to which she will be subjected.

The right to exercise one's procreative powers is not identical with the right to have as many children as one wants through the use of those powers. In a situation of last resort, society might very well decide to ration the number of children per family and try to provide some just means, like a lottery, for deciding who will be permitted to reproduce more than two children. This limits the right to choose how many children one will have but not the right to choose to have one or two children of one's own. Ketchel's proposal threatens this right, since by the use of sterilants that reduce everyone's fertility some people are involuntarily made infertile. Of course, if Ketchel can prevent or offset such mishaps, his proposal could be used as a method of rationing.

The right to have a choice regarding the exercise of one's procreative powers and to be able to retain the capacity to procreate is as fundamental as the right to life.* Choosing to have a child of one's own is a choice as to one's own genetic continuity. One should be free to express one's gratitude to one's parents and to honor their desire for continuity in the human community; one should be free to seek a place in the memory of future generations. If our lives are to be deprived of any choices in establishing

---

*To say a right is "fundamental" means, in this context, that it is the kind of right that is recognizable as universal, that is, a right belonging to every human being qua human being, as it is in the United Nations, "Universal Declaration of Human Rights," articles 1-3 (United Nations General Assembly, 1961). It would be recognized as such by an ideal observer who is fully informed and impartial, and who can vividly imagine how his actions affect others. For a full description of such an ideal moral judge, see Firth (1952). Furthermore, a fundamental right has a prima facie claim upon us. See Ewing (1947) for his arguments against absolutistic theories of rights. A fundamental right, therefore, always has some claim on us, but there may be circumstances in which a particular fundamental right cannot be honored because of a conflict between more than one individual or more than one fundamental right. When one person, for example, attacks another, the person who is attacked may justifiably defend his right to life even when this might necessitate taking the life of the aggressor. In the example cited earlier, the right to free speech is justifiably abrogated in instances when, as in the case of falsely shouting fire in a crowded theatre, it seriously threatens the right to life of a great many people.

312

these links to the past and the future, we have lost a great deal of what life is all about and, indeed, we have lost the most predictable way known to us of extending our lives on this earth. Very few people achieve immortality on earth in other ways. Compulsory, irreversible sterilization, I would contend, is not an ethically acceptable method of curbing birth rates.

Our draft system is often used as an analogy for justifying the use of compulsion to meet the needs of society. A just war, fought with just means, as a last resort, and in self-defense, would seem to justify conscription. But even in this situation, conscientious objectors are exempted from military service. Population policies should make a similar provision for those who cannot in good conscience submit to sterilization, or have an abortion, or stay for other reasons within a given rationing scheme. Presumably, when population problems are a clear and present danger, most people will wish to limit the number of their children. Precedents in human history are now well known; hunter-gather societies now being studied in the deserts of Africa keep their populations at levels that guarantee them ample food and leisure for what they regard as the good life (Thomas, Harold, unpublished manuscript). They have what modern societies will need to develop, namely a very keen appreciation of the limits of their environment and their own technical capacities to benefit from it without harming it.

Although I believe it is wise to sort out in advance what forms of compulsion would be least evil as last resorts, I consider any compulsory control of birth rates unjustifiable now and in the indefinite future for at least three reasons. First, famines and environmental deterioration are not exclusively a function of population growth rates; second, more practical and ethically acceptable alternatives to compulsion exist and have not yet been sufficiently tested; and third, there are distinct benefits associated with small families which can be facilitated and the knowledge of which can be more widely disseminated.

Questions of Benefits and Harms

Nutritional deficiencies and ecological imbalances will not be eradicated simply by reducing or even halting growth rates. To overcome these harms, agricultural development and pollution

313

abatement will be necessary even if zero growth rates were to be immediately achieved throughout the world. The reasons for this are thoroughly discussed elsewhere (Revelle, 1968:362-391; Goldsmith, et al., 1967:1-135; Revelle, 1969).*

Rapid population growth rates do make it more difficult to feed people, to prevent environmental deterioration, and to maintain the quality of life in other ways. Are there population policies that are more beneficial than harmful and which do not involve injustices or serious threats to human freedom? I wish to suggest some.

In a country like the United States, birth rates have been dropping for the past decade. We have time to see how much more can be done by extending voluntary family planning** by providing health services where needed to improve infant and maternal care, by educating people to the bad consequences of continued population growth for the nation as well as the individual family, and by improving educational and job opportunities for everyone, especially blacks, women, and other currently disadvantaged groups.

What about the situation in less developed countries? On the basis of intensive research over a period of seven years in the Punjab region of India, Gordon and Wyon hypothesize that people in such an area would be motivated to reduce their birth rates if mortality rates for infants and children were sharply decreased, local social units were stimulated to measure their own population dynamics and to draw inferences from them concerning their own welfare and aspirations, and efficient methods of birth control were introduced (Wyon and Gordon, 1967:24-28). Initiating these conditions would substantially increase the opportunities to reduce family size without undue fear, to assess more precisely how fertility affects families and their community, and to plan family size more effectively. Whether birth rates would be markedly lowered by bringing about these conditions alone would depend not simply upon the extent to which people in that region stand to benefit from a reduction in fertility but also upon the

---

*See also Joseph L. Fisher and Neal Potter, "The effects of population growth on resource adequacy and quality," and "The consequences of rapid population growth," in NAS, 1971.

**Liberalized abortion laws are among the methods now being advocated. For a thorough discussion of the wide variety of ethical issues raised by abortion, see Potter (Cutler, 1968).

extent to which they actually perceive such benefits, both social and economic, and believe they are attainable.

Gathering and disseminating information is, therefore, a crucial aspect of this proposal. Without accurate information, a sense of group responsibility cannot exist on a rational basis and will have no perceptible dividend to the individual members. The proposal of Gordon and Wyon assumes that rational and purposeful behavior exists already to some degree and can be modified in the direction of lower fertility by certain modifications in the environment which make small families beneficial and more attainable.

Looking at the total ecological context within which population problems arise in the less developed countries—especially the factors of undernourishment, poverty, and lack of opportunity—some writers have suggested that nothing less than substantial technological, social, and economic changes would provide the conditions under which birth rates can be sufficiently reduced (Revelle, 1969). These changes include industrialization, urbanization, and modern market agriculture. In the demographic history of the West such an environment certainly has been associated with sharp declines in birth rates. Urbanization and industrialization, accompanied as they are by rising levels of literacy, better communications, increased economic opportunities, improved health care, lower infant mortality rates, higher status for women, and higher costs of bearing and rearing children, may be necessary to provide the incentives and the means to control population growth. In these terms, a population policy is an overall social and economic development policy (NAS, 1971).

These two policies would not violate any of our ethical criteria. They would enhance human freedom and encourage responsible community behavior. Indeed, on the face of it they do not violate any of the normative or meta-ethical criteria we have introduced in this essay. Both would increase the elements in the decision-making process of individual couples that contribute to making the morally best decision. They would increase knowledge of the facts, stimulate the imagination of people concerning the effects of reproductive decisions, and encourage impartiality by fostering more universal loyalties that go beyond one's own interests and passions, and those of one's own group.

Gordon and Wyon's proposal has the advantage of introducing a minimum of disruption into a culture. It may, by the same token,

315

be inadequate to induce the requisite behavior without further transformations of the social and economic lot of the people involved. Each of these ethically acceptable population policy proposals relies upon the voluntary decisions of individual couples. Several writers have contended recently that population policies *cannot* rely upon individual couples pursuing their own benefits to satisfy the needs of society (Davis, 1969:730-739; Hardin, 1969:1243-1248; Ehrlich and Ehrlich, 1970; Blake, 1969:522-529).

Hardin, for example, has argued that in matters of reproduction individual interests are definitely incompatible with collective interests and, therefore, population growth rates will have to be regulated by society (Hardin, 1969:1243-1248). How cogent is this argument?

His argument rests on what he calls "the tragedy of the commons." Where a finite amount of grazing land is available to a number of sheepherders, each sheepherder will add sheep to his own flock, ultimately amassing a larger total number of sheep than the land will sustain. Although each individual sheepherder is aware of this fact, his immediate decisions are determined, nonetheless, by the profit he contemplates from adding another sheep to his flock. The knowledge that the commons will at some point be overgrazed, if everyone does this, does not suffice to deter him.

All of this seems reasonable enough when one is talking about sheep. But does the analogy extend to decisions of parents regarding the number of their children? Are the benefits of adding a child to our own families even roughly comparable with the benefits that come from enhancing our economic status?

In discussing freedom, I took the view that children are one means of extending our own selfhood into the future, of obtaining some kind of personal continuity. Children are also a way of replenishing the human community in which we hope to live on as a cherished memory. One child surviving into adulthood and having children of his own will suffice to maintain our own continuity. If our self-interest is extensive enough to embrace a concern for the continuation of society and of the species, two or three children will be enough.

However, in some circumstances we may feel disquieted about limiting ourselves to two or three children. When, for example, we

316

live under conditions in which infant mortality is high, we may very well want to have one or two extra children to be sure that two will survive us, or at least will live to have children of their own.

A second set of satisfactions and opportunities is associated with childbearing and child rearing. To the extent that having a child is a quest for the experience of rearing a child, it is not clear that relatively large families are best. For those satisfactions that come from the quality and frequency of one's contacts with one's own children, small families are preferable to large families. In very large families, the older children, not the parents, obtain most of the satisfactions of playing, of training, and of other forms of intimate interaction with the younger ones. Parental contacts with children in a large family are more likely to occur as disruptions for a busy mother than as opportunities for a show of affection and an exchange of ideas.

The benefits of bearing children are somewhat more ambiguous. At present there is no sure knowledge as to the strength of the drive to bear a child and what role this plays in the number people have. The desire to have the experience of giving birth may be satisfied with the birth of one child. Some women, however, may covet the repetition of this kind of experience.* One psychoanalyst has expressed his amazement that the desire to bear children is so easily and quickly satiated (Wyatt, 1967:29-56). Such satiation may result from the long period of dependency typical of human offspring, as well as from the physical exertion, pain, and risks of childbirth itself. Whatever joys may be associated with our children, there are also lifelong concerns and anxieties.

Spacing the interval between births is good for both children and parents (NAS, 1971). It enhances the intellectual development of children and the health and tranquility of mothers. Even in societies where average family size is relatively large, spacing is extensively practiced (Wyon and Gordon, 1967:24-28).

A fourth element in reproductive decisions, not present in decisions to add a profit-making sheep to our flock, has been

---

*Some women seem to have a strong unconscious urge to bear children even while practicing birth control. Dr. Hilton Salhanick has observed that some women practicing the rhythm method will break or lose their thermometers at the critical juncture in their menstrual cycle.

317

observed by Rainwater.* In his intensive studies of working-class parents, he found that among those who had more children than they professed to want there were parents who reported that they had exceeded their own family-size ideals because they did not wish to be seen as selfish by their neighbors. This desire to be seen as an unselfish, kind, and public-spirited person could be used to bring about a wider acceptance of small family-size ideals. In view of the social problems generated by rapid rates of population growth, generous impulses can now best be exhibited by having only the children that society considers desirable or necessary.

Of course, Hardin might contend that the shepherd who adds to his flock is not deterred by the possibility that such additions will be seen as selfish by other shepherds using the same grazing land. In his case, however, *selfishness* and profit are linked; but in child-bearing and child rearing, *unselfishness* is linked with benefit.

Where children serve to provide a substitute for a social security system or where they bring economic profit through their labor, the situation begins more nearly to approximate the one depicted by Hardin. Nevertheless, the constraints that we have cited obtain even in the rural villages of less developed countries where children are often economic assets. There are some recent indications that in areas where agricultural productivity is increasing, birth rates are coming down, for example in certain areas of India (Wyon, 1969). Given the history of the demographic transition in developed nations, this should hardly come as a surprise. If adding children were like adding sheep to one's flock, however, birth rates should be going up. Surely Hardin's analogy is at best an uncertain one, and, at worst, inappropriate.**

Davis and Blake have also expressed the belief that individual couples will not voluntarily provide for the collective interests of society but will, given the strongly positive public attitude toward parenthood and especially toward motherhood, persist in having relatively large families (Davis, 1969:730-739; Blake, 1969:522-529). Like Hardin, they do not take into account any of the four constraining factors we have cited.

---

*See Rainwater 1960 and 1965, particularly chapters five and six, in which the concern for unselfish parenthood is documented for the middle class as well as the working class.

**This is not to deny the existence of interests that may in the long run keep family size just high enough to prove troublesome.

One could argue, contrary to Davis and Blake, that we would do well to think of motherhood even more positively and to emphasize the tremendous responsibility entailed by it. If, much more than they now do, societies came to measure the quality of parenthood and motherhood by the achievements and the quality of life of children, the constraints on family size would operate even more effectively. If the concern of parents is for the best possible development of their children, then it is important to space children widely, to expose them as much as possible to the stimuli and warm support of parental interaction, and to be a model of unselfish restraint in keeping down the size of one's family. Responsible parenthood of this kind would include living in accord with whatever national fertility goals may become morally desirable or necessary to maintain the quality of human life and guarantee a future for the human species.

Davis and Blake have stressed the need to improve the status of women by providing better and more extensive opportunities for employment and for contributions to society in ways other than through childbearing and child rearing. Employment for women and opportunities to make a variety of contributions to the human community extend the freedom of women. Better and more extensive education for women also has the effect of contributing to the quality of mothering as well as to other forms of self-realization.

It would seem to be a shortsighted policy to attack the institution of motherhood and parenthood generally. Stressing the quality of mothering and parenthood and, at the same time, providing women with alternative forms of vocation and self-realization would appear to be a morally and demographically superior policy.

To claim, as I have, that individual couples and their children benefit in certain ways from keeping families small is not to claim that these benefits will necessarily suffice to offset other forces that now keep many families large enough to maintain rates of population growth rapid enough to be troublesome to certain countries. I am maintaining, however, that to mitigate these latter forces, it is helpful to study, facilitate, and make known the benefits associated with small families; and to expose some of the fallacies of assuming that individual couples who actively seek the satisfaction of childbearing and child rearing will generally benefit most by having relatively large families or even as many children as they can afford.

Veracity and Meta-Ethical Criteria as Practical Guidelines

There are certain practical guidelines that should be part of the formulation and implementation of population policies. Generally, these guidelines draw in a special way upon the norm of veracity, i.e., truth-telling, and promise-keeping, and the meta-ethical criteria specified earlier.

Knowing the Facts

An ideal program that would evoke the voluntary response of the people affected by it would make an honest case for the reproductive behavior called for in the policy. Parents need to know what benefits will accrue to them from limiting the number of their children. Evaluations of population policy recommendations, therefore, must include specific designations of what counts as a population problem and of what interests individuals and societies have in their children. Research is definitely needed to explore more fully the significance and meaning of children to parents in a wide variety of circumstances.

Often, in discussions of population policy, there are allusions to the use of propaganda. This word threatens to create a credibility gap. If by propaganda we mean trying to persuade people that a certain policy is in their interest, without giving them the facts that will allow them to decide whether it *is* actually in their interest, we violate the canons of veracity. Moreover, we do not satisfy the criterion of giving people as many of the facts as possible, and hence do not respect their potential to make a morally correct decision and to act upon it.

Vividly Imagining How Others Are Affected by Our Actions

In some of the literature, there is a distinct elitist strain, implying that only certain people are in a position to formulate population policy and that the rest of mankind must be propagandized, won over by incentives, or compelled to act in ways considered to be desirable by the experts. In contrast to such

320

elitism, ethically acceptable population policies should be based on sympathetic understanding of the conditions of life and of the aspirations of the people who will be affected. To guarantee this, many voices must be heard.

Black people in the United States are among those who are making apparent the value of wide and diverse participation in the planning process and thereby extending the actualization of democratic ideals and the humanization of social institutions. Ways must always be sought to assure that vivid images of how people live, and of what they feel and desire, will guide and shape the planners and their work.

Universalizing Loyalties: Impartiality

To strive for impartiality or universal loyalties is to strive to discount the influence upon our moral judgments of particular interests and passions. For example, we demand of a judge that he not try his own son and that he disqualify himself in an antitrust suit involving a company in which he is a significant shareholder. Similarly, both our constitutional provisions for separate branches of government and our continuing quest for fair judicial process are attempts to minimize the effect of particular interests or passions by providing representation of diverse interests, while at the same time assuring equitable checks and balances.

Problems of rapid population growth make the need for impartiality, our third meta-ethical criterion, concretely explicit. Though survival values within our species are strong and tenacious, they are usually individualized and tied to relatively small interest groups representing one's social, ethnic, and national identity. For the survival of such groups many would, under certain circumstances, make sacrifices and even die. But population policies, though they must attend to the needs and interests of particular regions and population groups, should endeavor to ascertain and foster the best interests of the entire human species in its total ecological setting, a task that embraces attention to other species and material resources as well. The goals of population policies go beyond the boundaries our societal and national interests set for us.

In defining these goals, population policies would fail utterly to improve the human condition and enlist its deepest loyalties were

they to diminish, rather than augment, the extent to which bene-
ficence, freedom, distributive justice, and veracity are realized on
the earth. These are not moral luxuries: our survival, and the
worth of that survival, depend upon their effective implementation. As the demograher Ansley Coale has so sagely observed,
"preoccupation with population growth should not serve to justify
measures more dangerous or of higher social cost than population
growth itself" (Coale, 1968:467). It would be the ultimate irony
of history if through our population policies we should lose
precisely what we seek to save, namely, human rights and welfare.

References

Baier, Kurt
1958   The Moral Point of View. Ithaca, New
                York: Cornell University Press.

Berelson, Bernard
1969   "Beyond family planning." Studies in Family
                Planning 38 (February):1-16.

Berelson, Bernard (ed.)
1966   Family Planning and Population Programs. Chi-
                cago: University of Chicago Press.

Berelson, Bernard, et al. (eds.)
1969   Family Planning Programs: An International
                Survey. New York: Basic Books.

Blake, Judith
1969   "Population policies for Americans: is the gov-
                ernment being misled?" Science 164 :522-529.

Bogue, Donald J.
1966   Principles of Demography. New York: John
                Wiley and Sons.

Boulding, Kenneth
1964   The Meaning of the Twentieth Century: The
                Great Transition. New York: Harper and Row.

Brandt, Richard B.
  1959   Ethical Theory. Englewood Cliffs, New
                  Jersey: Prentice-Hall.

Carritt, E. F.
  1935   Morals and Politics. Clarendon: Oxford Press.

Coale, Ansley
  1968   "Should the United States start a campaign for
                  fewer births?" Population Index Vol. 34 No. 4
                  (October-December):467.

Cobb, John C., Harry M. Raulet, and Paul Harper
  1965   An I.U.D. Field Trial in Lulliani, West Pakistan.
                  A paper presented at the American Public
                  Health Association (October 21).

Coles, Robert
  1964   Children of Crisis. Boston: Atlantic-Little
                  Brown.

Cutler, Donald (ed.)
  1968   "The abortion debate," by Ralph B. Potter Jr. in
                  The Religious Situation 1968. Boston: Beacon
                  Press.

Davis, Kingsley
  1969   "Population policy: will current programs
                  succeed?" Science 158:730-739.

Dialogues of Plato, The
  1937   Translated by B. Jowlett. Vol. 1:332-334. New
                  York: Random House.

Ehrlich, Paul, and Anne Ehrlich
  1970   Population, Resources, and Environment: Issues
                  in Human Ecology. San Francisco, Califor-
                  nia: W. H. Freeman and Company.

Ewing, A. C.
1947   The Individual, the State and World Government. London: Macmillan.

Firth, Roderick
1952   "Ethical absolutism and the ideal observer." Phil Phenomenol Res 12:317-345.

Frankena, William
1963   Ethics. Englewood Cliffs, New Jersey: Prentice-Hall.

Hardin, Garrett
1969   "The tragedy of the commons." Science 162:1243-1248.

Hare, R. M.
1963   Freedom and Reason. Clarendon: Oxford Press.

Holmes, Oliver Wendell Jr.
1919   Shenkwin vs. United States.

Ketchel, Melvin M.
1968   "Fertility control agents as a possible solution to the world population problem." Perspect Biol Med 11:687-703.

Liebenstein, Harvey
1969   "Population growth and the development of underdeveloped countries." Harvard Medical School Alumni Association Bulletin 41:29-33.

Mandelbaum, Maurice
1955   The Phenomenology of Moral Experience. Glencoe, Illinois: The Free Press.

NAS (National Academy of Sciences)
1971   Rapid Population Growth: Consequences and Policy Implications. Baltimore: The Johns Hopkins Press.

Nortman, Dorothy
1969   "Population and family planning programs: a
            fact book." Reports on Population/Family
            Planning. Population Council, New York (De-
            cember).

Ohlin, Goran
1967   Population Control and Economic Development.
            Paris: Development Centre of the Organization
            for Economic Cooperation and Development.

President's Science Advisory Committee
1967   "Population and nutritional demands," by Grace
            Goldsmith in the World Food Problem, Report
            of the Panel on the World Food Supply. Vol. 2.

Rainwater, Lee
1960   And the Poor Get Children. Chicago: Quad-
            rangle Books.

1965   Family Design. Chicago: Aldine Publishing Com-
            pany.

Rawls, John
1958   "Justice as Fairness." Phil Rev 67:164-194.

Revelle, Roger
1968   "International cooperation in food and popula-
            tion." International Org 22:362-391.

1969   Effects of Population Growth on Natural Re-
            sources and the Environment. Hearings before
            the Reuss Subcommittee on Conservation and
            Natural Resources. Washington: U.S. Govern-
            ment Printing Office.

Ross, W. D.
1930   The Right and the Good. Clarendon: Oxford
            Press.

Samuel, T. J.
   1966   The strengthening of the motivation for family
                limitation in India." Journal of Family Welfare
                13:12-14.

Spengler, Joseph
   1969   "Population problem: in search of a solution."
                Science 166 (December 5):1234-1238.

United Nations General Assembly
   1961   "Universal declaration of human rights." Article
                16 in Richard Brandt, Value and Obligation.
                New York: Harcourt, Brace and World.

Wyon, John B.
   1969   "Population pressure in rural Punjab, India,
                1952 to 1969." A paper presented at the Sev-
                enth Conference of the Industrial Council for
                Tropical Health. Boston: Harvard School of
                Public Health (October).

Wyon, John B., and John E. Gordon
   1967   "The Khanna study." Harvard Medical School
                Alumni Association Bulletin 41: 24-28.

Woodside, Moya,
   1950   Sterilization in North Carolina. Chapel
                Hill: University of North Carolina Press.

Wyatt, Frederick
   1967   "Clinical notes on the motives of reproduction."
                Soc. Issues 23:29-56.

CONTRIBUTORS

Contributors

HOWARD M. BAHR is professor of sociology and chairman of the Department of Rural Sociology at Washington State University. His interest in population problems dates from his doctoral studies at the University of Texas, where he held a National Defense Education Act fellowship in demography and human ecology. He has taught at Columbia University, Brooklyn College, New York University, and the University of Texas. His academic specialties are urban problems, deviant behavior, demography and human ecology, and race and minority relations. Professor Bahr's research experience includes two large-scale studies of aged and homeless people in New York City conducted under the auspices of Columbia University's Bureau of Applied Social Research. Since 1969 he has collaborated with Bruce Chadwick in a series of studies of ethnic relations in the Northwest, with a dominant focus on Indian-white relationships in urban areas. He is the author of *Disaffiliated Man: Essays and Bibliography on Skid Row, Vagrancy, and Outsiders* (1970) and *Native Americans Today: Sociological Perspectives* (1972, with Bruce Chadwick and Robert Day), as well as a monograph, *Old Men Drunk and Sober,* coauthored by Theodore Caplow and soon to be published by New York University Press. His articles have appeared in *Social Forces, Social Problems, Journal of Marriage and the Family,*

Public Opinion Quarterly, The American Sociologist, and other social science journals.

HAROLD J. BARNETT is professor of economics at Washington University, St. Louis. Formerly he did research at Resources for the Future, RAND Corporation, and the U. S. Departments of Interior, State, and Treasury. From 1952-55 he headed the economics staff of the RAND Corporation, and for the following four years was director of economic growth studies for Resources for the Future, Inc. His graduate degrees in economics are from Harvard University. He taught at Wayne State University before moving to Washington University, and has been chairman of the economics departments at both Wayne State and Washington University. His research and writings in natural resources date from the 1940s. He is author of *Energy Uses and Supplies* (1950), *Malthusianism and Conservation* (1959), *Research and Development, Economic Growth, and National Security* (1960), *Scarcity and Growth* (with C. Morse, 1963, 1965), and of many monographs and articles in environmental economics, economics of energy, economic development, and other applied fields. He has been a member of the Executive Committee on Behavioral Sciences of the National Academy of Science and has served as consultant to President's Materials Policy Commission, President's Cabinet Committee on Energy Policy, National Research Council, United Kingdom National Board for Prices and Incomes, and other agencies.

R. W. BEHAN teaches resource policy, administration, and management at the University of Montana School of Forestry, where he is associate professor of resource policy. His background includes administrative experience in the preservation of natural resources as well as academic experience. From 1957 to 1963 he worked for the U.S. Forest Service in Alaska; among the positions he occupied there was assistant forest supervisor of Chugach National Forest. Since joining the staff at the University of Montana in 1963, he has served as a consultant for the Forest Service. He received his Ph.D. in forestry from the University of California at Berkeley. He was a member of the Select Committee of the University of Montana (the Bolle Committee), which undertook a policy study of the management of the Bitter Root

330

National Forest for the Committee on Interior and Insular Affairs of the U.S. Senate, and is one of the authors of their report, *A University View of the Forest Service*. With Richard Weddle he edited the volume *Ecology, Economics and Environment* (1971), and he is presently writing a book tentatively titled *The Conservation Liturgy*. His articles have appeared in *American Forests*, *Journal of Natural Resources*, *Journal of Forestry*, *Midwest Review of Public Administration*, and other professional journals.

BRUCE A. CHADWICK is assistant professor of sociology and assistant rural sociologist at Washington State University. In September, 1972, Professor Chadwick is moving to Brigham Young University where he will be associate professor in the Department of Sociology. He obtained his B.A. (cum laude), M.A. and Ph.D. from Washington University, St. Louis. His academic and research specialties include social psychology, child development, minority relations, and urban problems. Professor Chadwick served as director of the Washington State University Seattle Urban Research Station. He has conducted three research projects which established experimental schools as part of the testing of theories of learning as applied to aggressive and/or underachieving students.

He has also directed several studies concerning racial and ethnic relations on the WSU campus and in communities in Washington state. At present he is collaborating with Howard Bahr in two major projects concerning native Americans' adjustment to living in cities. One of these projects is to develop an out-reach legal and social aid service utilizing Indian people trained as legal paraprofessionals. He is coauthor of *Native Americans Today: Sociological Perspectives* (with Howard Bahr and Robert Day). His articles have appeared in *Social Psychology*, *Journal of Applied Behavior Analysis*, *Social Science Quarterly*, and other social science journals.

ARTHUR J. DYCK is Mary B. Saltonstall Professor of Population Ethics, Harvard School of Public Health. Since 1965, he has been a member of the Harvard Center for Population Studies and the Harvard Divinity School faculty. His Ph.D., in religious ethics, is from Harvard University; he also holds master's degrees in psychology and philosophy from the University of Kansas. His articles have appeared in *Social Biology, Journal of Reproductive Medicine, New England Journal of Medicine, Harvard Theological Review,* and other journals, and he has contributed chapters to the following books: *Rapid Population Growth* (1971), *Toward Social Change* (1971), *Experimentation with Human Subjects* (1970), *Updating Life and Death* (1970), and *The Religious Situation: 1968.* He is under contract with Harvard University Press for a book tentatively titled *An Ethical Analysis of Population Policies.* Also under way is a book on ethical theory, *Moral Evaluations and Reality.*

W. FARRELL EDWARDS is professor of physics and coordinator of general education at Utah State University, where he has been a faculty member since completing his graduate studies at the California Institute of Technology. He has also taught at Los Angeles State College. From 1966-71 he was head of the Physics Department at Utah State, and from 1968-71 he served as chairman of the Committee for the Assessment of Undergraduate Education. His present research interests in physics are electromagnetic theory and relativity, and his articles have appeared in *Science, Bulletin of the American Physical Society, Nuclear Physics, American Journal of Physics,* and other scientific journals. Professor Edwards is a coauthor of the text *Fundamentals of Physics* (1970).

R. BUCKMINSTER FULLER has been described as "one of the most extraordinary Americans of our era." He is a designer, an architect, an inventor, a philosopher, and a poet. His many inventions include the Dymaxion house and the three-wheeled Dymaxion car, but he is probably best known for the geodesic dome. He has founded several companies and served as consultant to many governmental and private agencies. He presently occupies a professorship with life tenure at Southern Illinois University, but he spends much of his time traveling and is in great demand as a lecturer. He has served as a visiting professor and lecturer at Cornell University, Yale, the University of Michigan, Massachusetts Institute of Technology, Princeton, Washington University in St. Louis, the University of California at Berkeley, and many other universities in the United States. In addition, he has presented his ideas at invited addresses throughout the world, at universities in

Japan, Burma, India, Pakistan, Kenya, South Africa, Great Britain, West Germany, Italy, Holland, and many other nations. He has received countless awards, including honorary doctorates from the University of North Carolina, University of Michigan, Washington University, University of Colorado, Clemson University, Rollins College, New Mexico University, and Southern Illinois University. In 1961-62 he was Charles Eliot Norton Professor at Harvard, and since 1964 he has written for and edited the "Notes on the Future" column in *Saturday Review* magazine. His books include *Nine Chains to the Moon* (1938), *No More Second Hand God* (1962), *Education Automation* (1962), *Unfinished Epic of Industrialization* (1963), *Ideas and Integrities* (1963), and *Intuition* (1972).

B. DELWORTH GARDNER is professor and head of the Department of Economics at Utah State University. He received his Ph.D. from the University of Chicago, and taught at Brigham Young University and Colorado State University before joining the faculty at Utah State University. In 1965 he was Visiting Professor of Agricultural Economics at the University of California, Berkeley. As consultant to USAID in Bolivia, he conducted an evaluation of the Bolivian rural development and agricultural programs and a study of the future of wheat production and milling in Bolivia. He has also done research in Ecuador. A former president of the Western Agricultural Economics Association, Professor Gardner has also served as a Visiting Scholar for Resources for the Future, Inc., and in 1971 he served on a task force in rural development for the National Academy of Science. His major research specialties include the economics of water transfer and use, the role of water in regional development, optimal rural settlement patterns and uses of rural land. Professor Gardner is one of the contributors to the edited volume, *Extractive Resources and Taxation* (1969), and a coauthor of *The Role of Water in Regional Economic Development* (1971), a comprehensive report prepared for the National Water Commission. His many articles have appeared in such journals as *Journal of Farm Economics*, *Natural Resources Journal*, *Land Economics*, and *American Journal of Agricultural Economics*.

ELVIS J. HOLT is assistant professor of environmental physiology

333

at Purdue University. He received his Ph.D. from Purdue in 1969. He lists undergraduate education as his dominant interest, and teaches courses in environmental biology, human anatomy, and physiology. He has conducted research on physiological responses to thermal stress and on water in the city ecosystem. He has published in the *American Biology Teacher* and presently is engaged in a research project, "The Biology of Lake Michigan."

PHILLIP R. KUNZ received his Ph.D. in sociology from the University of Michigan. Presently associate professor of sociology at Brigham Young University, he also has taught at the University of Michigan, Eastern Michigan University, and the University of Wyoming. His fields of specialization include marriage and family studies, social organization, and population. His books include *Utah in Numbers: Comparisons, Discussion, and Trends* (1969) and *Complex Organizations and Their Environments* (1971; both books were written in collaboration with Merlin Brinkerhoff) and *Man in His Social Environment* (1970, with Spencer Condie). Professor Kunz's research interests have been extremely broad, and he has written articles on parental discipline and achievement demands, divorce patterns, occupational aspirations, immigration and socialization, romantic love, organizational stability, childlessness, the sociology of religion, complex organizations, and child rearing. His works have appeared in *American Journal of Sociology, Journal of Marriage and the Family, The Family Coordinator, Rural Sociology, The Sociological Review*, and other journals.

PHILIP F. LOW (Ph.D., Iowa State University) is professor of agronomy at Purdue University and President (1972) of the Soil Science Society of America. His work in soil chemistry is internationally known and acclaimed. In 1963 the American Society of Agronomy presented him its Soil Science Achievement Award, an award given annually to the person regarded by the Society as having made the greatest research contribution to soil science in the preceding five years. Later, Professor Low was chosen from among the past seven winners of the Award as the Society's first nominee for a national honor. He has received many other awards for his pioneering research, and has lectured and participated in symposia at universities and scientific organizations throughout the world. He is presently a consulting editor for the journal *Soil*

334

Science and has been associate editor of *Clays and Clay Minerals.* He has taught at Hebrew University of Jerusalem, University of California at Berkeley, North Carolina State University, and the University of Florida. Professor Low is a prolific writer, and his articles have appeared in *Soil Science, Soil Science Society of America Proceedings, Science, Water Resources Research, Nature,* and many other journals. He is presently writing a book on the physical chemistry of soils.

EVAN T. PETERSON is professor of sociology and chairman of the Department of Sociology at Brigham Young University. He received his Ph.D. from the University of Michigan in 1959. He has taught at the University of Michigan, Mississippi State University, San Diego State College, and Arizona State University. Professor Peterson has specialized in research methods, family sociology, and medical sociology. He has been Public Health Service Research Fellow at the University of Michigan, associate director of the United States Public Health Research Project at Mississippi State University, associate research professor of nursing at the University of Utah, and a sociological consultant for the Engineering Corporation of America at Phoenix, Arizona. His works date since 1953 and have appeared in many reports, studies, anthologies, and journals including *Marriage and Family Living* and *Journal of Health and Social Behavior.* He is coauthor of *Introductory Sociology* (1960 and 1961) and *Working with Families with Health Problems* (1966), and author of *Notes on Methods of Sociological Research* (1969).

DARWIN L. THOMAS is assistant professor of sociology at Washington State University. He will join the Department of Child Development and Family Relationships at Brigham Young University as associate professor in September, 1972. He was the recipient of a National Institute of Mental Health fellowship in the sociology of the family at the University of Minnesota, where he completed his Ph.D. degree in 1968. In addition he was awarded a Comparative Sociology Research Fellowship at Indiana University (Summer, 1967). A recipient of two National Science Foundation research grants as well as grants from the University of Minnesota and Washington State University, he has conducted a large scale comparative study of socialization, drawing primary data from

335

young people in New York City; San Juan, Puerto Rico; Merida, Yucatan; Bonn, Germany; and Seville, Spain. His writings have appeared in *American Sociological Review, Journal of Marriage and the Family, International Journal of Comparative Sociology, Sociometry, Social Forces, Journal of Comparative Family Studies, Social Science,* and *Sociological Symposium,* and he is presently completing a monograph entitled *Family Socialization and the Adolescent.*

BEN WATTENBERG, a writer who specializes in demographic and political topics, has been acclaimed for the book, *This U. S. A.: An Unexpected Family Portrait of 194,067,296 Americans Drawn from the Census* (1965), which he wrote with Richard M. Scammon. More recently, he collaborated with Mr. Scammon on one of the most influential political books of the past decade, *The Real Majority* (1970), which was described as "a splendidly incisive and intelligent analysis of the American electorate" by *Saturday Review.* A graduate of Hobart College, Mr. Wattenberg was Assistant to the President under President Johnson, and has since devoted himself to writing, consulting, lecturing, and working as a campaign analyst and advisor for Senator Humphrey and Senator Jackson. In 1969, he was a lecturer for the United States Information Service in India and the Near East. He is presently working on a book which will reflect the changing characteristics of the American public as revealed in the 1970 census and in recent public opinion polls. He is also under contract to write a book on world population, using demographic data from United Nations agencies. His articles have appeared in many newspapers and magazines, including *U. S. News and World Report, Ladies Home Journal, Newsday,* and *The Washington Post.*

INDEX

Index

tion of, 40n
Benefits and harms question, 265, 313-320
Bentham, Jeremy, political philosophy of, 48
Big business, 248-249
Biological factors, 269-271
Biological scientists, 285
Birth control, 23, 29, 38, 59, 257, 270, 274-275, 287, 289, 292, 293, 294, 317n
  compulsory, 118, 287, 294
  LDS Church statement on, 167
  sterilization and abortion, 289
  voluntary, 289, 292, 293, 294
Birth control chemicals, 20, 113-114
Birth control laws of Connecticut, 309
Birthrate, 50, 62, 110, 257, 289, 304
Birthrates, 34, 46-47, 49, 113, 311-313, 319
  and family planning, 49
  and population myopia, 103
"The Black Death" (William Langer), 178
Black, Eugene, 103
"Blockbuster" policy, 104
Brazil and population density, 21
Bronze, 106, 108
Building industry, 244
Buying, world, 248

C

Calories, 72
Capitalism, 198, 250, 270
Capital, 116
Catholics and birth control, 292
Census Bureau of United States:
  on future population, 23
  on population stability, survey of, 27

Census data, 134, 181
Center for the Study of Democratic Institutions, conferences of, 6-7
Change, elements of, 263
Childbearing, benefits of, 317
Child density, 161-162
Children, 115, 160-161, 310-311
  advantages due to, 37-38, 40, 47, 308, 316, 318
  and crowding, 45
  disadvantages due to, 39-40, 284
  licenses to have, 294
  of low income families, 40
  rights of, 11
  and social costs, 39-40
Childspacing, 287, 293
  and intellectual development of children, 317
Chile, high death rate in, 274
Church of Jesus Christ of Latter-day Saints, The, statement on population control, 167
Circles and human welfare, 123-125
City population of the United States, 22
Club of Rome, 87-88
Coal, 56-57, 93-94, 96, 106-107, 254
Coale, Ansley, 6
Coercive measures, 264-265
Colombia, protein starvation in, 72
Communications industry, 245
"Completed fertility," 27
Compulsory controls, 264-265, 306-307, 313
Congestion, population crowding, 45-46
Conservation, 102, 120
Conservationists' premise on natural resources, 97
Consumerism, 111
Consumers and environmental

343

344

Hydrogen, for energy production, 95

I

Ideological statements and "facts," 268
Ideology, 9, 280-283
Incentive programs, 264, 306, 315
Income per capita, determinants of, 42
India:
    and birth control methods, 314
    crop yield in, 63, 70
    and Green Revolution, 56
    and the "population explosion," 19
    and reduced birth rates, 314
Individual interests vs. collective interests, 316
Individual rights, 264-265, 310
Indus plains and underground water, 66
Industrial changes, effects of, 44
Industrialization, technological tools of, 247
Industrial network, worldwide, 247-248
Industrial pollution and technology, 124
Industrial process, "ephemeralization" of, 248
Industrial Revolution, 50, 106
Infant mortality, averages of, 115, 306, 317
Insects and food supply, 222-223
Institutional ecology, 126
Interaction between parent and child, quality of, 134
Internalizing the costs and circles, 125
International Cooperation Year (1965) and design science, 246

International Rice Research Institute in the Philippines, 63
Invisible evolutionary systems, 244
Invisible techno-economic world-social-force fields, 243-244
Irrigation, 56, 68-69, 78
Iron, 57, 96-97, 106
Iron age and technology, 108
Iron ore, 97

J

Japan:
    and population control, 285
    and population density, 8
    rice yield in, 63-64
Jefferson, Thomas, political philosophy, 48
Jevons, W. S., 34
Jones, Edmund, 42
Juvenile delinquency and population density, 6

K

Ketchel, Dr. Melvin, 30
Keyfitz, Professor Nathan, 114
Kuhn, Thomas, 4-5

L

Labor, organized, 248-249
Lake Erie, 24, 29
Langer, William, 178
Land. See also Resources, land
    arid, 67
    changes in use, 70-72
    damage to, 201
    disfigurement of, 44
    pollution of, 117, 120, 124
    production of, 279
    uninhabitable areas of, in United States, 21
    unused, 21

345

348

crop production, 59, 62, 64, 69-70

Yosemite and crowding, 29

Young, Gale, statement on rain-making, 67

Z

Zero growth rate, 311, 314

Zero per capita energy consumption growth, 254, 255, 256, 257

Zero population growth, 29, 255, 258, 268, 294

as basic premise of recent neo-Malthusian movement, 4

dangers of, 10

as eliminator of pollution, 197

Zinc, 56, 96

Zoning, 204-205

18-303